THE DISSENT CHANNEL

THE DISSENT CHANNEL

...

AMERICAN DIPLOMACY
IN A DISHONEST AGE

Elizabeth Shackelford

PUBLICAFFAIRS

New York

PublicAffairs
Hachette Book Group
1290 Avenue of the Americas, New York, NY 10104
www.publicaffairsbooks.com
@Public_Affairs

Printed in the United States of America

First Edition: May 2020

Published by PublicAffairs, an imprint of Perseus Books, LLC, a subsidiary of Hachette Book Group, Inc. The PublicAffairs name and logo is a trademark of the Hachette Book Group.

The Hachette Speakers Bureau provides a wide range of authors for speaking events. To find out more, go to www.hachettespeakersbureau.com or call (866) 376-6591.

The opinions and characterizations in this piece are those of the author and do not necessarily represent those of the US government.

The publisher is not responsible for websites (or their content) that are not owned by the publisher.

Print book interior design by Jeff Williams.

Library of Congress Cataloging-in-Publication Data has been applied for.

ISBNs: 978-1-5417-2448-8 (hardcover), 978-1-5417-2447-1 (ebook)

LSC-C

10 9 8 7 6 5 4 3 2 1

To my grandpa, Paul Bergstrom,
who inspired me to travel and
encouraged me to write.
I might have become an entirely
different person without him.

Contents

Author's Note

IN 1971, THE US DEPARTMENT OF STATE ESTABLISHED THE Dissent Channel, an official avenue for expressing dissent within the department. Disappointment and disgust with our foreign policy during the Vietnam War had led to hundreds of resignations, revealing unprecedented levels of professional discontent. With the White House shaping foreign policy decisions to influence narrow political goals and domestic policy ends, career diplomats felt helpless, watching a barrage of far-reaching consequences unfold. But the administration had no intention of changing its direction. The Dissent Channel was the bureaucratic solution. The Foreign Affairs Manual outlines its purpose and process:

> It is Department of State policy that all U.S. citizen employees, foreign and domestic, be able to express dissenting or alternative views on substantive issues of policy, in a manner which ensures serious, high-level review and response.

It is considered an option of last resort, to be used after all other "routine channels" have been attempted.

In an institution staffed with polite professionals tasked with minimizing conflict and managing discord (we're diplomats, after all), its use is rare. As it is a carefully guarded internal tool, its public discussion is even rarer. If you've heard of it at all, it was probably from the leaked dissent cable in 2017 opposing the Muslim travel ban, which more than one thousand State Department employees signed. Or in 2016, when a few dozen diplomats signed a dissent urging strikes against the Assad regime in Syria.

Usually, however, dissents are conducted quietly, politely, within the walls of the department, *all protocols observed*. Diplomats who have filed a dissent can tell themselves they've done everything in their power that they could do.

Unfortunately, those dissents are often prescient, laying out in plain language the dangers of a foreign policy driven by inertia, domestic politics, short-term thinking, and overly narrow interpretations of the national interest. Often, these are lessons we've learned before. Dissents don't typically identify problems no one saw coming. They usually identify problems we willfully chose to ignore.

What follows is one story of a problem we ignored, repeatedly and over a long period of time, which the decisions and actions of the US government not only failed to stop, but helped precipitate. It is a story of impunity, of unchecked violence against civilians, of abuses that occurred on our watch by a government we continued to legitimize. It illuminates a long-standing American trend of failing to look at long-term consequences in our foreign policy. I learned firsthand about the consequences of our failure to take a stand for the values of human rights and justice, when doing so could make a difference. This is the story of how America failed the people of a small country and how it did so by failing itself.

This book reflects the author's best recollections and understanding of the events portrayed. While the author has had the benefit of extensive contemporaneous notes, journals, and correspondence to fact-check and enhance these recollections, others will inevitably have different memories of some of these events. Some names have been changed, some events compressed, and some dialogue re-created, but the author has endeavored at every stage to capture all events as truthfully and accurately as possible.

Juba

July 2013

WITH THE FOURTEEN-HOUR FLIGHT FROM WASHINGTON behind me, I had just a short hop from Addis Ababa to Juba before I'd arrive in my new home. As I sat at the crowded gate awaiting boarding, I overheard the Ethiopian check-in attendant ask a tall, thin man if he had a nationality. The question sounded odd to me, but the man took it in stride. "I am South Sudanese," he responded, as an obvious matter of fact.

"You only have this Sudanese passport though?" asked the attendant, looking at the rough and aged travel document. "How long have you been away?"

"Four years," the tall man replied. The attendant reflected on this for a moment and said, "I cannot guarantee they will honor this and allow you in. But welcome home."

South Sudan: the world's newest country. Many of my colleagues, friends, and family were shocked that I volunteered for the assignment, even more so that it was my top choice. I was coming out of a prime posting in Europe, which some friends had hoped might steer me away from a fixation on less glamorous places. Having left the development world behind when I joined the Foreign Service, I had options now, and a directed assignment to Europe gave me a first step on a career path winding through pleasant places to live—the

1

kind your friends and family want to visit. No one would be visiting me in Juba. My parents weren't thrilled with my choice, but they knew me better than anyone. They had tried to dissuade me from a move to South Africa when I was nineteen. When that failed, they simply came to terms with my life choices, and now they expected nothing less.

An unsourced one-page backgrounder provided in my welcome packet began with a description of Juba as a place "where the only time you don't feel sweaty is 5 minutes after you've had a wash (if you have any water to wash with)." The rest of the sheet read:

Climate: Mostly 100 to 120 degrees Fahrenheit

Morning air: rather dusty

Evening air: extremely dusty

Getting Around: Juba has one tarmac road built in 1972 that today consists of a patchwork of potholes. All other roads are built of other potholes, dust and layers of plastic bottles and other rubbish.

Money: Take all money you think you will need with you, since credit cards are not accepted and there are no reliable banks.

Accommodation, Food and Health: Allegedly, Juba is the 2nd most expensive city in the world. Resist the urge to convert prices, otherwise you will not buy anything. Also expect rather erratic pricing. For example, a jar of Nutella will cost you $21, but a pack of 24 cans of Carlsberg will set you back only $18.

If staying in a guest house that provides food, expect ugali and beans for every meal. Other vegetables don't exist here.

Juba has a hospital. Make sure you go between 11 am and 1 pm during which time you might have a chance of receiving treatment. Don't count on it though, especially not on Wednesdays. Probably safer not to get sick.

Community: A large variety of soldiers can be seen in Juba. Don't take photos. Really, don't.

If you arrange to meet a local, expect them to arrive anytime in the four hours following the time you arranged to meet.

Even among those who worked in hardship posts around the world, Juba had a reputation for being a backwater, but that didn't dampen my enthusiasm as a new arrival. When I first joined the Foreign Service, my friends in the orientation class and I often discussed dream postings as we waited anxiously for our first directed assignments. I remember a lunch conversation in the Foreign Service Institute cafeteria in September 2010. "If you had your first choice of anywhere, where would you go?" My answer was clear: Juba. I wanted to be in Africa. I wanted to experience diplomacy on the front lines. I wanted to help a post-conflict country find stability and prosperity. I was naive.

I was looking for a real challenge, something unique. Juba was it. When we received the bid list of available postings at the end of that week, I scrolled quickly through the alphabetical names of cities, but no Juba this round. I'd have to wait, but I didn't give up. I felt fairly confident that much would remain to be done in South Sudan in the years to come. At least I had that right.

Two years later, I was sitting in Warsaw after six months of Polish language training and my first year on assignment when the bid list for my second assignment was released, and there it was: Juba. I assumed it would be competitive and didn't hold out hope that I'd get my first pick. Like first postings for career US diplomats, the second is also directed: you indicate your top preferences, and the service assigns positions as it sees fit, often with little rhyme or reason. Those fluent in Mandarin might be sent to months of Spanish language training for a border posting in Mexico. It wasn't for us to question the needs of the service. We served where we were sent.

I received my assignment a few months later: Juba. I had no idea what I was in for.

SOUTH SUDAN WAS born into dire circumstances. It scored bottom of the barrel on nearly every development indicator, and the population was still recovering from literally decades of war. Nation building from square one: the greatest of diplomatic and development challenges, to be sure. South Sudan had just secured its independence in 2011, so not only was it the world's newest country, but ours was America's newest embassy too.

South Sudan was my dream assignment, but I knew relatively little about the country's history at first. I knew the stakes were high—it was at a critical juncture in its national development—and that our team in-country was small. I hoped and expected that—unlike in more high-profile conflict postings such as Afghanistan and Iraq, with dozens of Foreign Service Officers—I'd have significant responsibility and be part of real policy conversations, even as a junior officer. This was exciting but intimidating as well, so I wanted to be as prepared as possible.

In the year leading up to my assignment, I devoured every book and paper I could find on South Sudan. The national narrative I came away with was dominated by the elation of independence in 2011 and hinged on a fairly straightforward tale of good versus evil.

I'd started my research by looking into Sudan under colonialism and the role of the British in drawing the boundary lines for what the country would become at independence in 1956. The country was divided by significant differences between a primarily Muslim north, culturally more Arab influenced and aligned with North Africa, and the East African and Christian south. The north and south were administered separately under British colonial rule until 1946, at which point they were merged into a single administrative unit as the British government prepared the region for self-rule. So the story goes, this did not sit well with southerners concerned about being marginalized and oppressed by their northern leaders in the new republic. By Sudan's independence in 1956, the new country was already facing civil war.

From 1955 to 2005, Sudan's population suffered two civil wars separated by an eleven-year cease-fire, from 1972 to 1983. The first war killed approximately five hundred thousand and the second was estimated at as many as two million, mostly civilians. Both civil wars were often described as the southern population seeking greater autonomy and more representation from an oppressive government dominated by the Muslim north in the capital, Khartoum. I would come to learn that the wars were a bit more complicated than that.

The second war ended in 2005 with the Comprehensive Peace Agreement (CPA). Under this agreement, the south would hold a referendum, after six years of autonomy, to determine whether it would remain part of Sudan or become independent. Dr. John Garang, the leader of the Sudan People's Liberation Army (SPLA), signed the CPA on behalf of the south. He was considered the founding father of the movement, but had Dr. John lived, the outcome might well have been different. He was a strong proponent of a new united Sudan, in which the minority groups (including the southerners) would have equal rights and would leverage their collective strength into greater political power, but his death in a mysterious helicopter crash, only three weeks after signing the CPA, paved the way for secessionists to take hold of the movement. Dr. John's deputy Salva Kiir, who inherited the leadership role, was a committed secessionist, and by 2011 secession was a fait accompli.

On July 9, 2011, amid great jubilation and cheering crowds unfazed by the baking sun beating down on the ceremony in the John Garang Mausoleum in Juba, the flag of Sudan was lowered and the flag of this new nation raised, with bands of black, red, and green stretching out from a blue triangle on which was centered a yellow star. The black band represented the people; indeed, the name Sudan, a term recorded since the twelfth century, meant "land of the black people." The red represented the blood shed by southerners in decades of war. The green, the country's lush landscape of grasslands, wetlands, and forests. The star stood for unity and sat on a blue background representing the mighty life-giving Nile. The flag's symbolism was strong and unifying, at least on that day.

Dignitaries from around the world joined this important occasion, including Sudanese president Omar al-Bashir and United Nations secretary-general Ban Ki-moon. A large US delegation sat in the VIP area. US ambassador to the UN Susan Rice headed up the group of Americans and delivered remarks to the overflowing crowd, welcoming the new country to the community of nations and calling it "a day of triumph for all who cherish the right of people every-where to govern themselves in liberty and law." She went on to say, "We remain mindful of the challenges that await us. No true friend would offer false comfort . . . but the republic of South Sudan is being born amid great hopes, the hope that you will guarantee the rights of all citizens, shelter the vulnerable, and bring prosperity to all cor-ners of your land." To great applause, she stated, "My government will stand with you. . . . So long as you seek a more perfect union, you will never be alone." It all sounded just and right and as though we, the United States, were ready to be the guarantors of this justness and rightness.

Nation building was an unpopular concept in 2013, particularly in America following a decade of expensive folly in Iraq and Afghan-istan. I was not convinced our foreign interventions weren't doing more harm than good, but in South Sudan I saw a combination of factors no other damaged, post-conflict country could claim. De-spite lacking real strategic importance for the United States, South Sudan garnered an outsize interest from both the White House and Congress, with a corresponding level of US support rarely seen on the African continent (or anywhere of such little international conse-quence, for that matter). In all my reading, South Sudan's formation was cast as a Cinderella story of sorts, with the United States playing a key role negotiating the glass slipper. But why?

If this all seemed an overly simplified view of history, that's be-cause it was. Yet it was the one we chose to guide our intervention. South Sudan had oil, but, contrary to popular conspiracy theory, that wasn't what was driving US interest. Tireless lobbying efforts by American Evangelicals, who had championed the plight of the south-ern Christians against Muslim domination from the north since the 1990s, had built strong bipartisan support for the country. The Evan-gelicals were joined by advocates of democracy and human rights who were keen to end Africa's longest-running civil war. American investment in the south had spanned more than two decades be-fore independence. With this much interest in the country's success, backed by nearly $700 million in aid each year, could this be a place where we could get it right? If not here, if not under these circumstances, could we ever?

As I flew into South Sudan for the first time, this was the question on my mind. My view from the plane was mostly blocked by the wing and propeller, but what I saw as we soared over the landscape of this new state looked lush, green, flat, and ... empty. This was what I had envisioned, after all: a blank slate, but a fertile one, where democracy was only starting to take shape and the possibilities were endless. What I couldn't see from cruising altitude were the many obstacles to progress already deeply rooted in the dark, rich soil.

THE SMELL OF burning trash was the first thing I noticed upon disembarking. A South Sudanese fixer with a big smile and an enormous gap between his front teeth picked me up planeside and whisked me through the decrepit VIP lounge, also smelling rather ripe. As we made our way past a line of passengers and a few large couches in the dimly lit lounge and out to the parking lot, past drivers waiting by large SUVs, I noticed something else: I felt small. The South Sudanese were famously tall, particularly the Dinka and Nuer, the country's two largest ethnic groups. Even women routinely surpassed a height of six feet. But it wasn't just their stature. No one appeared obese, but the locals were thick, strong, with a presence that seemed to fill up the space around them. The big men on the big couches in the lounge were emblematic, the physical manifestation of a political scene dominated by shows of strength and masculinity. I was slim and, at five feet, five inches, marginally above average height for an American woman. In South Sudan, I immediately felt pocket-size.

We reached James, my new boss, who was waiting in the parking lot outside. He, too, towered above me. By the time I met our similarly statured deputy chief of mission, Mike, a few hours later, I wondered if they had assigned an average-size American here by mistake.

James was an American diplomat right out of central casting. His neat, dark suit contrasted starkly with the sun-bleached dirtscape and ramshackle facilities of the airport. He was clean-cut bordering on preppy, and his dark-rimmed glasses gave him a studious appearance. He looked polite and inoffensive in every possible way, easily the person you would choose to deliver a difficult message respectfully, all protocols observed. James had the skills and reputation to succeed anywhere. He'd proven this with a coveted position in the White House National Security Council a few years prior. But he'd opted to follow his passion and focus on Africa, in some of the most difficult places with the greatest need, starting in the Peace Corps more than a decade and a half ago. He was passionate about using US diplomacy—the most powerful tool he could access—to improve lives. The role of a diplomat, however, wasn't the same as an activist, and James had worked hard to develop the skills and finesse necessary to balance advocacy with other US priorities. I'd learn quickly that James was a well-meaning boss and a team player, always giving credit where credit was due, never one to grandstand and never one to rock the boat.

We piled into an armored embassy vehicle, and James used the quick drive—less than ten minutes across this glorified village-turned-capital—to update me on the latest local news. As we cruised along the rough but bustling Airport Road, passing nondescript shop fronts and unmarked compounds, I noticed a lot of construction underway. New country, new opportunities. Juba looked like a boomtown of the old Wild West sort. I listened intently to what James had to say.

"Welcome to Juba! It's been quite a week. We've had a curfew of 8 p.m. since President Kiir sacked his VP and entire cabinet last week. That's the time the evening news comes on local TV, so it's a precaution in case any new, controversial presidential decrees are announced. It's stayed pretty quiet, but the city is still tense. I'll drop you off at the residence, and you should just settle in the rest of today. Rest up. Trust me, you'll have plenty of time to work."

We arrived at the American residential compound. It was walled off from the rest of the neighborhood, but the adjacent compounds looked similar from the outside. All I could see gazing down the steep dirt road were more walls on either side. A block down, the road deteriorated so much it effectively disappeared. At the gate, guards opened the hood of the car to search for anything unusual and test for explosive residue, and then they used a long handle with a round mirror attached to the end to search underneath the vehicle. Once we were cleared to disembark inside the compound, James walked me across a gravel parking lot to the front desk before hurrying back to the embassy.

It was the middle of the afternoon on a workday, so the compound, which resembled a low-budget summer camp facility, was empty and quiet but for a couple of cleaners and a manager for the company that provided life-support services. The manager showed me to unit 12A, three shipping containers converted into a small apartment with a compact screened-in porch attached to the front. My new home faced the back wall of the compound. It looked functional and was more spacious than I'd expected, but it felt cold and impersonal inside. Metal walls aren't particularly homey. I turned off the wall-mounted AC unit—the cold air was shocking in the sultry climate—and sat down on an unnaturally stiff, beige couch. Little did I know, my full-size couch, uncomfortable though it may have been, was the envy of container dwellers far and wide.

Unlike most US missions around the world, our residences in Juba were not fully furnished with the standard-issue expensive but unattractive Drexel Heritage Queen Anne collection, replete with brass fixtures, cheap dark-cherry veneer, and an abundance of overly stylized curlicues. I expected the American-size furniture—shipped worldwide from North Carolina at great taxpayer expense, thanks to the Buy American Act—simply wouldn't fit in these small spaces. I wasn't sad not to see it, though I was a bit surprised that each unit looked like it was decorated from items found on street corners outside frat houses after the semester ends. Full-size couches were a hot-ticket item, apparently.

It was time to learn a new job and a new country, get a new routine, and figure out where to get groceries, where to run, and what was both culturally and climate appropriate to wear. I didn't want to rest the afternoon away; I'd been anticipating this arrival for a year. I was ready to dive into the new gig, so I logged in to the computer in my unit. Blackberries were in short supply in Juba—like everything else, I'd learn—so I wouldn't be issued one. It was 2013, and I felt like I was the last person alive without a smartphone. I wasn't yet sure if it was a blessing or a curse, but at least I could read official email at home. A good thing, right?

As James said, it had been an eventful period, so I wanted to catch up on the recent news. I found Secretary of State John Kerry's statement on South Sudan's second anniversary of independence, given only a couple of weeks earlier.

> *I will never forget the moment I shared with the people of South Sudan as the world witnessed the birth of a new nation. I saw long lines of people waiting for hours, reveling in the privilege of voting for their freedom. When I mentioned to some voters the need to be patient and remain in line despite the delays, they said, "We have waited 55 years, we can wait a few more hours." Today their wait is over and South Sudan is an independent nation. But we all know that much work remains to be done.... We have an obligation to do more to make sure that we've helped free people give birth to a lasting and successful nation.*

But other news on the country's second anniversary lacked Secretary Kerry's optimistic sheen. A July 9 *Guardian* article reported on the situation: "As South Sudan began to confront the challenge of running a country without enough schools, hospitals or roads, the unity that had underpinned the referendum and declaration of independence dissolved. More than 2,000 mothers die for every 100,000 live births and 75 of every 1,000 babies will not survive their first birthday."

By now, the elation of South Sudan's independence was beginning to fade in the face of a harsh reality. The patience citizens had displayed while waiting to cast their ballots was waning as it became more evident that the new country had nothing to offer them. Government services were still almost nonexistent. Conflict, corruption, extreme poverty, and violence were rampant. Political leadership squabbled over power, wasting little time addressing the grievances of its people, and President Kiir's tolerance for any limitations to his own authority was increasingly strained. The SPLA, the ragtag militia previously revered in the independence struggle, had become a predatory national army, with human rights abuses too widespread to attribute to the growing pains of a new government with a rebel force in transition. The SPLA and the Sudan People's Liberation Movement (SPLM) began as the military and political wings of the rebellion, and even the nomenclature revealed that the leadership of this new nation had struggled to remake itself from a rebel movement into a national government.

As the capital and seat of government, Juba was in better shape than the rest of the country, but I would learn it wasn't doing that well either. Getting by in Juba was expensive because the economy was a mess and nearly everything was imported. The heavy international presence did its part to warp the market, with expats who earned danger pay willing to shell out a lot for very little. Battered fruits and vegetables were costly, brought in overland from Uganda. Gas was expensive and often in short supply. Yet the political leadership sat pretty, squabbling with each other as they lived lavish lifestyles behind the walls of their expansive compounds, robbing the country blind.

The discrepancy wasn't lost on the local population. Juba sprawled with construction—hotels and new camps to house the development set and the army of white SUVs they rode in on—but for all the international aid, the payoff for the average South Sudanese appeared minimal, if there was any at all. To the South Sudanese population, it seemed the aid bounty could only be benefiting the corrupt, as it wasn't making their lives any better.

The US government was investing more than any other donor. Washington's high-level interest continued, but there seemed to be no measure of critical self-reflection: our patience persisted and our course of support was set. Embassy staff on the ground continued to inform Washington of the need for a more cautious optimism, recognizing that results of diplomatic efforts were slow and often partial. But the overall message remained one of hope, which translated to giving the South Sudanese authorities the benefit of the doubt, regardless of the mounting case for skepticism.

It was the beginning of my time here, though, and I wanted to be hopeful too, so I fought my inner skeptic. Years of working in development in Africa before I joined the State Department had left me doubting the innate benefits of hundreds of millions of dollars in aid. In fact, I became a diplomat because of my growing conviction that international aid's greatest utility was as a lever for more effective diplomacy, an investment to be granted or withheld in furtherance of the values we believed made the world more stable and prosperous: human rights, democracy, the rule of law. After all, if it wouldn't be used toward a beneficial end, why invest taxpayer dollars? It was an unpopular position in development circles, but I believed this was how we could really make a difference. This method of pressure and consequences, aid contingent upon positive outcomes and good behavior, however, didn't fit well with our optimistic foreign policy approach in South Sudan. We were friends, and friends don't barter for better behavior. Friends don't judge. Friends are accepting and forgiving. In this country, friends expected unconditional love. In this country, we gave it.

As I read through media updates and internal situation reports in my new container home, I was not yet privy to the curious nature of our bilateral relationship with South Sudan, but I did realize that this was a pivotal time. The team we'd been rooting for seemed to have split in two, and a battle inside the country's ruling political party was underway.

President Salva Kiir's recent government shake-up was dramatic, but, as analysts in Washington told me during consultation meetings ahead of my arrival, something dramatic was overdue. State Department colleagues had explained that Kiir's popularity had been waning with growing public disappointment at widespread graft, ongoing insecurity, and a lack of government services. Kiir had stripped his vice president, Riek Machar, of key powers in April, as Machar was becoming a vocal critic of Kiir's leadership, and everyone had been waiting for the other shoe to drop.

Riek Machar was a charismatic man and the most obvious political threat to President Kiir. He did not hide his ambitions for the
presidency. Machar filled up a room, in more ways than one. He was
robust in stature, bordering on portly. Tall and lean during his fighting years, opulence and the sedentary lifestyle of governing had filled
him out. His face, now round and cheeky, gave a softer impression
than it did during his days in the bush, but the significant gap between his front teeth remained his most noticeable feature.

Post–shake-up, a group of influential politicians, patronizingly
referred to as the "Garang Boys," were mostly lining up with Machar,
a Nuer. The Garang Boys were those who had been within the close
ranks of the late Dr. John Garang during the war, and they had
been involved in international politics for decades. Several had held
leadership positions inside the SPLM. Well educated and worldly
(Machar himself has a PhD in philosophy from a British university),
these men had spent considerable time in metropolitan capitals in
Europe and North America; they were as comfortable discussing
economics in a men's club in London as they were sipping weak tea
in the shade of an acacia tree. They were not only relatable to the
diplomatic set but locally credible too, having spent years on the
front lines of the liberation struggle. The group hailed from a variety
of ethnicities, which was a healthy turn in a country attempting to
establish a nonethnic national identity. Despite Kiir's efforts to iso-
late them, Machar and his allies in discontent had plenty of political
cards left to play. They didn't want to risk appearing to instigate violence, which would delegitimize their side to potential international
supporters, and they took pains to avoid an ethnic characterization
of the dispute or any incendiary language.

Kiir was from a different stock entirely. Soft-spoken, with none of
the charisma of Machar or the late Dr. John, Kiir joined the southern
rebels at an early age during the first Sudan civil war and was brought
into the Sudanese Army after a peace agreement was signed in 1972.
While in the army, he graduated from the Sudan Military College
and shortly thereafter joined Dr. John in defecting to the rebel SPLA,
where he rose through the ranks to become the leader's deputy. Like

Dr. John, Kiir was a Dinka and, as the heir apparent, easily secured the position of SPLM candidate for president of the semiautonomous region. The region then voted overwhelmingly for independence in a referendum the following year.

Kiir had no experience beyond East Africa and Khartoum until 2005, when he visited Washington for the first time. The transition from fighting in the bush to hobnobbing with diplomats and world leaders didn't come naturally to a lifetime soldier more at ease in combat camouflage than expensive Italian suits. President George W. Bush's gift of a black cowboy hat during Kiir's first White House visit in 2006 was integral to helping Kiir rebrand his image, and it became the trademark piece of his new politician's uniform. (The hat also conveniently concealed a receding hairline that he has hidden from public view for years.) Kiir, too, was not as svelte as he had been during the war, but he wore the extra weight more subtly than Machar, which gave him the impression of substantially greater height, though both men were characteristically tall.

Although Kiir had learned to dress for his new role, he hadn't left the old one far behind. Shortly after sacking his cabinet in July, Kiir visited his home region of Greater Bahr el Ghazal and told a crowd of Dinka supporters that "the 'Tiger' had now taken out its claws and was ready to crush their faces. Blood will flow." The Tiger—Kiir's nom de guerre in the bush war—had grown bored of political checks and balances. He was a warrior ready to fight. This was apparent to anyone willing to see it.

But, in 2013, who was he at war with? During this same event, Kiir made several references to 1991, evoking memories of the Bor massacre during the second civil war, when Nuer fighters under Machar killed approximately two thousand Dinka civilians, just a few months after Machar had broken ranks with the SPLA. Machar later acknowledged and publicly apologized for his role in the bloodshed, but the scars from this and other atrocities ran deep.

I'd come to learn that at various times during that war, enmities between the Nuer and Dinka exceeded even their hatred of the north. South Sudan's two largest tribes were both traditional herding

communities that migrated in search of water and grazing grounds during the dry season. This had long led to traditional conflicts over cattle and land. Decades of civil war and the proliferation of heavy weapons had exacerbated these clashes, and both sides had routinely capitalized on them, feeding existing animosities and distrust to motivate fighting forces. The Dinka-Nuer conflict was conveniently dropped from South Sudan's official creation myth, which lauded how the two southern sides came together ahead of a jubilant independence. But injustices were never addressed, the wounds never healed, and the history never forgotten.

ON THIS FIRST night in Juba, James had planned to meet me for dinner at the small residential compound restaurant the expats affectionately called the *Tukul* (a local term that refers to the country's ubiquitous round mud huts) to catch me up on developments. But with the announcement of the new cabinet appointments, he was tied up at the embassy until late. I went to dinner alone around 7 p.m., armed with my notebook and reading material. Juba was so close to the equator that the sun had already set—more or less a reliable seven to seven of daylight year-round—so I made my way across campus in the fading light. The staff in the Tukul were friendly, but jet lag had kicked in hard and the depressing fluorescent glow inside sapped the last bit of my waning enthusiasm for the day. CNN played in the background, and the few other people dining watched it mindlessly. Everyone had a tired look about them. I'd arrived on the early side of the new rotation of staff for the summer, so many of these people were probably awaiting an imminent departure. I was tired, too, and no one at the four or five other tables in the room made an introduction, so I stared at the TV as I ate an unidentifiable pasta dish and ruminated on the contradictory pictures of South Sudan forming in my head.

After dinner I made my way back across the dark compound, past the small pool and the dark, empty bar to my stark, metal home, unit 12A. I crawled into bed, a hard mattress with cheap sheets under a dingy mosquito net, but sleep wouldn't come. I couldn't figure out what was really going on under the surface. In the months leading up to my move, I'd read books and reports to prepare, but the history and the present simply weren't adding up.

I found it hard to judge how serious the political situation was now. When the ruling political party was everything, and it was in crisis, what did that mean for . . . everything else? Was the shake-up inevitable given Machar's naked ambitions to replace Kiir at the top? Even if he now represented himself as an alternative, Machar could use a reminder that he and others critical of Kiir had held powerful positions for several years—the government's failings were theirs too.

On the surface, international partners seemed more concerned with Machar's instigation than Kiir's manipulation to consolidate his control. The West, South Sudan's neighbors—*everyone* had backed Kiir as the heir to the liberation struggle. Everyone wanted him to succeed, willed it to be so, needed him to be everything hoped for South Sudan. But was our faith in him still warranted?

I wondered what Kiir was willing to do to retain power and what we would tolerate from him. As it turned out, the answer to both questions was just about anything.

2

Muddying the Narrative

I WOKE UP EARLY AFTER A FITFUL NIGHT'S SLEEP IN MY NEW home. The sun was just starting to creep up in the sky, but the air was already thick and warm. My navy pantsuit, painstakingly packed to prevent wrinkles during the long journey from Washington, would not stay crisp in this heat for long. I quietly congratulated myself for remembering to pack ground coffee and my travel mug as I poured a cup and got ready to go. My shipment wouldn't arrive for several weeks, so I carried the essentials with me. I was already tired, and I knew from experience that jet lag would render me somewhat useless sometime around lunch.

I walked across the quiet residential compound in the soft morning light to catch the first shuttle van to the embassy. I hopped in, and we drove to the exit at the southwest corner of the compound. The guard moved slowly from his position, manually opening the gate, and our van inched forward, passing the guard house and onto the dirt road outside.

I sipped my coffee, hoping to ward off any contagious effects of the guard's slow pace. I naturally walk and talk quickly, often coming across as though I'm in a hurry—and usually I am. These traits would come to amuse my South Sudanese colleagues and counterparts, with their flexible African timelines, long greetings, and unhurried strolls.

We exited the compound and drove at a crawling pace for about thirty seconds over a lopsided dirt road to the embassy, located only one long block away on a parallel street. The embassy was nothing more than a small US Agency for International Development (USAID) compound repurposed in 2011 upon independence and the arrival of our first ambassador to South Sudan. It looked small and soft compared to the austere and fortresslike appearance adopted by most of our embassies across the globe. Some colleagues I met in the van directed me to my desk in the main chancery building, where I logged in to start sifting through the emails that had piled up in the weeks ahead of my arrival.

While I had been unpacking and settling in on the residential compound yesterday, James and our South Sudanese political assistant, Chol, had been hard at work at the office. Chol was an affable and well-connected South Sudanese American dual national whose easy manner belied his remarkable life story of survival and success. Chol had escaped the civil war in his homeland in what is now South Sudan by walking out on foot as a child, one of thousands of the "lost boys" who endured perilous journeys to reach refugee camps beyond the conflict's borders. After several years, Chol secured asylum status and a ticket to the United States, where he was determined to take advantage of every opportunity, soon graduating from college. After South Sudan achieved its independence, like so many other hopeful South Sudanese, he returned to help his homeland in its early, challenging years.

Chol floated easily between the American and South Sudanese cultures and understood how to work effectively in both, making him a critical member of the team. His currency was his ability to reach anyone in the country quickly, and I was shocked to learn we had no regularly updated contact database otherwise—that was a big bet on a single individual, no matter how exceptional.

Once James and Chol arrived at the embassy, they filled me in on what they'd learned thus far. Kiir's new cabinet was receiving mixed reviews, and the usual political heavyweights were largely absent. Some observers optimistically lauded it as a sign that Kiir was taking allegations of poor governance and corruption seriously, touting some of the appointees as true technocrats put in place to tackle difficult reforms.

But a closer look raised questions regarding motive. Chol and James had reviewed the new cabinet members one by one and discovered that Kiir had dismissed all of the Garang Boys and replaced them with politicians known to have closer ties to Sudan's leadership in Khartoum and clearer loyalties to Kiir himself. This combination struck me as odd. Ties to Kiir *and* Khartoum seemed incompatible. I was suspicious, but I was new, so maybe I just didn't understand all the dynamics yet. I kept my thoughts to myself. The team reported it back to Washington with little commentary.

Many of those replaced were the SPLM's core members, including much of the party's leadership. While the cabinet's regional distribution suggested diversity, there were ethnicity concerns. More than half of the ministers—ten of the eighteen—were Dinka, with only four Nuer and four Equatorians, a significant but smaller collection of minority ethnic groups from the Equatoria region.

Concerns about tribalism and Dinka domination of the government were not new. But although South Sudan's international champions tried not to pay this much mind, the South Sudanese certainly did. When I asked an Equatorian colleague about these ethnic dynamics, he painted a stark picture. "Here, you have nothing unless you are Dinka. They control business, government, jobs. At least in Khartoum, I could compete. We had a chance. We were not the second-class citizens we are in Juba." I was starting to understand the complexities. But nostalgia for Khartoum here in the south?

To some South Sudanese, at least, the biggest enemy didn't reside up north; it was here at home. Already the most basic facts I thought I knew about Sudan's civil war and the new country's celebrated origins were beginning to unravel.

I WAS FASCINATED by the latest political drama and longed to better understand it, but James was our lead on national political matters, and it was time to dive into my own portfolios. Given our limited staffing in the embassy, I wore two separate hats. I was our sole consular officer, which primarily involved helping American citizens out of crises, as well as our human rights officer in the political section. Though these two jobs were unrelated, the consular work would reveal a lot about the human rights situation in the country, from prison conditions to arbitrary arrests, from harassment of journalists to health care. On my first day at the embassy, I was keen to check out the infamous "consular closet"—my second office located inside a literal closet in the cafeteria, for lack of any other space on the compound—but it was locked, and I couldn't find anyone who knew the door code to get in. My predecessor Oliver had left weeks ago, and the person covering for him had gone on leave yesterday. My attempt at consular duties foiled, I turned my attention to the human rights issue on everyone's mind: the situation in Jonglei state.

Oliver was well known in Juba's human rights and diplomatic community for his passionate and effective advocacy on Jonglei. I had big shoes to fill. At his suggestion, I'd read up on it before I arrived, but not much stuck, and now I found myself swimming in acronyms, names, and geography I couldn't get straight. The atrocities were a laundry list, mere numbers that seemed physically and intellectually distant. I might as well have been reading about events on the moon; it all felt abstract from where I sat in Juba. I had no faces to pair with names. I couldn't see Jonglei or visualize its people. It would be months before I would have an opportunity to see the state myself, and not seeing it made it hard to grasp, to understand, or even to be outraged.

I revisited my notes. The state of Jonglei was huge and empty, mostly inaccessible, larger than Pennsylvania and with marginal development even by South Sudan's low standards. Since 2012, the SPLA had been engaged in a violent counterinsurgency campaign against the Murle, a minority ethnic group of seminomadic people whose economy consisted primarily of cattle raiding. Violence in Jonglei was cyclical, and while much of it related to the conflicts of the civil wars, some of it was discrete and local. Murle attacked

Lou Nuer communities (a subtribe of the Nuer), raided cattle, killed people, abducted women and children. Lou Nuer responded in turn. Rinse, repeat. Cattle raiding was a long-standing practice in both communities, but, just as it had done with conflicts between the Nuer and the Dinka, the ready availability of cheap weapons during the war had dramatically changed the nature and consequences of the practice. Both sides had killed hundreds, maybe thousands, prior to and since the country's independence.

Sifting through my inbox, I saw that I already had an invitation to next week's Jonglei crisis meeting. I didn't have much time to get smart on the subject before it would be time to meet the experts.

MY FIRST WEEK at the embassy was a total blur, and I ended up with little time to devote to studying up on Jonglei. I hoped James could join me for the meeting, to introduce me and provide some template of behavior for me to follow, but he was busy in a meeting with the ambassador. I would be on my own representing the US position.

The Jonglei crisis meeting was an after-hours, once-a-week get-together with a coterie of NGO, humanitarian, and mid-level diplomatic personnel. Over room-temperature wine and chips, experts would sit at a long table in a poorly lit office room in an NGO compound on one of Juba's nondescript dirt alleyways to engage in a Chatham House Rules comparison of notes and strategies for stopping the violence and helping those in need. Small photos of South Sudanese herders, huts, and cows, worn with age and exposure, were hung at random locations and odd heights around the room, with a few maps interspersed in between. I wondered if they were placed to mask cracks or mold on the walls.

"Hi, I'm the new Oliver." It was an easy shorthand to use, and I'd learned that if I introduced myself any other way, that moniker usually came back to me in the reply. The group quickly did a round of introductions to accommodate the new arrival and then got down to business. I scribbled down names alongside shorthand descriptions—ponytail, blazer, plaid shirt, glasses—of the dozen or so people at the table in an attempt to keep identities straight. Names had never been my forte, which was a serious handicap in the diplo- macy business.

I sipped wine out of a plastic cup and listened. Plaid Shirt gave a readout from a recent trip to Jonglei to assess the humanitarian impact of fighting in July. Thousands of Lou Nuer fighters report- edly mobilized for revenge attacks against several Murle commu- nities, adding to the tens of thousands of Murle already displaced. Six months of steady conflict had emptied the population centers in Pibor county, Jonglei's largest, so even finding the victims of abuse was a challenge. The "missing Murle" had been the topic of hu- manitarian talk for weeks. An upcoming Human Rights Watch re- port would provide the most detailed public assessment so far, but many of the experts in the room were worried that it wouldn't go far enough. To those who'd seen the cost of the violence firsthand, Human Rights Watch—one of the most prominent advocacy groups in the world—was letting the government off easy.

The one positive sign, everyone agreed, was that the "interna- tional community" was finally speaking out. In South Sudan, the "international community" generally referred to the United Nations and the major donor countries, including the United States, the United Kingdom, and Norway, which were collectively referred to here as the "Troika." Everyone seemed pleased that the United States and the UN had released statements in July condemning the ongo- ing violence and calling out the government for failing to prevent it. Since the statements both focused on the South Sudanese gov- ernment's inaction, rather than any intentional contribution to bad acts, it struck me that—even more so than Human Rights Watch— we were delivering a tepid rebuke at best.

But I stayed quiet. I wasn't ready to speak up on the issues, and every question or comment I had was couched in self-doubt. I was facing a steep learning curve, and the stakes were high. The US gov- ernment had power and influence; my job was to inform its ad- vocacy, which could save lives. I believed that what I reported to

Washington would have consequences, so I was deliberate. I wanted to get it right.

But what I'd be reporting back wasn't new. Why hadn't it spurred harsher words or more action yet? I asked myself why we were such reluctant enforcers of our values and interests in a country where our opinions should carry tremendous weight, given the hundreds of millions of dollars we provided in aid and our pivotal role in South Sudan's push for independence. Back in Washington, even NGOs and advocacy groups were hesitant to cast stones, though their very purpose was to draw attention to crimes against the world's weak and vulnerable.

The simple answer was that no one seemed willing to muddy the narrative that had led to an independent South Sudan. The fight against Khartoum was something everyone could get behind, and everyone did—Congress, Christians, Hollywood. The struggle of the Christian David in the south versus the Muslim Goliath in the north was something Americans could grasp and care about. Movie stars helped give the dull, dusty advocacy camp some shine and prime-time coverage, but to generate that level of interest and support for a backwater just northeast of Conrad's setting for *Heart of Darkness*, they needed a simple but compelling story line: a sympathetic pro-tagonist against an obvious foe. Khartoum bad; Juba good. It sold well, and it had sticking power. For years, South Sudan's many Western friends refused to admit a more complicated story line. We conveniently glossed over the pieces that didn't fit.

The United States' reaction to the violence in Jonglei, while delayed, was our harshest public rebuke of this partner to date. It wasn't for a lack of targets. In the coming weeks, I'd learn more about the violence and atrocities committed by southerners during the war, the very southerners now running the country, and about the ongoing violence since independence, which included several civilian massacres that occurred with tacit approval or explicit participation by government forces. It seemed as though South Sudan's many champions had wiped the slate clean with independence, as though history only began that day, conveniently looking past years of brutal violence the new country's liberators had unleashed on each other and their population.

In the second half of 2013, many diplomatic leaders in Juba—from the UN, the United States, and other Western countries—still glossed over the cracks in the foundation of this creation myth. They raised alarm about the political turmoil but looked for reasons to remain optimistic. They wanted Kiir to stabilize the political situation, but they took pains to avoid making him look bad to leadership or the public back home. Our confidence in him was his currency.

Meanwhile, my job drew me to these cracks. I worked often with South Sudan's human rights advocates. At their insistence, we met in dark corners at unpopular venues, tables away from the nearest perked ear. Most didn't want to come to the embassy, lest it alert the National Security Service (NSS) to their affiliations. They told tales of harassment and targeting, homes stormed by NSS or plainclothes officers at all hours, laptops confiscated, arrests, threatening phone calls and text messages. They viewed the government as the enemy, and the government felt the same way about them as it fixated on maintaining its positive image and international optimism. This wasn't the behavior I'd expected of a country we supported so wholeheartedly.

The picture I started to see in South Sudan wasn't optimistic at all. It was a picture of entrenched bad behavior. Would the history of internal conflict inhibit the new country? What would our ongoing support mean in the long run? And why weren't we making a bigger deal about all of this? These were the questions I started to ask myself.

But mostly I wondered, *Who are the good guys here?*

Human Rights

America's Just Not That into You

I want to speak to you today about the strands that connect our actions overseas with our essential character as a nation. I believe we can have a foreign policy that is democratic, that is based on fundamental values, and that uses power and influence, which we have, for humane purposes.

FAIRLY EARLY IN HIS PRESIDENCY, DURING A 1977 COM-mencement address at the University of Notre Dame, Jimmy Carter outlined a new approach to foreign policy, one grounded in morality and human rights. Carter believed wholeheartedly that the very existence of the United States was based on the value of the individual and the rights demanded by that intrinsic value. He believed in our duty to live up to these principles, at home and overseas. It was also the dominant theme of his farewell address in 1981:

America did not invent human rights. In a very real sense, it is the other way round.... Our American values are not luxuries but necessities—not the salt in our bread but the bread itself. Our common vision of a free and just society is our greatest source of cohesion at home and strength abroad—greater even than the bounty of our material blessings. Remember these words: "We hold these truths to be self-evident, that all men are created equal; that they are endowed by their creator with certain inalienable rights; that among these are life liberty and the pursuit of happiness." This vision still grips the imagination of the world.

I wasn't yet born when President Carter gave his commencement address and was only a toddler when he left office, but I grew up believing in his image of America. Somehow, along the way, I missed that it was merely aspirational.

Despite living through the human rights assault of the early years of the war on terror and despite growing up in Mississippi, the beating heart of our country's segregation movement, I had retained a rosy picture of America's human rights record. The blots on our history were isolated incidents, not reflective of who we were. I joined the Foreign Service because I believed America was great and special and I wanted to be part of the civilian army bringing our greatness and specialness to others around the world. I did this, and believed our government did this, in the name of making our country—and the world—safer and better for all. I bought the State Department's mission statement hook, line, his sinker.

How embarrassing for me. Even worse, I, like many of us, believed I was well-informed. Like that high-maintenance friend who's convinced she's low-maintenance, or the Georgetown Prep kid who went straight to Harvard on his parents' dime and thinks he pulled himself up by his bootstraps.

I had studied international law, the history of the United Nations, and US engagement in postcolonial independence movements. What I didn't do was a critical deep dive into the history of human rights in our foreign policy—not until the present state of it became clear to me in South Sudan. When US foreign policy was considered as a whole, what I thought were the exceptions were in fact the rule.

The history of human rights in US foreign policy is a fraught one, and the role they play today in our international endeavors is at best inconsistent. While Donald Trump's administration has been the most blatant in its dismissal of the subject, this has been the case for decades.

Human rights were in vogue after World War II and the focal point of some of the most important international laws and institutions that emerged during that period. The United States was a key architect of this new international system but remained wary of it. We were born with an independent streak, after all, which left us skeptical of handing too much authority over to "group projects." So the United States continued to go its own way, regardless of international obligations. We acted covertly, unilaterally, and often unjustly in countries around the world in the name of whatever made sense at the time. We didn't let growing international consensus on human rights constrain us—though we expected it to constrain others. Sure, other big countries acted similarly with impunity, but we were the only ones with the balls to pretend we were still a shining city on the hill. Call it "American exceptionalism."

Then came President Jimmy Carter. His record was mixed when it came to action, but he embraced human rights, putting them front and center in our foreign policy like no one had before, and he endeavored to make that mean something. He proposed human rights as a fundamentally American concept, one that would both inform and constrain our foreign activities.

The shift was dramatic, particularly in contrast to the dark Kissinger years that preceded it. Henry Kissinger, who served as national security advisor and secretary of state under presidents Richard Nixon and Gerald Ford, was—to put it mildly—dismissive of the human rights agenda. Put less mildly, Kissinger was downright Machiavellian. Under Kissinger's direction, we not only turned a blind eye to allies' violent abuses but at times encouraged them, such as in Argentina and Chile, and ordered our own in Vietnam and Cambodia. When Carter came to office, we had a reputation to repair. (This seems to happen a lot, doesn't it?)

President Carter wasn't just a bleeding heart. He genuinely believed in the long-term benefits of a global and national framework founded in justice and equality; therefore, a focus on human rights was in our nation's self-interest. He also recognized that the pragmatic case for human rights went well beyond reputation concerns. When you ignore human rights, you ignore core problems that will later come to bite you in the foreign policy ass. Balancing human rights with other interests ensures we remain clear-eyed about the people we're dealing with, whether allies or enemies. It deters us from that temptation to see them as what we want or need them to be at any particular moment in time.

Where I had been naive—assuming that this human rights identity we espoused was our guiding principle—Carter had been clever. He didn't buy into our rhetoric but tried to use it to make this identity come true. The timing made sense. In the aftermath of Vietnam, the American public wanted our country to do better and to look better in the world. Following this trend, Congress passed a series of laws in the 1970s institutionalizing human rights in foreign policy for the first time. These laws established a new human rights bureau in the State Department (which was then, and still remains, a black sheep in the State Department family) and linked some US foreign assistance to human rights performance. Just to be clear, before that legislation, we didn't even pretend to care about the human rights record of regimes we generously supported. See: South Korea in the 1950s, Brazil in the 1960s, Chile and Argentina in the 1970s, Saudi Arabia, Israel, and Pakistan. The new legislation gave Carter a legal foundation to build on, and it was his focus that gave human rights a public prominence and formal place in our foreign policy lexicon that had not previously existed. As his modest legacy, the human rights implications of our foreign policy actions had to be considered moving forward. We would continue to push human rights aside when it suited us, but someone would at least ask about the human rights implications of our actions—whether in a congressional committee or a windowless basement office in a State Department annex in Foggy Bottom.

President Ronald Reagan wasn't much of a fan of the direction Carter had taken, and he made that clear from the start. In a Trumpian move, he nominated Ernest Lefever, an avid critic of the legislation establishing the State Department's human rights bureau, to be assistant secretary for the very bureau that he didn't believe should exist. Congress overwhelmingly rejected the nomination, in the kind of bipartisan effort we now only read about in history books. Reagan ultimately surrendered, allowing human rights to retain a role in foreign policy as a component of our national interest, but his remained an à la carte approach that failed to prevent the United States from propping up abusive dictators who were otherwise allies in the Cold War campaign. George H. W. Bush adopted a similarly pragmatic approach, incorporating human rights into his repertoire when useful but downplaying or ignoring such issues in the face of competing interests.

Bill Clinton's legacy on human rights was, in a sense, great expectations disappointed. He entered office with strong rhetoric that was ultimately not matched by his policy decisions. It is impossible to consider his human rights legacy without understanding the impact of the Battle of Mogadishu during Operation Restore Hope in Somalia in 1993. Somalia was the first US military intervention based solely on humanitarian needs, and it would be the last for a long time to come. You might be thinking, *What about all those other times we intervened to stop a humanitarian crisis? Like Haiti in 1994, Bosnia in 1995, Kosovo in 1999, or Libya in 2011?* Humanitarian disasters tend to go hand in hand with failed governance, horrific economic downturns, a breakdown in trade, massive refugee flows, and other destabilizing factors that threaten the prosperity and security of neighbors, allies, and trade partners. We intervene for many reasons, but it's generally because we fear an immediate or eventual negative impact on our economy or security or the economy or security of our close partners. In Somalia, we went in to help a UN humanitarian mission because it seemed the right thing to do.

This Somalia intervention ended in spectacular failure, with the downing of two US Black Hawk helicopters and the gruesome deaths of eighteen American soldiers. After this incident, interest in human rights as a national priority came crashing down too, leaving the Clinton administration hamstrung in the face of future moral crises, from Rwanda to the Balkans. Moving forward, President Clinton contorted enthusiastically to find other grounds to justify his foreign interventions.

Human rights as a stand-alone national interest took a hit with Somalia, but the norm continued to limp along. By this stage, no president had consistently applied the same standard of human rights to allies, enemies, and the United States, but no president after Carter could ignore human rights either. International standards were coalescing, and the United States was recognizing them.

And then came 9/11.

Norms that had been well established in international law and practice, if not always respected, were now at risk. Throughout the 1980s and 1990s, we'd at least pretended to follow the rules and tried to hide it if we didn't. After 9/11, we didn't even bother. The George W. Bush administration didn't gloss over the fact that human rights would not impede its actions in the name of security. Nothing would. I could give you a laundry list of offenses, both inside and outside the country, all of which were being executed vigorously, absent accountability, and with the full endorsement of the White House. But to understand our moral failure in the W years, it's enough to consider that the administration fought tooth and nail to preserve its manufactured "legal" grounds for government-conducted torture.

While the Barack Obama administration sought to undo some of the damage done by W, such as attempting (unsuccessfully) to close the prison at Guantanamo Bay, it skipped the reckoning entirely. Choosing instead to "look forward," the Obama administration blocked any attempts at accountability for the torture, lies, and cover-ups that occurred under W in the name of counterterrorism. The takeaway: rule breaking with impunity lives on. But I'm sure the CIA learned its lesson absent literally any consequences. Consider Gina Haspel, who, for her role overseeing one of the CIA's infamous black sites and destroying evidence of its activities in the face of potential legal consequences, earned the harsh rebuke of appointment and Senate confirmation as director of the entire agency in 2018.

Obama also embraced some of the dark practices he inherited from W, in particular the drone program, which he expanded dramatically. Targeted assassinations of "suspected terrorists" are conducted regularly with little oversight or scrutiny. Most Americans have no idea how many countries US drones are flying over to drop bombs on the regular, at times based on little more than a strong hunch that a particular bad guy should be below. "Very few civilian casualties," they say, but it's easier to be certain about that when your definition of "militant" is deep and wide (any military-age males in a strike zone qualify) and when no one else has access to any of the relevant information or indicators. Our drone practice is a black box, continuing its stealthy expansion under President Trump and making us look less than noble in countries across the world, where explosions rain from the blue sky, at times flattening weddings, funerals, and other community events.

What's worse is that the American public doesn't seem to care. Protests and even questions about our ongoing misadventures overseas have dissipated. If there is a bright side to this whole Trump era, perhaps it's that many Americans have been jostled awake and have started again to reflect and consider: What is it that we stand for anyway?

So where does that leave us?

When I arrived in South Sudan, I didn't get it, but then I started to.

Stretched

August 2013

I FINALLY TRACKED DOWN THE DOOR CODE TO THE CONSULAR closet. Opening it was like lifting the lid on a Pandora's box of problems. This was the control room from which the Department of State endeavors to protect the interests and safety of Americans who find themselves in South Sudan. I was surprised to find that we didn't have a dedicated and experienced consular officer at the helm in such a challenging and potentially dangerous environment, but then we didn't even have a real room to work from. The closet didn't exactly shout "national priority." You'd be hard-pressed to describe it as a functional work space. It was, however, a vivid reflection of how much the US government valued the day-to-day work of the Department of State.

Consular services are a significant and critical part of the department's portfolio. Unless you've found yourself in trouble overseas, you probably don't think much about it. Before South Sudan, I hadn't either, to be honest. Like many of my colleagues who came into the Foreign Service as political officers, I had a low opinion of consular work. The consular requirement was one of the reasons I'd waited years to apply for the Foreign Service; I couldn't imagine wasting a year or two issuing visas and documents to customers through a service window. But every Foreign Service Officer was required to do at least one year, sometimes two. This was necessary simply to manage the workload each year, which consisted worldwide of more than thirteen million visa applications, ten thousand AmCit (American citizen) prison visits, ten thousand deaths overseas, and fifty thousand emergency passports.

I had already met my consular requirement. In Warsaw, I served on the visa line, interviewing about eighty visa applicants a day, in Polish. I was ready to focus on political work, so when I learned from my predecessor Oliver a few months before my arrival that my position included all of the consular services as well, I was surprised. The job description for the position I bid on—political officer covering human rights—failed to mention that rather significant detail.

"It's only supposed to be about 40 percent of your time," Oliver had said of my consular duties. "But if there's a death or an arrest case, consular becomes all you can do."

What bothered me most was that I had no idea what I was doing. Consular work in South Sudan consisted mostly of emergency services for American citizens. I'd never done that before and had no senior consular officer at the embassy to guide me. Thankfully, expectations seemed low.

In May 2013, the Office of the Inspector General (OIG) had conducted a thorough inspection of Embassy Juba, reviewing protection of personnel, facilities, and sensitive information; security; effectiveness of the mission in achieving goals; and management efficiencies. Before my arrival, I'd read the OIG report on the recommendation of a desk officer in Consular Affairs back in Washington. She'd worked with Oliver closely over the last year as he established consular services in our new embassy, and she'd suggested that the report would give me a good idea of the challenges I'd face.

Embassy Juba didn't score well. The forty-page document detailed a wide variety of failings, from shocking security shortcomings, particularly in the wake of the recent attack on the US facility in Benghazi, to facility shortfalls so extreme that the mission was unable to accommodate the staff needed to effectively promote US interests or manage an assistance program that had grown to $1.6 billion.

"Personnel and the integrity of our programs are at risk," the report noted ominously. The urgency of fulfilling the State Department's mission here again seemed lacking, as did our concern with the security and well-being of our personnel.

When I muscled open the door to the consular closet, it really hit me how painfully accurate that report was. But I'm not a high-maintenance person, and Juba was a hardship post—expeditionary, even. Working out of a closet couldn't be that bad. There were perks. Lunch delivery was ridiculously easy. Anyone I needed to see was likely to pass by. Quickly, I grew accustomed to spending hours in the closet just off the cafeteria, away from my desk in the chancery building across the compound.

Like my predecessor, I established a habit during my first days of going into the entryway of the access control area—before the security screening for the embassy compound—and sitting on the bench next to the people seeking consular services. We had no service window or dedicated consular meeting space, so this was the best option for meeting with the public. The area was small, with a run-down appearance not unlike the waiting areas in Juba's own poorly constructed and crumbling ministry buildings. A security guard sat in a chair by the door, and any more than one person in the anteroom gave it a crowded feel. A tall, wooden display stand housed yellowing passport application forms, job applications, and USAID promotional materials. When members of the public or embassy guests arrived, they would check in at the guard window directly across from the door before waiting for someone to collect them. Here, on a rickety bench, I advised American citizens and others on filling out applications, listened to their concerns about missing relatives or arrested colleagues, administered oaths, and collected fees and documents, all while other embassy staff and visitors moved back and forth through the passageway, in one door and out the other.

Initially I didn't worry too much about the fact that I was beyond the "hard line" of security. Terrorism threats weren't the likely dangers here. Then, one day, a few weeks after I arrived, the guards called my desk in the chancery building to tell me that an American citizen was looking for help with a passport application. As I walked across the parking area to the compound's controlled access entry point where the American was waiting, the other half of my consular team, Gio, intercepted me.

Gio was a tall, thin, gentle Equatorian. He had tremendous compassion and wisdom and an unending reserve of calm. While I operated in an almost perpetual state of frantic nervousness, he inexplicably never sounded alarmed. He was too great a figure, physically and metaphorically, for the literal closet in which we worked.

"I don't think you should go see this American," Gio said to me out in the parking area, in his usual understated manner. As it turns out, "this American" was a drunk dual-national SPLA soldier casually carrying his AK-47 on his shoulder, and Gio had it under control. He had a guard kindly explain to this American that guns weren't allowed on the premises, here's a passport application form, come back when you're more sober—without the weapon, please.

Back in the office, I told James what had happened. Technically, I reported to our deputy chief of mission, Mike, on consular matters, but there was little effective oversight. Everyone was overworked, and no one seemed aware of how we conducted appointments anyway. Consular services were generally an afterthought. This incident served as a gentle reminder of why we had a worldwide policy of using security screening for public visitors to our embassies and why we didn't send our staff outside the "hard line" to meet them. We redoubled our efforts to get a working microphone, as recommended by the OIG report, so I could conduct interviews from inside the entryway guard booth. In the meantime, I reverted to yelling at applicants and American citizens through thick bulletproof glass.

The consular closet itself posed challenges and security concerns. The ceiling crumbled a bit more with each rain or heavy wind, and the debris and dust mucked up the printer and contributed to a persistent cough. I never tested it, but I was pretty sure I could dig through the decrepit plaster wall with a sharp spoon. To fit both of us inside the closet, Gio and I wedged in two chairs back-to-back at the two crowded workstations, and one of us had to leave the closet if we needed to swap our positions based on which computer we needed to use. I was grateful that my one consular colleague was an eminently polite, thoughtful, and quiet man, though it might have benefitted the working space if his legs weren't quite so long.

I took to doing as much of the consular work as I could before and after regular working hours and on weekends. I was at the office most days from 6 or 7 a.m. to 9 p.m. anyway (usually rushing back just before the Tukul kitchen closed), and it was nice to have a bit of space—to be able to sit back in my chair without hitting someone else's back.

It was a learning-by-doing experience for me. My brief training in Washington hadn't addressed a wide range of tasks—including the special printing processes for visas and passports—that US officers rarely did themselves, since most embassies had dedicated local consular teams that managed and executed those systems. Our online programs were unreliable and prone to crashing, and we had no IT assistance at the embassy familiar with consular systems. Outside regular eastern standard time zone working hours, which overlapped little with our own, the IT help desk in Washington was staffed with what might generously be called the B team. They might as well have looped a recording asking you to call back during normal business hours if you'd already tried rebooting your computer. Since my consular "section" only handled emergency services for American citizens, every time I faced a new task, I was teaching it to myself on an emergency timeline. The first emergency passport I issued was for an American woman who was sick and evacuating for urgent medical treatment. I had a few hours to figure it out before her flight. The first two hours involved learning that I needed a laminator to finish a passport print job, finding the laminator hidden in a drawer, and getting a passport book stuck in the laminator because I didn't know how to use it.

Phone a friend became my lifeline of choice. I called up Suzanne, my consular mentor in Nairobi, for the fourth time that week. I first met Suzanne in Lagos, Nigeria, in 2011, when I volunteered to fill a gap in her visa section there for a few weeks, and we became fast friends. Her fun-loving, laid-back nature obscured her extensive consular expertise and problem-solving skills. I couldn't be happier to have her only a same-time-zone phone call away. Suzanne's section in Nairobi was much larger, so she had seen a lot.

Suzanne was the one to alert me to the need for the laminator and then directed me to a surprising YouTube video that explained how to open it with a screwdriver to remove stuck material. I guess I wasn't the first person to have this problem. In the third hour, I was scouring the embassy compound to locate a screwdriver, which I found in the maintenance dock where a mechanic was working on one of our large armored vehicles. As I sat on the dusty floor of the consular closet dismantling a machine I'd only just learned I had, I wondered if I'd ever get my head above the consular water enough to do the job I had actually signed up for, which was political reporting and advocacy on human rights.

But this was the State Department, and the needs of the service didn't really align with the resources we had available. We'd do the best we could with what we had, but we certainly could have used a lot more.

5

Do Less with Less, Do More with War

I ENTERED THE FOREIGN SERVICE IN SEPTEMBER 2010 WITH about one hundred colleagues, all crammed into a single small classroom at the Foreign Service Institute in Arlington, Virginia, for "A-100," Foreign Service orientation. A-100 is named for the room number in the Eisenhower Executive Office Building in Washington, DC, (formerly the State, War, and Navy Building) where the first Foreign Service class met in 1925. The State Department is the oldest federal agency, originally deemed the Department of Foreign Affairs at its inception in 1789, but this first class of officers was the beginning of the department's professional diplomatic corps. Our founding fathers hadn't been particularly fond of foreign entanglements, so perhaps they didn't see the need for a skill set in this area.

The Foreign Service Act of 1924 established a personnel system of rotating assignments and merit-based promotions, and a salary scale that was tenable for those who actually had to work for a living. For decades to come, well-heeled white men from "good" families sporting Ivy League educations would continue to be overrepresented in the service, but the door had cracked open, and a slow shift was to come. At a glacial pace, growing numbers of women and minorities entered and began moving up the ranks (albeit still less often than their white male counterparts, even to this day). By 1972, a female Foreign Service Officer didn't even have to resign to get married!

When I joined, the class was a six-week-long crash course in how to be a diplomat, and women made up about 40 percent of the unprecedentedly large new classes. The A-100 room was suitable for perhaps a class of sixty. Tables and chairs were crammed in in a manner that would induce the envy of modern airlines. We were so tightly packed that complex choreography was required for a single person to escape the middle of a row, and we were one of several A-100 classes in 2010. That year saw 727 new Foreign Service Officer hires.

We were one year into Secretary of State Hillary Clinton's hiring surge, dubbed Diplomacy 3.0. This initiative was intended to reverse the damage that prior administrations, including the secretary's husband's, had inflicted on our diplomatic readiness through massive budget cuts and general neglect. The goal was to increase the number of Foreign Service Officers by 25 percent. Clinton's State Department was on track to do so, and I benefited directly from the initiative. What had previously often been a multiyear slog to get into the Foreign Service had accelerated rapidly. In eight months, I had taken the Foreign Service exam, executed the required written essays, passed the famously complex daylong oral assessment (complete with the despised group exercise portion and the case study, which most applicants fail simply by not completing it in time), received my conditional acceptance letter, and passed both the security clearance and the medical clearance.

Diplomacy 3.0 was halfway to its goal when along came the 2013 budget sequestration (a fancy term for automatic budget cuts). In order to reach a détente with the Republican Congress in 2011 over the debt-ceiling crisis, President Obama had signed the Budget Control Act, which included a provision for sequestration in 2013, should Congress not agree to alternative methods to reduce the deficit. The exact provisions of the sequestration were complex, but essentially it required large mandatory cuts in spending across the government with little consideration to priorities, order, or consequence.

The hope was that because this option was so reckless and poorly conceived, surely it would scare Congress into agreement on something. Alas, it did not. With no consensus on the Hill, sequestration was unleashed with dizzying effect. Across much of the government, long-standing budget plans and programs were hit with an indelicate axe, and State was no exception. New hires that year dropped to 291—roughly on par with annual attrition. The service size was now static. The hiring surge came to a halt, and State continued to limp along with inadequate staffing and resources for the tasks it was called upon to complete.

When the Trump administration proposed a 30 percent cut to the core budget of State and USAID in 2017, it was met with the rarest of unicorns in the Trump era: bipartisan condemnation from Congress. Senators across the aisle were outraged. Senate majority leader Mitch McConnell and Senator Lindsey Graham, both stalwarts of the Republican establishment, vocally opposed the cuts, with Senator Graham declaring it would "cost influence" and "put lives at risk."

But, the truth is, the Foreign Service had seen this before, and we knew what a 30 percent budget cut looked like.* Under pressure first in the mid-1980s and then under President Clinton's deficit-reduction plans beginning in 1993, the civilian international affairs budget had been ruthlessly slashed. Consulates, embassies, libraries, aid missions, and cultural centers were shuttered and more than two thousand employees cut. The total budget for civilian international programs fell by 51 percent between 1984 and 1996, adjusting for inflation. As Secretary of State Warren Christopher detailed to a House appropriations subcommittee, this budget crunch led to less-than-ideal conditions for our diplomatic personnel, such as "sewer gas" seeping through the walls of the US Embassy in Beijing.

------

* These details were captured in a June 3, 1996, *Washington Post* article by Thomas Lippman, "U.S. Diplomacy's Presence Shrinking." Thanks to *Diplopundit* for highlighting this gem. "The Last Time @StateDept Had a 27% Budget Cut, Congress Killed ACDA and USIA," *Diplopundit*, March 31, 2017, https://diplopundit.net/2017/03/31/the-last-time-statedept-had-a-27-budget-cut-congress-killed-acda-and-usia/.

Sadly not much changed in twenty intervening years, and the results of the cuts in the 1990s mirrored my own experiences overseas: the crumbling exterior security wall at the residence in Juba, long in line for an upgrade, which subsequently collapsed in a heavy rain in 2014, or the stubborn mold problem throughout our bunker in Mogadishu in 2016 and 2017, which left many of us with a persistent hacking cough. The bunker smelled like sewage as well, and we all slept on bunk beds in shared rooms, but none of that bothered me as much as the repeated sinus infections. All a far cry from the cocktail parties and fancy European residences many Americans picture when they think of diplomats at work.

The decline of our civilian foreign affairs agencies began with the end of the Cold War, as politicians prioritized domestic issues. Nuanced international influence, cultural and historical understanding, durable relationships, negotiation skills, language skills, and the like no longer seemed pressing. The slash-and-burn tactics progressed through the 1990s with little fanfare or objection, and with the consent of both a Democratic White House and a Republican Congress. By the end of the decade, the Arms Control and Disarmament Agency, which had led US strategy on these critical security issues for nearly forty years, and the US Information Agency, a key tool in our battle for hearts and minds for nearly fifty, were both shuttered, with their few remaining staff rolled into a State Department already overextended and under-resourced for its existing responsibilities.

After a decade of declining interest and investment in the State Department, 9/11 was a wake-up call. The understaffed, undertrained, and under-resourced State Department was poorly positioned to face the complex foreign policy challenges that lay ahead.

George W. Bush's secretary of state Colin Powell rushed to rebuild a diplomatic corps fit for the challenge, but the rebuild was conducted in a military frame of mind. Secretary Powell was, by any measure, a strong and committed leader, but he was also a four-star general, and these were times of war. The military's influence across our government expanded, and the State Department was reborn a counterterrorism institution.

But by the time a crisis hits, you're already behind. You don't create a diplomat overnight. You don't learn languages or cultures in a day. You don't build influence in an afternoon. You don't come to understand the complexities of a region's politics, social structure, ethnic dynamics, and history in a two-day seminar. Our expertise was decimated. We could scramble to add bodies, but we couldn't replace experience.

Even as Powell increased the number of staff, newbies with little expertise were quickly siphoned off to the massively expanding "stabilization" missions of Iraq and Afghanistan. Eventually, every Foreign Service Officer, regardless of background or expertise, was expected to "do your time" in one of these dangerous hardship locations, leaving the rest of the world still understaffed and overlooked. Entire books are dedicated to the folly of these missions,* but suffice it to say it wasn't our diplomats' or military's finest hour.

We were finally on our way to a better place when the 2013 sequestration foiled Secretary Clinton's painstaking efforts to build a Foreign Service commensurate with the foreign policy challenges we faced. The State Department is staffed with many extraordinary and dedicated people, but even the extraordinary have limits. I expect it's hard for the average American to understand the concrete impact of an inadequate civilian foreign affairs budget. In Juba, it meant we didn't have enough drivers and vehicles, which meant I often missed important meetings and events for no reason other than I couldn't get a ride. This might not sound like a big deal, until you realize how expensive it is to keep us on the ground in dangerous places. Trust me, you don't want us streaming cat videos in our container homes or lounging by the pool on the taxpayer's dollar. It meant our consular section was located in a crumbling cafeteria closet with sensitive material, including personal information in passport applications, insufficiently secured. It meant people seeking a visa to travel to the United States had to go to another country to get it. It meant long

---

* My personal favorite is Peter Van Buren's *We Meant Well: How I Helped Lose the Battle for the Hearts and Minds of the Iraqi People* (New York: Metropolitan Books, 2011).

waits for visa interviews in many countries, which meant fewer visitors spending money in our economy.

It also meant long hours and hardship conditions for all our staff. We were overextended as a matter of course, and we began to think this pace was normal. We requested weekend meetings so often that the South Sudanese Ministry of Foreign Affairs sent us an official diplomatic note presenting "its compliments" and reminding us that Saturdays and Sundays are not workdays in South Sudan. It meant I had the workload and responsibilities of three people, even as an inexperienced junior officer.

One important leadership lesson I learned in Juba was that employees need balance in ordinary times so they have reserves to draw on in times of crisis. This might not be necessary in an accounting firm or retail business, but it is when your mandate includes responding to situations affecting hundreds of thousands of lives.

When the crisis hit in Juba, we were already running on empty.

THE IMPACT OF State's enduring budget woes was magnified by the parallel militarization of everything post-9/11. Facing several boundless, borderless, and undefined wars, our military became all-consuming. The Pentagon's budget expanded repeatedly while all others contracted or stood still.

I've worked and lived closely with military personnel in difficult parts of the world during dangerous times. They've been colleagues, friends, and confidantes. Marines have stood guard at every embassy where I've worked, both as a Foreign Service Officer and a USAID contractor. The Army and Air Force's East African Response Force would secure our embassy and residence in Juba during the early months of the war, making it possible for us to maintain a diplomatic footprint and evacuate Americans in need. Members of the military were also my Christmas and New Year's companions, all of us celebrating together since we couldn't be with our families. US troops came under fire in Bor, South Sudan, while trying to evacuate US citizens. In Somalia, I would work alongside military colleagues who were risking their lives as they labored diligently toward the same goal as we did: to help stabilize this country far from home in order to reduce the threat of terrorism.

I have the utmost respect for our troops, their sacrifices, and those of their families. I believe, however, that their interests and our national interests would be better served if our civilian foreign affairs budget was commensurate with the increasing defense budget and expanding military activities, rather than sacrificed to it.

The Defense Department is resource rich, with far greater capacity to execute missions and programs than the State Department or USAID and a staffing level that outnumbers its civilian counterparts by one hundred to one.* The cycle only reinforces itself. As our civilian foreign affairs agencies became less and less able to meet growing demands due to diminishing resources, the White House and Congress increasingly look to the military to do more. When troops are all you have to spare, that's who you send.

In the early Iraq and Afghanistan reconstruction days, it happened out of necessity. The military moved into the development and governance space because they had people on the ground in far greater numbers than anyone else, and they had the money to fund the projects. In 2005, Secretary of Defense Donald Rumsfeld made this mission creep official, signing Directive 3000.05 declaring "stability operations" a core military mission.**

AFRICOM, the new geographic combatant command established in 2007 to cover Africa, embodied the Pentagon's new holistic approach to stability operations. It was initially billed as an interagency command, even attempting to secure a USAID official in a senior position to demonstrate its seriousness about the "whole of government" approach, but the experiment failed. While

---

* Rosa Brooks, *How Everything Became War and the Military Became Everything* (New York: Simon & Schuster, 2016), 91. As the title suggests, this book provides a fantastic deep dive into the militarization of everything. Rachel Maddow's book *Drift: The Unmooring of American Military Power* (New York: Broadway Books, 2012) is another good examination of the subject.

** Brooks, *How Everything Became War*, 79.

AFRICOM's leadership did include one civilian—a senior Foreign Service Officer in the position of deputy to the commander for civil-military engagement—it was a decidedly military endeavor. Well-meaning though it was, AFRICOM was an exercise in the military taking the lead in areas where it had no business doing so. But since the Pentagon is the only one with the money and resources, that's where we ended up. Before long, AFRICOM was active across the continent, constructing classrooms, researching sexual violence and mental health, vaccinating cattle, constructing hospital wards, and promoting HIV screening. AFRICOM represented the total militarization of our foreign policy, and its reach quickly went well beyond the locales of any war on terror exception. And the more the military stepped in and expanded its role, the more marginalized the State Department and USAID became.

What did it matter who was doing it, as long as the work was getting done? Whether it's public diplomacy being conducted by an officer in uniform, or veterinary assistance provided by troops in fatigues, the manner in which foreign policy is conducted, its impact, and the image it offers to the outside world are all very different when done by the military rather than by diplomatic and development professionals. Besides, as a State colleague once put it, "Only screwed up countries have military supremacy with a lack of civilian control."

6

The Blue House

August–September 2013

AS THE SOLE CONSULAR OFFICER IN OUR MISSION, I HAD A certain set of regular responsibilities, but I was also the receptacle for most of the unwanted issues and misfit requests that came by anyone in the embassy.

An American citizen was in a business dispute with a South Sudanese company? Call Lizzy. A bank shut down the account of an American citizen working in South Sudan because he purchased books online from Amazon while sitting in Juba, and the bank mistakenly thought this violated Treasury Department sanctions against the *other* Sudan? Call Lizzy. A blind American missionary got stuck at a military roadblock after dark following an ambush outside Juba? You get the idea.

The two biggest files in my consular email folder were "Arrests" and "Deaths," but arrested Americans would dominate my first couple of months on the job (a modest consolation). Americans have a lot of misconceptions about the role of an embassy if they are arrested overseas. It's limited. Though many Foreign Service Officers—myself included—are lawyers, we're not your legal representation, and we encourage you to hire a lawyer of your own. We don't argue your innocence or advocate for your release. We look out for your physical welfare and lobby for your due process under the law of the country you are in. If the law says you have a right to a lawyer, a right to be informed of the charges against you, and a right to be released if no charges are levied against you, we'll advocate for the country to respect its own laws regarding those rights.

In South Sudan, the laws on the books are pretty good regarding the rights of those under arrest. The country's transitional constitution of 2011 was penned with the help of Western legal scholars, after all. But laws and customs differ significantly, and the nascent justice system tended to rely more on customs. These norms often tripped up Americans doing business or missionary work in South Sudan. Custom, for example, tended to focus more on financially compensating victims than on proving guilt. Add that to the rampant corruption problem in every aspect of governance, and I found my schedule quickly filled with prison visits.

My first arrest case in Juba wasn't just about money. The central authority at issue was the mysterious National Security Service, South Sudan's sinister intelligence agency, and politics appeared to be involved. In 2013, no laws or regulations governed the agency's activities or powers, and it had no enumerated arrest authority, but that didn't stop its officers from harassing and detaining people—citizens and foreigners alike—for weeks, months, or years. The South Sudanese approach to intelligence and intimidation was right out of the Khartoum playbook, suggesting that "do as has been done to you" was their guiding light.

A young South Sudanese woman, Lora, showed up at the embassy one Friday afternoon in August to report that her boyfriend, Deng, a US-South Sudanese dual national, had been picked up by the NSS. The embassy, as with most offices in Juba, closed midday on Fridays, but I was still at work—the first of many Friday afternoon embassy softball games I'd miss during my tenure. I sat down on the bench in the entryway of the embassy to hear Lora's story. NSS officers had come to Deng's house that morning and gave no explanation for taking him away. Lora hadn't been able to reach or see him since he was taken, and the family thought it might be part of an effort to intimidate his cousin Pagan Amum, the former chairman of the ruling political party who had been ousted by President Kiir in July and was a key political opponent of the increasingly paranoid president. ("Cousin"—like "brother"—was used loosely in South Sudanese culture, so the proximity of relation was entirely unclear. At the same time, family was defined broadly and came with strong ties, so the nature of the blood relation wasn't particularly important.)

"What is the embassy going to do about this?" Lora asked, though it didn't sound like a question. She was clearly upset, but she wasn't cowering; she was demanding answers and my help finding them. Her attitude was confident, bordering on entitled—I wasn't sure if I was impressed or annoyed.

With the NSS involved, I couldn't just walk up to Juba's prison or police station and demand to see Deng. The NSS had a series of unmarked offices and houses around town where they kept detainees, and they weren't exactly transparent about whom they kept or where. I worked with colleagues at the embassy to track down a number for someone in the minister of national security's office who could help. On Saturday morning, I was still trying to get someone to pick up my call, but I also had plans for my first real outing in Juba: rock climbing on Jebel Kujur, just southwest of town. At about two thousand feet, it wasn't a particularly impressive mountain, but I had heard the granite rock face just below the summit offered some pretty good routes and, in the morning hours, even boasted shade from an otherwise punishing sun. This was supposed to be my first real day off since I had arrived, and a little time outdoors seemed like the stress relief I needed.

I met up early at the Tukul with one of my security colleagues, who was trying to help me track Deng down. "It feels irresponsible to go climbing when we haven't found this AmCit yet," I confessed.

"Go, enjoy. You haven't taken a breath since you got here last month," he told me. "You have your phone with you, right? I'll let you know if I get anywhere, and we can send a car to pick you up if we need to." It was true. There was little else I could do myself at that stage, so I grabbed my climbing shoes and harness from my unit and headed outside the gate to meet my ride. My colleague reached me a few hours later with a new number to call. I was surprised it had taken nearly twenty-four hours to even get the government to acknowledge they were holding Deng. He was an American citizen, after all. Wasn't this exactly the kind of straightforward situation our close relationship with the South Sudanese government should facilitate?

I wasn't sure what to expect when I called the number. "Is this Daniel?" Daniel was the NSS officer who was supposed to be my liaison now. "Yes," was all he said at first. "This is Elizabeth with the US Embassy. Can I come to see the American citizen Deng?"

"But it is the weekend. We cannot see him today. Let us try on Monday." Monday seemed like a long way away for someone who was being held in uncertain conditions. Daniel confirmed Deng was at the NSS headquarters, but he revealed little else.

"He has been held for twenty-four hours at this point. We would just like to check on his well-being."

"He is fine!" Daniel said insistently.

"His family would like to see that he is okay," I replied.

"Let his family come," Daniel said, but he was noncommittal on details. I wasn't sure if it was the quality of my cheap cell phone or of Daniel's conversation, but I had trouble pinning him down on specifics. By the end of the call, it was clear the NSS wouldn't let the family see Deng until Monday either, but Daniel agreed to allow them to drop off some personal items and food for him in the meantime. In the absence of basic standards of care, many NSS detainees relied on their families to feed them.

I dialed Lora to give her the news. Not what she was hoping to hear, but she seemed mildly relieved to know Deng's location. She and the family would head there shortly, she said, to take him some things. She'd let me know if they faced any trouble.

ON MONDAY, DANIEL agreed to allow me to meet with Deng in the presence of several NSS officers. NSS headquarters, where Deng was being held, was locally known as the Blue House. Several stories tall, it was adorned with reflective blue-hued glass to ensure that no prying eyes could see what went on inside. The bright, shiny building looked out of place surrounded by the hard, tan packed dirt of the parking area, perimeter wall, and wide road before it. Despite looking like a rather mundane office complex, something about the compound always unleashed goosebumps on the back of my neck. I felt it even just driving by. The air was heavy with the ghosts of people whose stories simply disappeared behind those walls.

As with many government complexes in the country, and indeed across the continent, it was not entirely clear where to go and what to do on arrival. The embassy's political assistant, Chol, had joined me today to help navigate this unclear process. Chol always knew which phones to call and which doors to knock on to get the inside scoop on political developments. He usually enjoyed being in the middle of the action, but this was too close to the NSS for anyone's comfort. Normally jovial and all smiles, Chol, too, was on edge.

We were stopped at the gate as we turned off the wide dirt road at the compound's entrance. The road ran all the way to the foot of the compound wall. Nothing broke up the landscape, so, despite little traffic in this area, anywhere you stopped a vehicle on this block seemed inappropriate. The Blue House did not give off a welcoming vibe.

There was no obvious way in, so I walked up to an armed guard at the gate and said I was there for an appointment. "I'm here to see Officer Daniel?" I realized I didn't even have his last name. One officer, manning a small group of plastic chairs on the other side of the wall, suggested I call Daniel on his cell and ask him to come and collect me. I did, and Daniel said he'd be out shortly. The officer then invited us to enter the compound through the large black gate, but in the parking area we were still outside in the midmorning sun. The air was thick, hot, and sticky. I was sweating in my dark suit.

The officer waved the other loitering guards off the chairs so we could sit. The men moved slowly, like reluctant cats, but otherwise barely registered our presence. He handed me a giant weathered notebook in which to write my name and contact information. No other visitors had signed in that day.

Daniel arrived a few minutes later and greeted me with an enthusiastic handshake and a smile, like an old friend. I wasn't sure if this should make me more or less comfortable. He probably understood, far better than I did, just how much we'd be seeing of each other over the coming months.

Chol and I followed Daniel up slippery tile stairs and into the building. My eyes struggled to adjust from the bright sunny parking lot to the dark hallway inside. I didn't see much as we were led down the hall to a small windowless office with wooden chairs by the door that reminded me of an old elementary classroom. Daniel directed us to the school chairs and introduced me to an older uniformed man, presumably his boss, who sat opposite us behind a dusty wooden desk in a large black office chair that looked new, contrasting starkly with the rest of the decor.

I explained to the older officer that we were not there as Deng's lawyers or to make his case but only to ensure he received fair treatment under the law, which included being released if no charges were levied against him. The older officer encouraged me to relax, said they'd give him due process in due time, but that the "investigation committee" had not yet concluded its findings.

Daniel walked in with Deng, a tall, thick man who looked younger than I expected—and who was very happy to see someone from the embassy. Chol stood up from his chair so Deng could sit down beside me. I introduced myself, and he gave me a hearty handshake with both hands, dwarfing mine. Then an awkward quiet returned to the room.

I asked him if he'd been mistreated, how was his health, what did he need? They were treating him okay, he said, but what else would he say in front of his captors? I was relieved, though, that he looked to be in generally good health.

I reiterated our expectations that the NSS follow the country's own laws and constitution and allow Deng to speak to a lawyer and release him if he wasn't promptly charged. The officer in charge merely reiterated that the investigation committee had ongoing work. He agreed to let us return the following day to bring Deng a mosquito net for his small cell, per his request. We ended the meeting fairly quickly, as Deng didn't have much to say in the officers' presence, and we had little more to offer if we couldn't get him out. He seemed in good spirits, though, and everyone walked away feeling somewhat relieved after a weekend of uncertainty.

That was the end of our friendly treatment. The next day, we were given the runaround, with no one, including Daniel, even taking our calls. It took days to get another answer, and even then it was more stonewalling. No lawyer, no charges, no explanation for why this American citizen was being held, against even the laws of South Sudan. I tried to raise alarm at the embassy, but for the first week, the feedback I got was essentially, "At least they aren't torturing him." I felt somehow this didn't fully meet our obligations in what appeared to be a case of political detention of an American citizen by a friendly country. I was surprised, too, that we couldn't simply shake him loose. What about the constitution? What about our influence? What about our friendship? What about our hundreds of millions of dollars of aid? How could this country that relies so heavily on US support be so unresponsive to our priorities, when responding to our priorities would cost so little and would even align with its own laws?

Soon, though, we were getting pressure from Washington, since Deng's cousin back in Iowa had raised the arrest with Senator Chuck Grassley's office, and senators always take the fate of their constituents in foreign countries very seriously. After about a week of being stonewalled, we delivered a diplomatic note to the minister of national security, formally requesting a meeting with the ambassador to raise our concerns about Deng's case. This led to an answered phone call, but then the runaround continued, back and forth for another two weeks. Three weeks of detention for an American citizen held without charge in the prison of an agency that didn't even have authority to detain! It seemed like a lot of work for something that shouldn't have been so hard among friends. Then, with little fanfare and no explanation of the outcome, after four weeks of detention,

Deng was released. Did they drop charges? He was never charged, so no. Was he cleared of . . . something? Hard to tell.

In the context of a place like South Sudan, detention without charge for several weeks barely hit the radar of human rights violations, but Deng was an American citizen on whose behalf the US government was lobbying hard. And I'd been dealing with two other similar cases at the same time. I looked back at the State Department's 2012 human rights report on South Sudan, which cited in staid language the three most serious human rights problems in the country: "Security force abuses, including extrajudicial killings, torture, rape, intimidation, and other inhuman treatment of civilians; lack of access to justice, including arbitrary arrest, prolonged pretrial detention, and corruption within the justice sector; and conflict-related abuses, including continuing abuse and displacement of civilians." In this context, I suppose, "at least they aren't torturing him" was a fair baseline. I knew the United States was engaged heavily in training and supporting the country's security forces and working with the justice system, both military and civilian. But were we making things better or just propping up abusive systems? At this stage, I couldn't be sure.

CASES OF AMERICANS arrested, harassed, ill, or missing didn't let up during my first few months in South Sudan. The NSS in particular had a knack for picking up Americans late on Fridays; they seemed intent on bringing chaos to my catch-up weekends. These experiences were highly traumatizing, particularly for the Americans who were not as familiar as some of the dual nationals with the security forces' loose relationship with civil liberties. But they became routine occurrences for me; the Blue House started to lose its mystique, and a four-to-six-week stint inside became standard. Like my colleagues who had been in country longer, I started to see my own threshold for the government's bad behavior increase. Arrests remained a regular part of my weekend existence, but I didn't let them bother me as much. If I was not on the phone with the NSS or at the Blue House, I might see one of my NSS contacts lurking in the corner of a restaurant during a meal. They were everywhere, and not so secretive about it. This, too, became normal to me.

While handling one case of a naive American businesswoman whom the NSS brought in for questioning about her ambitious (and ill-advised) solar energy business plans, I asked an officer why he was following her in the first place. "I was assigned to her hotel." He was very matter-of-fact about something I would assume to be covert, or at least not advertised. He explained that officers were assigned to every hotel that foreigners frequent, just to keep an eye out for anything fishy (a different standard, I suspected, than probable cause). This officer didn't like how the American had answered questions in her registration at the hotel. His concern led to about a week of questioning, some of which I joined at her request, and then the NSS officers strongly encouraged her to leave the country. She seemed more clueless than anything else, but cluelessness in Juba was dangerous. Given what I knew about the security forces' abuses, I recommended she heed the officers' advice, and I breathed a sigh of relief when she departed the country. By then, I was well aware of the limitations of the embassy's rescue skills.

Even as it started to become standard fare for me, I remained surprised at the brazenness of the South Sudanese authorities. The United States was a donor country with a close relationship to the South Sudanese government, having played such a pivotal role in the country's creation and continuing to provide much ongoing support. Nevertheless, the United States wielded little influence, even in simple scenarios that would be civil cases in more developed legal systems. It would cost the authorities little to simply follow their own due process at our behest, but the government, it appeared to me, had learned that it need not heed our warnings, pressure, requests, or queries. We, on the other hand, remained unconditionally supportive of the South Sudanese administration, regardless of bad acts or impunity. We told ourselves this was important to maintain access and influence. But what influence and to what end? And what lessons were these supposed friends learning in the meantime? If they could ignore our small-scale asks, how could we possibly rely on them when the stakes were high, whether for direct US interests or in taking the challenging steps needed for South Sudan's own stability and prosperity? And if we couldn't, why were we bothering?

To me, it didn't feel like friendship. It felt like our bilateral relationship was a one-way street.

Open for Business

September–October 2013

AS A YOUNG DIPLOMAT, I WAS LEARNING THAT EFFECTIVE diplomacy relied on timely access to sound information and an ability to persuade. One didn't get far on either front without relationships, and rock climbing with humanitarian actors who had extensive reach and deep experience across the country was a good reminder that relationships were built after-hours, over activities and beers, not meetings and notebooks. I was more of an information gatherer at this stage, so I needed to build relationships with the people who had the information. For the human rights portfolio, this meant the UN personnel and the advocacy and NGO officers who knew South Sudan and its recent history intimately, traveled around the country often, and were frequently the first on the ground after an attack or incident occurred.

These were serious people working on serious problems. They worked long days nearly every day and were not likely to show up at the crag on Saturday mornings. I had to find a way to make myself worth their time.

I learned the lesson of leverage early: having something other people want but don't have could get me what I wanted. My parents graciously sent me to college with a car. It seemed like cheating at the time, but that was my ticket to early friendships in my dorm, as a series of road trips to concerts across the southeast would demonstrate.

On Juba's hot, humid, and generally dull weekends, the US residence pool was my leverage. It was in poor shape and in dire need of a paint job, but it was a nice asset for Juba. I became shameless about using it as a lure. My target was the Atrocities Crowd, the shorthand I used for the serious set of expats who joined the weekly Jonglei crisis discussions and who had been tracking atrocities in this country since before it existed. I'd need a different approach to build trust with the South Sudanese human rights activists, but this was a start.

Two weekends in a row, I put out the invitation for Sunday afternoon at the pool. The dedicated extracurricular-ists of the climbing community showed up with bells on, as did a few more diplomats from other missions. This crowd worked hard and played hard, managing to prioritize both. If there was an event in Juba—holiday party, charity event, burger night, national day for a random Southeast Asian country—a certain subset of expats always appeared. It got too hot to climb by early afternoon, and other events tended to happen in the evening, so what better way to spend the time than a dip in a pool, a cold beer, and a debate on how to address ongoing impunity in the SPLA?

But I wasn't yet getting traction with the Atrocities Crowd. About a dozen expats—mostly Europeans, Americans, and a South African or two—made up the core of this seemingly impenetrable group of international experts. The polite regrets came in one by one. "So sorry, humanitarian crisis near Lekuangole. Can't make it this time!" "High-level visitor in from Brussels, next time though!" "Got cleared for the UN flight to Bor last minute, maybe drinks next weekend?" Apparently it was easier to entice this group to a work meeting on a Sunday afternoon than anything resembling fun.

But my invitations spurred reciprocity, and by late September I finally had my in. I'd been invited to Dina's "fakewell" party. Dina was a longtime South Sudan watcher who'd held a variety of positions over the years in Juba, and she was at the heart of the Atrocities Crowd. I smiled when I got an email early in the week from Casie, another longtime South Sudan analyst: "We're still hearing about the improved situation in Pibor. I was curious if your team is hearing the same. Fair warning, I may try to pick your brain at Dina's fakewell on Saturday. But I promise to avoid work talk after the first beer or two."

The social and professional worlds were never far apart in tense conflict environments like South Sudan. I got dual-use emails all the time:

"Hey Lizzy, would love to catch up over drinks. Maybe Logali House this Friday? Oh, and if my new passport is ready, maybe you can bring it?"

"I'd love to join dinner tomorrow with the girls, thanks for the invite! Are you going to the British reception to mark the 11th World Day Against the Death Penalty? Maybe we can share a ride after."

"I have some questions about child soldiers and hear you might be tracking developments. Will you be at that farewell at the UN Thursday night?"

But Dina's "fakewell" invite and Casie's email promised more excitement than the usual working social event. The guests wouldn't be just fellow diplomats passing through as generalists, trained to learn each place an inch deep, just enough to speak intelligently on a wide variety of issues. This was the in-group for conflict tracking and analysis, a bunch of conflict-zone nerds whose cocktail conversation drifted from the latest needs assessment for civilians affected by raids up-country to interrupted food distribution and expectations for the upcoming "fighting season." It was unclear that they ever fully trusted those of us just passing through—or the motivations of the governments and international organizations we served.

Dina was saying farewell to her position with an international conflict-prevention NGO. She was petite, with an impressively infectious smile and positive energy for someone whose job was essentially to track and respond to atrocities. She sported a pixie cut and a tomboy style that seemed both effortless and too cool for Juba. Her next steps weren't yet clear, but no one believed she'd be gone for long—hence the "fakewell." (In fact, she'd return in a few weeks as co-ordinator for the South Sudan NGO Forum.)

The "fakewell" became the standard branding for the event at which we bid farewell to a member of the community who would shortly return to Juba under a different title. This wouldn't be the last one I'd attend. South Sudan could be a dark place if you worked on these issues, but apparently it was a hard place to leave. While some humanitarians and advocates would leave for months or even years at a time—often for other garden spots like Iraq and Syria—no one's door to South Sudan ever seemed to fully close. The country got under your skin, like those ubiquitous parasites common in this part of the world. The locals knew it was true. "Once you drink from the Nile, you are destined to return," they'd say.

Dina's party marked the first time I'd seen so many of this set outside a meeting environment. The compound was charming, with soft lighting around a pool and real furniture in the apartment, just off the courtyard. Sipping a glass of wine by the kitchen island, I spotted photos of friends and family, art on the walls—real walls, not metallic siding. Suddenly, it was clear to me that many expats here were living real lives, lives very unlike my artificial existence on the US compound, where Foreign Service Officers observed time-bound deployments from container homes.

Would this compound look so charming in the light of day? I wasn't sure, but it seemed so tonight, in part due to the warmth of the community. These people knew each other, dated each other, had watched each other develop and change over time, crossing paths around the world over the years. Many had grown up professionally together. I felt like an imposter, watching from the outside, as though a window separated me from the conversations right in front of me.

I didn't usually go to social events on my own. The security, military, and intelligence specialists were the only ones in the embassy allowed to drive themselves around Juba; the rest of us were relegated to sharing the embassy's perpetually under-resourced motor pool. "Can't get a car" was a common excuse for not showing up to all sorts of events. But I had worked out a ride share with colleagues heading to a nearby location, so here I was, on my own, no social safety net to cling to. I had a couple more glasses of wine for a boost of liquid confidence and entertained my new friends with my latest crazy consular tales, a reliable crowd-pleaser.

"So this young American guy shows up outside the embassy late on Friday afternoon. It's ALWAYS Friday afternoon when the Americans in trouble come calling. He says Jesus told him to go to Uganda to save the children. Sounds like he might have seen that documentary on the 'Machine Gun Preacher' or something. He gets to Uganda on a one-way ticket and goes to a seminary that he thinks will just take him in. Turns out he has no tuition money, so they don't. He then makes his way up to the border and into South Sudan. I guess that was God's next suggestion. This guy shows up at the embassy. He wants US assistance getting home. He was robbed on the bus up to Juba, the gunmen took the $50 he had on him, so he's destitute. I reply, 'You're in a foreign war-torn country with no contacts, no return ticket, and no resources, and they took your fifty bucks, so *now* you're destitute?'"

We all knew that fifty bucks wouldn't have gotten him far in Juba, one of the most expensive cities in the world.

"I ask him what he wants to do. 'Well, this place is awful,' he said. 'Jesus said it's okay for me to go home now.'"

My small audience erupted in laughter at the punch line, and I assured them that this story, like all my consular stories, was true. "Could I really make this stuff up?"

I was tipsy and exhausted from extroversion by the time curfew was called. My armored chariot awaited me. As the heavy vehicle passed through the dark, broken backstreets of Juba, I reflected on the night and thought I'd made some headway. Even if I was still an outsider, I'd built a little more trust and a small reservoir of credit with the people who knew and saw what I needed to know and see. Turns out, I'd need that credit later.

IN OCTOBER, THE talk of the expat crowd in Juba was the upcoming Bradt book on South Sudan, the first commercial travel guide on the country. I dutifully preordered mine, due out in mid-December.

At a long wooden table on the back veranda of Logali House—a guesthouse and restaurant that became the place to be on Friday evenings—diplomats and humanitarians discussed the pros and cons of our edgy home opening up to tourists. The slow-moving ceiling fans did little more than stir the thick, humid air in swirls around a handful of tables dotted with expats, business people, and mid-ranking South Sudanese officials. Most conversations still had an air of business to them, but the mood lightened as the evening wore on and the empty bottles of Nile Special piled up on the tables.

"How could you do an entire book on this country? Most of it's inaccessible anyway," said an aid worker, recently frustrated by her own inability to get up-country.

"The country is beautiful. A lot to see. They say the wildlife migration here is bigger than the wildebeest migration of the Serengeti," a UN officer commented. "I'm looking forward to seeing what it has to say."

"But who is allowed to explore them? We aren't. And how many of those animals are still around since the last war? It's not easy to get there either, and certainly not safe. This country has zero tourism infrastructure," one of our embassy security officers chimed in.

"Or just infrastructure, for that matter," he added. "But, hey, you did the Nile boat cruise last weekend, so that's, what, about an hour?" The boat "cruise" consisted of a small wooden dinghy with an outboard motor attached, but tooling around on the river for a bit had been a major expat activity highlight. He thought for a moment and continued, "And the rock climbing nearby, right?"

"Yeah, only if you know how to avoid the SPLA by Jebel," one of the regular climbers replied, referencing our uncomfortable run-in with government soldiers recently at the start of the short hike up. The American climbers were still waiting to find out if the embassy would make this area off-limits now, a real blow to morale in a town with few leisure options not involving alcohol.

Tanaz, a fellow American and special assistant to the UN chief in South Sudan, chimed in. I considered her a good friend in Juba, though we talked more about seeing each other than we actually did, but we exchanged woeful "guess what happened to me today" emails regularly. She knew exactly what I was thinking.

"Lizzy, I guess this means you won't be out of a job this year."

"I spend half my time trying to get American investors, missionaries, and dual nationals out of trouble. The last thing I need is a bunch of clueless tourists running around," I muttered.

The beers were getting low, so someone headed to the bar to grab another round, but I glanced toward my American colleagues, with whom I had caught a ride that night. We silently agreed that it was time to head home. Curfew was approaching, and just thinking about American tourists haplessly descending on the country exhausted me.

A couple of weeks later, the upcoming travel guide was in the back of my mind as I undertook the routine consular task of updating the State Department's travel guidance for South Sudan. We updated travel advisories at least twice a year. We'd seen no significant security changes since the last update—no improvements, at least—so the language largely reflected what our guidance had been for the past couple of years. In light of the many recent arrest cases I'd had to handle, I tried to make that risk a bit clearer, but otherwise I left the existing language intact. If anything, the situation appeared less stable, particularly in Juba. Even the National Legislative Assembly had recently called out the government for the increase in violent crime in the capital city, including an armed attack on a humanitarian vehicle that left one worker dead, and another incident in which two Juba residents were killed in their home by nine men in police uniforms. Our South Sudanese staff in the embassy were also reporting break-ins and robberies on the rise in their neighborhoods, and most of the perpetrators were wearing government uniforms, suggesting some level of security-force complicity. An Interior Ministry representative told me that, in their defense, the police and soldiers weren't committing the crimes but might just be renting out their weapons and uniforms.

Our travel warning was already quite extreme. It was hard to improve on "Don't go there." I expected the draft to move through clearances in the embassy swiftly so I could forward it on to Washington to finalize. These ordinary consular tasks were usually a box-checking exercise when situations were relatively static, so I was surprised when James called me to his office to discuss it.

"The ambassador isn't going to clear this, Lizzy," James said. He reminded me that the US government was sponsoring the South Sudan investment conference coming up in December. Obviously, he explained, we wouldn't be inviting US investors if we also thought it necessary still to urge the public to "defer all travel to the country."

Ah, right, the country's first international investment conference, and USAID was a sponsor. How could I have forgotten? Our two-person economic affairs team and the Office of the US Special Envoy for Sudan and South Sudan (USSESSS—because the government always needs another cumbersome acronym) had been busy preparing for this historic event. The special envoy, Donald Booth, was even scheduled to fly from Washington to Juba to participate. Booth was a longtime career diplomat, having served as US ambassador already in Ethiopia, Liberia, and Zambia. His background in the service was economic affairs, so it didn't come as a surprise that he took a particular interest in business and investment as this nascent country's ticket out of instability. I wondered, though, how optimistic he would feel about this approach if he were here permanently. Government officials making millions in the black market off their own currency manipulations were enough for me to conclude that clean investment here would have a hard time. Our ambassador, Susan Page, had disapproved of supporting the initiative, but she had lost the argument with Washington. Widespread graft and lawlessness were minor details, apparently. South Sudan, the world's newest country, was open for business.

And it *was* open for business. Industries that capitalize on areas of conflict and risk were already taking advantage. We got regular inquiries from American companies about the landscape, and we welcomed them cautiously. Halliburton had registered a branch and was bidding on contracts, and ExxonMobil was negotiating an exploration agreement with the Ministry of Petroleum and Mining. South

Sudan boasted healthy oil reserves on which the government relied heavily. US companies were interested, though the oil sector here wasn't the most attractive. In addition to the long-standing conflict and insecurity, the crude was of a low quality and difficult to extract. But it was oil, and oil in dangerous places had a certain draw. The country also had enormous agricultural potential, and John Deere and Caterpillar were among the dealers visible in Juba. But I still wondered about the wisdom of actively promoting investment in the current political and security climate. We didn't need to encourage companies like Halliburton to explore dangerous places; that's what they do. But should we be trying to attract others?

I perched on the edge of the desk that belonged to Jimmy, the embassy's economic chief, as I considered the recent developments. Since Jimmy was not around, I took the opportunity to be candid about his portfolio.

"I totally agree, James, but I think that, of the two options on the table, we're picking the wrong one," I replied. "I haven't revised the travel advisory that much. It's basically the same warning we've had for years. Didn't you and the ambassador already approve this language earlier this year? You don't actually think things are improving, do you?"

Suggesting that the language was outdated, James noted that the security situation in Juba now was nothing like Iraq or Afghanistan, and the South Sudanese needed investments to get back on track.

As usual, James offered a reasonable argument. But I didn't see a country that ranks just above Afghanistan, North Korea, and Somalia on Transparency International's corruption perceptions index attracting much aboveboard investment, and I didn't understand why we would encourage it. The business environment was abysmal and the risks to investors were massive, both financially and personally. I thought of my conversation with an American investor I had visited in detention at the Juba police station recently, a discussion held through the bars of the cell because "the guy with the key" wasn't at work that day—a cell the investor shared with two dozen other men sitting body to body on a hard dirt floor, with a bucket for a toilet in the corner. This American had seen business opportunity in the region but ended up on the wrong side of a transportation accident. Though he was not present at the time and had only tangential ties to the goods onboard, he was assumed to have the money to pay for the injuries, so there he was. We pressed the government, the Ministry of Justice, and the investigator on the case for weeks. Exasperated and getting ill from the conditions, he eventually simply bribed his way out.

Remembering this angered me. It didn't feel like we were looking out for our own. It felt like we were conveniently buying the government's lies and therefore promoting them.

"Well, if the ambassador wants to attract more Americans here, maybe she'd like to be the one to visit them all in prison," I retorted. The travel warning was what I clung to when I couldn't get Americans out of trouble. We warned you, I'd think to myself. If Americans were warned and chose to take the risk anyway, I still felt bad, but not responsible. If we were feigning assurances that this was a good place to invest in, we were complicit in the harm they faced.

I was quietly fuming when I heard her. "I understand your concern, Lizzy, but James is right." The calm and measured voice came from right behind me in the doorway. It was the ambassador. I wasn't sure how long she'd been standing there, but I expected long enough. She acknowledged the recent arrests we'd been handling but commented that arrests were something we dealt with all over the world. She also noted that we were working closely with the government to improve all these challenges.

I internally recoiled in horror for a moment, blood rushing to my face with embarrassment as I turned around. I was sure this was a strike against me in the ambassador's mind, and I was convinced she already didn't think very highly of me.

Susan Page was the first US ambassador to South Sudan. She had a long history with the country prior to and through the independence process. From 2002 to 2005, she served as legal advisor to the Secretariat for Peace in Sudan, under the aegis of the regional body, the Intergovernmental Authority on Development (IGAD), leading negotiations for the Comprehensive Peace Agreement that would end the civil war. She was in the thick of it during the most consequential period leading up to the deal that created this country. Ambassador Page was well respected in diplomatic and South Sudanese circles alike and had a strong human rights background. Her presence in meetings and events was always weighty, despite her relatively small stature, particularly among the towering South Sudanese. She was social and outgoing as well, frequently joining the American staff at the bar on Friday nights or at Saturday barbecues, welcoming guests with a warm smile and enthusiasm, glass of red wine ever in hand. She was always keen to hear the latest gossip and was not one to turn down an edgy game of Cards Against Humanity. This endeared her to many of my working-level colleagues, but Ambassador Page and I had never really clicked.

I'd been thrilled to go to work for her, thinking that an experienced female ambassador in such a small post offered an incredible mentorship opportunity for me—an opportunity I planned to work hard to earn. But, over time, it became clear from comments she'd made to colleagues and in how she spoke to me in staff meetings that she didn't think I was up to my job. Since I'm a natural people pleaser and a perfectionist, her disapproval was a persistent source of anxiety for me. Walking home from late nights in the office on Fridays, I often found myself taking the long way around the back row of container units so I could avoid passing the bar and getting called over to a table of colleagues where the ambassador would hold court. I liked and respected her, but spending time with her after-hours just reminded me that regardless of how hard I worked, in her eyes, I couldn't deliver.

I was sinking into this familiar insecurity as I turned around, but when I looked in her face, cool and composed, I thought of the other faces I'd seen in Juba, behind bars, in interrogations, in unmarked NSS holding facilities hidden around town. At checkpoints, in morgues.

I'd often found myself questioning the ambassador's positions, particularly when it came to how seriously we took offenses and abuses by the South Sudanese government. But Ambassador Page had history and experience here that I lacked, so usually I begrudgingly deferred to her. I would learn that the ambassador was often begrudgingly deferring to Washington.

In this instance, however, I was glad I'd spoken my truth unfiltered in front of her—even unwittingly. I took a deep breath, trying not to betray any further emotion. I'd made my point, and there was little left to say.

"Yes, ma'am. I'll take another look at the language," I exhaled into the words, defeated but attempting to relay my skepticism anyway.

Does she really believe this? Does Washington? I'd only been here a few months, but it was glaringly obvious to me that the last thing South Sudan's most important international partner should be focusing on was an investment conference. What fictions were we telling ourselves in which this event made sense? The South Sudanese government had done nothing to improve the business environment to attract legitimate trade. It wasn't a priority for them, so why were we trying so hard to do it ourselves, particularly when it could put Americans and American interests at risk? It seemed obvious to me that keeping the economy shady worked well for those in power looking to make an easy corrupt buck.

It raised so many questions for me about our approach to South Sudan and our priorities here. And I wasn't the only one. Jimmy, the economic officer, was going through the motions; I knew he wasn't convinced. Rong, Jimmy's junior colleague, found the whole thing absurd. He went on leave in November and quit the Foreign Service, never to return. He had spent his last tour in Afghanistan, so this wasn't the first futile exercise he'd been a part of—but it was the last nail in the coffin.

AS TIME WENT on, I saw the physical manifestations of the corruption everywhere. Ministers and deputies sported expensive watches, handmade Italian suits, and fleets of fancy vehicles, even as they worked out of crumbling offices. Most offices offered few amenities beyond a new television, perpetually on in the background, as long as there was power or a generator running. Ministers and their staff were always on international travel, funded by some well-meaning donor, with healthy per diems, but they were gone so often it was unclear who, if anyone, was doing the work of building the nation. Money was being spent, but not on the country's needs.

I was only aware of one government official of modesty: Steven Wondu, the country's longtime auditor-general. Wondu was a tall, thin, quiet man with short-cropped hair and a thin mustache. He was Equatorian, kind and clever, a true technocrat determined to fight against the government's corruption, even if he was the only man doing so. His honesty and conviction earned him deep respect in the community of internationals in Juba. Wondu was the SPLM's first representative to the United States during the war with Sudan, and he maintained strong connections with and affinity for America. He was one of Ambassador Page's favorite contacts, a real friend even. I always enjoyed tagging along for meetings at his office, though I couldn't help but wonder why he stayed.

The government's leadership humored him, inexplicably allowing him to air the dirty laundry of the big men cashing in on the country's international spoils, at least to a point. Without prosecutorial authority, though, he had no power to address it. In 2012, Wondu released a damning report revealing gross mismanagement and corruption in the Ministry of Finance. He handed the findings over to the Ministry of Justice and the National Legislative Assembly, but, as with corruption findings from every other year, no one was brought to justice. Around the same time, President Kiir demonstrated his own robust commitment to addressing rampant corruption by sending a letter to seventy-five individuals inside or close to the government, asserting that $4 billion had been stolen from public coffers and politely asking if they would please return the money.

Other than Wondu, I was sad to learn that our "favorites" in the government all seemed to have dirty hands to varying degrees. Clem, our defense attaché, invited me to join dinner one night with the minister of national security, General Obuto Mamur Mete, a larger-than-life figure, physically and otherwise. "You'll love him. He's the real deal," Clem assured me. Having spent ample time at the Blue House, I was curious to meet the chief of the NSS, though our security colleagues cautioned me that he was more a figurehead than anything else these days—a sidelined war hero compensated with a title and ample opportunity to pilfer.

The sun was starting to dip down in the sky as we pulled into the monstrous compound in the Jebel neighborhood, just down a dirt road from the Blue House. Mamur met us in the large parking area in front of a nearly finished mansion, and I spotted a dozen or so armed men milling around the courtyard and outside the gate—guards, I presumed, though they weren't all in uniform. At the other end, I saw a sweeping multicar garage with a half-dozen monster vehicles, three of them tricked-out Humvees. These were the shiny civilian kind, made for show and driven by wealthy investment bankers at the height of a midlife crisis. Some were broken with flat tires, obviously not repairable in Juba, but still status symbols of a sort. *And this is one of the good guys?* I thought to myself, wondering how expensive it was to ship the cars in and which government account had covered it.

Clem introduced me to the towering general. He sported a big gold Rolex, and his soft, friendly face looked nothing like the hardened warrior I was expecting. He leaned over, peering into my face as he gave my hand a hearty shake, just before he grabbed me in a bear hug and lifted me off my feet. Clem and Major Mike, the embassy's security cooperation chief, laughed nervously, not sure how to respond. It felt like minutes before he set me down, abruptly turning to walk toward the corner of the parking lot, saying to no one in particular, "Have you seen my turtles? They're wonderful."

I looked at Clem and Major Mike. They both shrugged and followed Mamur. On the other side of the parking lot, Mamur pointed out a deep, narrow trough with eight giant Nile turtles inside. The turtles, soft-shelled and three feet or longer in length, were critically endangered in most of their former habitats; I didn't imagine the whims of a wealthy general were helping their population numbers. I knelt down by the trough trying to get a better look, and Mamur shouted something at some of his men in the courtyard. They brought over a pump and immediately started pumping water out of the trough and onto the pavement. To the extent they could show emotion, the turtles seemed alarmed, flapping slowly in the swirling water.

"What are they doing?" I asked urgently.

"The turtles will crawl out if there's no water. You can pet them!" I immediately regretted showing any interest in the animals. Sure enough, the beasts slowly made their way out of the trough one by one and crawled at a glacial pace across the pavement toward a grassy corner.

"Elizabeth, you can ride them!" the general shouted at me over the loud hum of the pump, still spilling water into the parking lot.

I looked again at Clem and Major Mike and got no more direction than additional shrugs. "No thank you," I said, horrified for the poor turtles, which moved awkwardly on the hard surface.

"Then I shall," said the general, and he marched toward the largest one and hopped in the air, crashing his feet onto the soft-shelled back of the poor turtle, which visibly flattened further and opened its beak with a silent scream.

"Please stop!" I couldn't help but say, and Mamur laughed and stepped off. The show now over, the men turned off the pump and started sweeping water back into the trough. I exhaled and reminded myself that this evening was an investment in this relationship. Hopefully, spending time with this jovial and at the very least marginally corrupt individual would aid me in future efforts to help American citizens nabbed by his organization. In any event, I was a captive audience, so I suggested we go inside for a drink before dinner. I could use one at this point.

Inside, we found seats on oversize couches in a living room with ultramodern decor. Mamur disappeared for a moment and returned with a massive bottle of Johnnie Walker Black Label. A magnum, they call it. "We shall slay Osama!" he proclaimed, apparently likening the oversize liquor bottle to a great American enemy. General Mamur placed the large bottle into a swiveling bottle holder prominently located in the center of his coffee table. Clearly it came as a set. I think I once saw something like it in an airport duty-free shop in Dubai. Mamur tipped the bottle over in dramatic gestures, filling the cocktail glasses far too generously. He handed a glass to each of my colleagues and then turned his head to me. He paused, stood upright again, and raised his hand with a pointed finger in the air. "WAIT!" Then he disappeared back to the kitchen area and emerged with a box of white wine. He grabbed a small stool and set it next to me, then placed the box of white wine on the stool with flour-ish—my dedicated ladies' beverage, I guess. "For the general!" He spat it out with punctuation as he saluted me. I hesitated a moment before taking a glass from the coffee table and filling it up. Mamur seemed pleased, though I noted that he poured nothing from either receptacle for himself.

Shortly after we sat down, the governor of Eastern Equatoria showed up. He seemed to be crashing the party unexpectedly, but he was welcomed with open arms. Mamur's wife, much younger, ar-rived as well, lamenting the absence of a social scene in Juba.

Mamur then spent the evening regaling us with stories of war from his brave glory days in the bush. This involved show-and-tell as he pulled up his pant leg and his shirt to show us still-lodged bullets and scars. There was a melancholy in his voice as we shifted the conversation back to the present. He said the right things, about the focus on training and professionalizing the forces, the need to respect civilians and the rule of law, but there was a disconnect be-tween the words and his eyes. Now I could see it for myself. This was a war hero sidelined. He had respect but no more influence, and he knew it, and it made him sad. He was an Equatorian, after all.

Dinner was abundant and delicious, looking more like a feast than a casual meal. Mamur mocked me throughout for eating "like a lit-tle bird," as many South Sudanese often did. Several African friends had long teased me for this style of eating, saying, "You Americans eat like goats, grazing all day. We eat like lions." The night was late, past curfew by the time we finished dinner. We had suggested a few times that we needed to leave. We were getting messages from Bob, our security chief, who was not keen for us to travel back past the heavily guarded Blue House after dark. But Mamur protested, each time presenting some new course long after we thought the feeding was through. When we finally extricated ourselves, he sent us back escorted by a Toyota truck with government plates, a half-dozen men piled into the back, mostly not in uniform, all casually carrying AK-47s. We followed the speeding truck in the dark, down unlit streets, past the ominous Blue House, cruising through checkpoints as the guards waved to their fellow armed countrymen. I wasn't sure if the escort enhanced our security or our risk, but we made it home without incident.

8

The Business of Diplomacy

ON WEDNESDAY MORNINGS IN THE US EMBASSY IN NAIROBI, the Kenya country team gathers in a conference room on the second floor of the chancery building for a quick weekly roundup of the embassy's activities. Representatives of all thirty-one US government agencies present in the country take a seat, along with the embassy's management officer and the ambassador's staff. In 2016 and 2017, I was a political officer with the US Mission to Somalia, but since Mission Somalia was housed inside Embassy Nairobi at the time, we had a seat at the table, and sometimes I filled it.

Having spent most of my time in the Foreign Service serving in smaller, "boutique" missions like South Sudan and Somalia, I didn't have a full appreciation of the scope and reach of US activities overseas until I moved into Embassy Nairobi. As our biggest embassy in Africa, Embassy Nairobi provided a more accurate reflection of the interplay of different stakeholders in our foreign affairs. And there were a lot of stakeholders. The country team meetings laid it out visually.

Most of the attendees were regulars. Irregulars, like myself, had to take subtle cues from those in the know to avoid looking foolish, speaking too long, or otherwise causing a delay. The unofficial seat assignments were sacrosanct, and violating them was the quickest path to pissing off the regulars. Don't expect anyone to guide you. Your test as someone who doesn't belong at the table is to figure out where you do belong. And do not, under any circumstances, show up after the ambassador.

The Mission Somalia representative was an unimportant place-holder. We interacted little with Embassy Nairobi on substance and primarily attended to make sure we were aware of any upcoming administrative actions that might affect us too. Otherwise, I paid attention simply out of curiosity.

What intrigued me most was how many different US government agencies were engaged in our commercial partnership with the country, and how varied those engagements were. The economic counselor, the commercial attaché, the agricultural attaché, USAID's economic growth and trade representative. In Kenya, these economic players were always busy with projects, trade delegations, visiting officials, or visiting businesses. Much of the work focused on increasing trade, in particular US exports, which worldwide make up about 13 percent of our country's gross domestic product and support millions of jobs.* About twenty government agencies play some role in supporting our exports overseas, involved in everything from providing information and counseling to US businesses, facilitating exports, funding studies, and financing and insuring trade, to advocating with foreign governments and negotiating and enforcing trade agreements.**

In 2017, the United States was the third-largest destination for Kenya's exports and the seventh-largest source of Kenyan imports.

---

* Trade Promotion Coordinating Committee, *Helping U.S. Businesses Increase Global Sales to Support Local Jobs: National Export Strategy 2016* (Washington, DC: National Export Initiative, 2016), www.trade.gov/publications /abstracts/national-export-strategy-2016.asp.

** Shayerah Ilias, Charles E. Hanrahan, and M. Angeles Villarreal, *U.S. Government Agencies Involved in Export Promotion: Overview and Issues for Congress* (Washington, DC: Congressional Research Service Report, 2013), https://fas.org/sgp/crs/misc/R41495.pdf.

We exported $454 million in American goods to the country, including aircraft, machinery, plastics, wheat, and other agricultural goods. US exports of agricultural products to Kenya totaled $74 million in 2017. The Department of Commerce estimates that these exports support five thousand jobs back home. We imported $572 million that same year.*

Kenya isn't a particularly unique or important economic partner to the United States, so try to imagine the level of engagement with a country that actually is. Nevertheless, the combination of our efforts in dozens of less important countries has an important cumulative impact on our economic health back home, and none of this happens on its own. It's the result of extensive work by many agencies and offices of the US government over the long term. All our partnerships take work and commitment to be productive, and their combined effect makes for a better US economy. Like Coca-Cola or McDonald's, America has a strong brand, but we still have to invest everywhere in building our market share. I was only starting to understand this when I got to Kenya in 2016. Had I understood the endgame better when I was in Juba, our economic focus might have been less surprising, at least.

In 2013, the special envoy's office and Embassy Juba's economic team were in the early stages of trying to normalize our economic relationship with South Sudan, mostly laying the groundwork for future trading potential. This involved, in part, trying to convince potential investors that Juba was normal (at least, normal enough). At that time, it was very hard to imagine a healthy trading relationship with South Sudan, such as what we had with Kenya, but the new country was open for business, and the US government wanted US businesses in on the ground floor. Our economic policy team declared "Forge ahead," as though peace was naturally and inevitably followed by an investor conference.

---

* "U.S. Relations with Kenya: Bilateral Relations Fact Sheet," Bureau of African Affairs, US State Department, September 4, 2018, www.state.gov/r/pa/ei/bgn/2962.htm.

Peace *is* typically followed by gamblers, though, and our economic team seemed to be angling for an outcome that gave risk-tolerant US businesses a leg up on the competition in exploiting emerging opportunities while facilitating the inflow of much-needed foreign currency to the struggling new nation. Where the economic officers saw opportunity, I saw a cascade of risks—risks to US citizen investors and the risk that we would multiply opportunities for graft and oppression.

But risky business is as American as apple pie and double standards. Capitalism is deep within our core. Our economic team in Juba was following a time-tested tradition of American diplomacy. Commercial interests and the prospects thereof have long driven foreign policy decisions. In the Barbary Wars of the early 1800s, one of our earliest overseas interventions, the US government sent the navy and then the Marines to North Africa to end pirate attacks on American merchant vessels. A naval expedition in 1853 to isolated Japan served the explicit purpose of opening up a foreign market to US business by force. The interests of American sugar-plantation owners, who wanted to avoid potential tariffs on imports to the United States, largely drove our annexation of Hawaii in 1898, and our actions across Latin America throughout the twentieth century were in defense of big fruit. Who knew there was a time when America's fruit companies could have taught the oil companies a thing or two about destructive capitalism and dirty wars?

The list goes on. Our "colonial" influence, such as it was, was always more economic than governmental, and our influence across the globe simply a modern Manifest Destiny. Let the sun never set on our multinational corporations.

With all our nasty human-rights-violating bedfellows during the decades of the Cold War, our actions make far more sense if you consider they were in the name of liberating markets, rather than people, from communism. At a basic—somewhat oversimplified—level, it's about creating business opportunities for American companies and promoting greater American prosperity. Our trademark optimism dictates that where there is opportunity, we will thrive. I honestly know of no particular company or companies whose interests were driving our commercial engagement in Juba. Our enthusiasm to encourage business there seemed ingrained.

Unrestrained capitalism, however, has long been one of the biggest challenges to our national interest in human rights. When human rights and capitalism come head-to-head in our foreign affairs, commercial interests typically prevail. This tension was visible in our South Sudan policy at the ground level, as we weighed our messaging on dangers in the country and human rights violations against our interest in progress on the economic front.

The answer, it seems, is to look to where economic interests and human rights intersect. Our economic and human rights officers could work in tandem in these areas rather than competing for primacy. In South Sudan, this could have involved offering to cosponsor an investment conference with the government in Juba in return for concrete progress on problems in the justice system (say, improving compliance with constitutional provisions on rights of the accused) or corruption (such as giving the auditor-general prosecutorial authority).

At the international level, better labor and environmental standards offer a broad opportunity for collaboration across economic and human rights interests. If businesses in other countries (including US multinationals operating overseas) must all comply with minimal standards in order to access US markets on equal terms, treating workers and the environment like expendable resources no longer gives a company a financial advantage in trade.

The Obama administration embraced this to an extent, realizing in the wake of the 2007 financial crisis that better labor and environmental standards worldwide would make it easier for America's workers to compete. In 2010, the administration brought the first-ever case under a trade agreement to enforce labor standards and workers' rights, in an effort to walk the walk. Without enforcement, labor-standards provisions were meaningless, after all. The United States challenged the Guatemalan government for failing to enforce the labor standards under the Central American-Dominican Republic

Free Trade Agreement. In 2017, however, the arbitration panel that heard the case found in favor of Guatemala, concluding that its failure to enforce its own labor laws was not "a sustained or recurring course of action or inaction" that was also "in a manner affecting trade."* Clearly, international enforcement has a long way to go.

But when it comes to the alliance of human rights and economic interests, we're now speeding in the wrong direction. The Trump administration has not only abandoned efforts to improve standards abroad but is enthusiastically rolling back all manner of such regulations and enforcement at home.

Corporate interests have won over the White House entirely. More than half of the twenty-one members of Trump's original cabinet were corporate executives, many of whom proudly had zero government experience. The very people who had been lobbying the government to gut regulations or finding creative ways to avoid them became the ones in charge of the agencies tasked with keeping their industries in check.

For now, complementary efforts by economic officers and human rights officers seem unlikely. For the many civilians deployed all around the globe from our wide-ranging government agencies involved in economic policy, corporate promotion and unfettered pursuit of American economic primacy will likely become dominant. What exactly that means on the front lines of diplomacy in an "America First" environment remains unclear.

Unfortunately, it will take many years, even decades, before Americans fully see and suffer the effects of Trump's retreat from global standards, both overseas and at home. Hopefully we will have an opportunity to start the turnaround sooner rather than later. In the meantime, I expect our economic officers and embassy country teams the world over will learn to double down on the no-holds-barred capitalism side of the diplomacy business. A world open for business indeed.

---

* "Trade Dispute Panel Issues Ruling in US-Guatemala Labour Law Case," International Centre for Trade and Sustainable Development, July 6, 2017, www.ictsd.org/bridges-news/bridges/news/trade-dispute-panel-issues-ruling -in-us-guatemala-labour-law-case.

9

The End of the Beginning

November–December 2013

"AFTER THE ARABS LEFT, I HAD TO LOOK FOR AN ENEMY. WE always need an enemy because that is our history, so we look for new enemies. That is what is dividing us. A tradition of revenge. We need to get over it." These were the only words I wrote down during a small human rights lawyers' conference I attended in Juba. They came from Minister of Interior Aleu Ayienyi Aleu, who opened the event. *Unsettling words from a close Kiir ally*, I thought, though it was unclear if his warning was to those making an enemy of Kiir or to Kiir for making an enemy of everyone else. Either way, it was prescient. The hunt for enemies was on. Clearly, no one was getting "over it."

Signs increasingly demonstrated that perhaps South Sudan's previously celebrated international partners—the United Nations, the United States, European countries—were fair game for the new enemies list. It seemed inconceivable. South Sudan, as much as any country on earth, had Western countries and international institutions to thank for its place in the world. Generous support from South Sudan's partners had kept it afloat. But that was no longer a narrative the South Sudanese government was embracing. Slowly, the story had shifted. International partners were meddling, colonial, threatening South Sudan's sovereignty. This tone came in private conversations more than public statements at this stage, but the sense that the UN and the West could no longer really be considered friends to South Sudan was starting to trickle down through the ranks. International partners were surprised, but we shouldn't have been—rallying your people against foreign threats is a tried-and-true tactic for flailing leaders.

EMILY, A COLLEAGUE from the human rights bureau in Washington, was visiting Juba for a few days, so we scheduled a series of meetings to give her a fuller assessment of the human rights situation at the time. First on the list was Diane, a senior officer for the UN Mission to South Sudan (UNMISS) and a mentor of mine. Diane didn't specifically work human rights issues, but her knowledge of the context was unparalleled, and I thought Emily ought to hear her assessment of the increasingly bad behavior of the South Sudanese government, which many UN and other diplomatic leaders seemed to be glossing over.

In a country where four to five years makes you an old hand, Diane had over a decade. She had been in South Sudan since long before South Sudan existed. When she joined, the UN mission's acronym ended in only one "S." Her Rolodex was populated with satellite phone numbers for war lords and rebels, all of whom she knew well. She was skeptical of those who looked for progress here in a matter of months. For this reason, she was honestly and sensibly skeptical about the government and its current relationship with its international partners. We met her at a rickety table in a quiet gazebo at "UN House," a sprawling compound that was relatively empty with a lot of green space and newer than the UNMISS main compound by the airport. It felt isolated on this side of town, and it was less popular with most UNMISS staff than the other location, though some appreciated the ability to speak more frankly here, given the privacy.

We were discussing SPLA impunity generally when Diane mentioned a recent attack on a UN officer in Juba, assuming we'd already heard. "It was only a matter of time, really," she said, upset but not particularly surprised. Emily and I looked at each other, wondering how we'd missed this news. "When did this happen?" I asked. Diane raised an eyebrow and pursed her lips. "Days ago." Then she walked us through it.

"A UN human resources officer, she's a neighbor of mine on the compound, midforties maybe. She was driving a UN vehicle, clearly marked and all, and turns onto Airport Road when she's rear-ended by an SPLA vehicle. Presidential Guard I think. The accident was minor, but the soldiers lost it. They pull her from the car and beat her, bash her head into the hood. Then they just leave her by the side of the road." This incident occurred in broad daylight only a few hundred meters from the UN gate.

Diane told us the victim was quickly evacuated from the country and undergoing treatment. I was shocked that I hadn't heard of this already, that it hadn't been reported in the news and publicly condemned.

Through its international military education and training program, the US military had trained dozens of SPLA officers in recent years, in everything from English language to personnel management, human rights to vehicle maintenance, command structures, and logistics. US contractors were restructuring the administrative and financial system at SPLA headquarters, and US military doctors were working alongside SPLA physicians at the army hospital in town. Despite all our efforts and dollars spent, clearly little had changed. The SPLA was a bush army, not a professional one. It would never be a national army with a national identity. As with most hopeless organizations, the army boasted a handful of solid, well-meaning individuals, the kind my military colleagues would cling to with hope, but these few couldn't alter the SPLA's fundamental nature, particularly in the absence of any interest at the highest levels to do so. The sensible ones never seemed to wield command, and growing swaths of ground troops—little more than kids in uniform—exhibited an arrogance and aggression that was chilling.

On the ride back across town, Emily and I were both in disbelief. "This seems like a pretty big deal. Shouldn't we say something?" I asked her. She understood the State Department and Washington far better than I did.

"Damn right we should, and why hasn't the UN?" Emily didn't hide her disbelief. It was a refreshing dose of emotion, which I often found lacking in my overly diplomatic colleagues at the embassy. "Maybe New York doesn't know," she surmised, wondering if the US Mission at the UN headquarters might still be unaware of what occurred.

Back in the office, I relayed the incident to James, and he, too, thought we should run it up to the chain. Maybe UN leadership had relayed this to Ambassador Page directly.

I followed James around the corner to her office. We didn't often take issues to Ambassador Page in person outside a scheduled meeting, but this incident seemed sufficiently important to bypass protocols. After all, if the SPLA could attack UN personnel in broad daylight just down the road, what did that mean for our own safety?

It wasn't clear if Ambassador Page was already aware, but she seemed less alarmed than we were. Since no Americans were involved, she said it would be up to the UN to decide how to respond. I'd later learn that Ambassador Page had had words with Hilde Johnson, the UN chief in South Sudan, about the incident directly, insisting Johnson couldn't just let it go. Johnson had replied dismissively, suggesting that the victim had been a problem at the mission anyway.

Maybe that's just how these things are addressed? I was shocked. But I was a newcomer to the multilateral world of the UN. Emily was skeptical, though, and I was quickly learning that she was my Washington-based alter ego. Before this trip, we were mere acquaintances, but after a few days of pounding the pavement together during her short sojourn to Juba, I knew this was someone whose values and priorities matched mine and whose instincts I could trust. She was wiser and more experienced than I was, but that experience hadn't tempered her passion for what was right. Moving forward, whenever colleagues in Juba minimized or explained away my concerns, an email or phone call to Emily became my gut check, my therapy, my encouragement to keep pushing back.

Emily sent an email to our UN mission in New York to find out what our colleagues there knew, if anything. They were unaware and shocked. The assault had happened days ago. Why weren't they told?

A UN representative in Juba would later tell James that per protocols, UNMISS sent a report to UN headquarters the same day and delivered a note verbale—an official diplomatic correspondence—to South Sudan's Ministry of Foreign Affairs two days later. They checked the boxes, she insisted. James had been concerned, but this appeared to answer his questions. All protocols were observed.

But most diplomats and humanitarians were disturbed by the incident, and even more so by the failure of the UN mission to publicly condemn it. Hilde Johnson was the UN special representative of the secretary-general, or SRSG in short. A longtime Norwegian politician, Johnson had served as a parliamentarian and then as minister of international development prior to taking up this UN posting. As minister, she was deeply engaged in the Sudan peace process, and that past seemed to have an outsize influence on how she managed the present. She believed the creation myth fully—she helped write it, after all. Johnson was a controversial figure in Juba, perhaps more so within her mission than anywhere else. While respected for her many years of dedication, both sides in the political battle underway viewed her as biased toward the other.

I asked several UN counterparts why reports of the attack on the UN officer were not more public, and everyone attributed it to Johnson's desire to limit negative press and avoid inviting more scrutiny or criticism of the government. Many were concerned that the failure to publicly address it could open up UN personnel to more abuse.

MEANWHILE, PRESIDENT KIIR continued to identify new enemies elsewhere and to shore up his defenses against them. His paranoia and distrust of those around him continued to grow; only his own Dinka kinsmen were exempt. His worries manifested in poor health, according to local press reports, though Kiir was rumored to be a heavy drinker, so that didn't help. If we had high-level visitors in town or the ambassador needed to deliver a message, we always aimed for meetings as early in the day as possible. Increasingly, anything after morning hours was likely to be canceled or, at best, muddled.

Public discontent with the government was increasing. South Sudan's people had been patient, but they were less forgiving than the country's international partners. The citizens were done accepting promises and now demanded results. Enthusiasm over independence had given way to disappointment that the government had failed to provide any services or benefits to the public, despite the ample availability of international aid. I asked our embassy drivers what the tone was in their neighborhoods. No one felt optimistic. When people saw their political leaders, their police, their army, they didn't see allies, protectors, or champions. They saw greed, lies, and danger.

Publicly, and often in reports to our capitals, South Sudan's friends continued to take pains to reinforce a hopeful fallacy of progress and a government trying to do the right thing. I witnessed this blind willingness to forgive even in our approach to the annual human rights report, the congressionally mandated document compiled in every country around the world specifically to highlight issues that each government, friendly or otherwise, needed to address. When the ambassador returned the draft to me with her handwritten edits, the changes she'd made seemed designed to soften indications of government culpability wherever possible.

This was an opportunity to sound the alarm. I knew Ambassador Page was increasingly worried about these trends too. She frequently raised concern about human rights abuses and corruption in meetings with officials at every level, so I was confused why she would pull our punches now.

After flipping through the first twenty pages of the draft and picking up the pattern, I walked to James's office next door and perched on the empty desk next to his. "I got the HRR edits back from the Ambo finally. Got a minute?"

I knew what it looked like to me, but I'd need his support if I was going to push back. I started with an easy one. "So she deleted 'clearly marked' describing the UN helicopter the SPLA shot down last year, James. That's the same language we used in last year's report, and she cleared it then. And it *was* clearly marked. I don't understand."

James reasoned with me calmly. He knew me well enough by then to know where this was going. I wondered if he and the ambassador had already spoken about the tenor of the report, or if he was simply channeling his inner Susan Page.

He said that the ambassador believed that the government wouldn't listen to us about anything if we beat them up about everything. Ever the consummate diplomat, James said we had to be balanced and pick our battles if we wanted to be effective. *James is the experienced diplomat. Should I be following his lead?* In this case, it just didn't sit right with me.

"The language on Jonglei is still really strong," James added.

"But the way she's tweaked the language keeps highlighting the aggression of the Murle rebels and downplaying the security force's role." I didn't see the utility in helping to smooth over the government's reputation.

He reminded me that there were two sides of the conflict. A violent insurgency was underway, after all.

"But we partner with the government. We provide them massive political and financial support. That's where our influence is. Aren't we supposed to hold them to the higher standard?"

James agreed with me in concept, but, for the public report, he seemed more concerned with the delivery of the message. He warned that if the government dismissed us as biased against them, they wouldn't be receptive to what we had to say. I knew this was the approach many in the UN's leadership took as well.

But, to me, it seemed clear the government hadn't been receptive to our messages for quite some time already. The friendly approach wasn't working. Ambassador Page and senior State Department and White House officials had strongly urged Kiir not to sack Vice President Machar earlier in the year, and those warnings fell on deaf ears. In 2012, they begged him not to shut down oil production due to a spat with Khartoum. He did. That same year, President Obama warned Kiir directly in a phone call not to send forces across the disputed border with Sudan. Kiir did it anyway, seizing oil fields and launching six months of armed conflict with his neighbor to the north.* No US advice or warnings had been heeded. It was unclear to me what influence we were trying to preserve. I left the conversation frustrated with the stubbornness of our supportive position and resigned that the report must make its way up the chain with the ambassador's moderating imprint.

MEANWHILE, KIIR APPEARED focused on nothing beyond his own power and survival as he expanded his meddling past politics and into the military. His growing paranoia led him to develop a private militia based at his personal farm in Luri, about twelve miles from Juba. This force, which Kiir insisted would be part of the Presidential Guard Tiger Division, was rumored to number in the thousands. This caused alarm within SPLA leadership, but all objections were ignored. Made up solely of Dinka from his home region, the "Luri Boys" began as Kiir's personal bodyguards but would become his war machine.

The political battle heated up even more later in the month. After returning from a trip to South Africa for medical appointments, Kiir announced that he was dissolving key leadership committees of the SPLM—a step up in his continued efforts to sideline political rivals. Shortly thereafter, Kiir backtracked, denying he even made the statement in the first place and suggesting that it was some kind of misunderstanding. He seemed to be testing the waters, seeing just how far he could push. No one called him on his lies.

---

* This incident was reported widely in the press. See Warren Strobel and Louis Charbonneau, "U.S. Was Slow to Lose Patience as South Sudan Unraveled," Reuters, January 14, 2014, www.reuters.com/article/us-usa-southsudan-id USBREA0D08R20140114, and Alan Boswell, "The Failed State Lobby," *Foreign Policy*, July 9, 2012, https://foreignpolicy.com/2012/07/09/the-failed-state -lobby/.

Our longing to see South Sudan through rose-colored glasses affected not only what we said publicly, but also what we told ourselves. James was still trying to get the ambassador's clearance for his "South Sudan at Two" cable. "Cable" was State Department terminology for an official report from a post overseas back to Washington, and it was common to draw up a lengthier analytical piece to comment on the direction and accomplishments of new governments at regular intervals in their administrations. In South Sudan's case, our assessment was of a new country.

James drafted his assessment as a warning, outlining the many challenges South Sudan still faced and cautiously recommending a course correction in our approach to Kiir's government before it was too late. James understood why the US government was taking a more cautious line publicly, but internally he saw the need for a frank assessment. The cable attributed challenges to a lack of resources, limited capacity, and the expected growing pains of a new state. It confirmed that the political space had narrowed since independence, and that the government was cracking down on free press and political opposition. It even admitted that diplomatic efforts to counter these trends had had little success, and it clearly called out the SPLA's human rights abuses in Jonglei. The ambassador's edits retained the enumeration of challenges yet shifted the tone to one of optimism: given how far the country had come in only two years, we should expect greater challenges ahead but remain steadfast in our commitment to the government (apparently regardless of its lack of commitment to its own people).

While the embassy's cable informed Washington of the warning signs, our reassurance that the overall picture in South Sudan was hopeful muddied the waters—to the extent anyone in Washington was concerned with our views at all. In fact, the White House's determined optimism seemed to exceed even the embassy's. Washington's engagement was shaped by then–national security advisor Susan Rice. Although she was a longtime champion of South Sudan, Rice had a mixed record on the continent and with many critics, particularly within the human rights community.

Rice's position on South Sudan would follow a well-established pattern. Since the 1990s, when Rice served in the National Security Council and then as assistant secretary of state for African affairs under President Bill Clinton, she had a tendency to cooperate with and support strongmen, long after their behaviors suggested we should do otherwise. Once she had chosen someone to support, her loyalty became unshakable. This was particularly evident with the war in eastern Congo, following the Rwandan genocide. Rwandan president Paul Kagame and Ugandan president Yoweri Museveni were both deeply engaged in destabilizing military action that had fueled a violent war in neighboring Congo for many years. Their actions, and accompanying human rights violations, were the subject of intense international scrutiny, but Rice's strategy was to look the other way and help them avoid overt criticism.[*]

In 2012, as US ambassador to the UN, Rice went further, actively blocking any mention of the neighboring countries' continued meddling in the ongoing war, and then delaying the release of a UN group of experts' report confirming that Rwanda was supporting the M23 rebel group. This would not be the last time Rice's position directly contradicted that of other State Department leadership or of our allies. It also wouldn't be the last time she actively worked to protect and shield from criticism the continent's bad actors while blithely conceding only to generic statements against violence.

Rice had also actively opposed the use of the word "genocide" during the Rwanda crisis in 1994, a move she later acknowledged as a mistake, saying that she would come down on the side of "dramatic action" if she ever faced a similar crisis again.[**] Yet she did not do so in the face of widespread violence in Congo, largely perpetrated and facilitated by leaders she continued to champion. In South Sudan,

---

[*] Armin Rosin, "The Controversial Africa Policy of Susan Rice," *Atlantic*, November 29, 2012, www.theatlantic.com/international/archive/2012/11/the -controversial-africa-policy-of-susan-rice/265752/.

[**] Elias Groll, "5 Highlights from Susan Rice's Diplomatic Career," *Foreign Policy*, June 5, 2013, https://foreignpolicy.com/2013/06/05/5-highlights-from -susan-rices-diplomatic-career/.

she would have another opportunity to live up to her pledge, and she would fail yet again.

While other key foreign policy advisors in the Obama admin-istration—including Samantha Power, who succeeded Rice at the UN—pushed for greater scrutiny and even sanctions in the face of some of Kiir's bad acts, Rice consistently stood in the way, and her position won the day. The justifications were varied: penalizing our friends could backfire and make it harder for them to succeed, and it won't achieve our aims, anyway. So we stayed on the steady path of support while occasionally warning the Kiir regime: "Don't do that again, or we'll do something, and we mean it."

But we never meant it. And Kiir knew that.

BACK IN NEW York, the UN Security Council didn't seem so for-giving, particularly when it came to attacks on the UN's own staff. This was a topic of much discussion when SRSG Johnson was called to brief the council directly, where she met their concerns with re-assurances; things were moving in the right direction, she asserted. She blamed the attack—and others like it on UN property and personnel—on the SPLA's lack of training and the enduring legacy of violence left over from the civil war. Declining the council's offer to take direct action to raise the profile of these incidents, Johnson insisted that the South Sudanese government only needed more time to respond and it would do the right thing.

At the embassy, we got the transcript by email from colleagues in New York, but I was curious to hear the reaction to Johnson's briefing from UN staff in Juba, so I headed over to the UNMISS tukul in the Tomping neighborhood near the airport. A peacekeeper hangout, the UNMISS tukul was populated at any time of day with an array of men in military attire. On Thursday nights, it became a raucous party complete with DJ. It was a good place to collect information on happenings across the country, since UN staff moved in and out of fifty-three bases and satellite locations across South Sudan. It was also the best place to catch the latest gossip from New York. Given the extreme male-to-female ratio, I avoided Thursday nights unless I took my own security colleagues as a buffer, but I found my way there at least once a week simply to listen.

I sat down at a table with a couple of younger UN officers. When I asked about Johnson's briefing in New York, they unleashed a torrent. "In broad daylight, right down the street, and she couldn't care less. She's out there defending them! 'Not to worry, Security Council, it's under control,'" a UN political officer quipped sarcastically. Then her voice dropped. "It's dangerous here. That was the Presidential Guard—Kiir's people. Hilde won't do anything to stop them, and they know it. They can do anything they want to us without consequence. It's terrifying."

Driving back to the embassy, we passed a couple of clusters of uniformed security forces, and I wondered how much Johnson's acquiescence had put us all at risk. UN personnel were being treated as enemies of the state and fair game, and the SPLA's soldiers weren't likely to distinguish one diplomatic plate from another. Juba had started to feel increasingly hostile. It was always dangerous, but somehow we had felt immune. What government would allow attacks on its partners? That would upset relations with its friends. But this was always a false sense of security, since the South Sudanese government simply didn't care, and now we knew it. The feeling that we were all vulnerable now was unnerving. I didn't sleep well that night. I didn't sleep well many nights thereafter.

ON DECEMBER 6, the mounting opposition to Kiir within the government culminated in a press conference led by former vice president Riek Machar, joined by a crowd of influential Garang Boys. We got the report from Chol, who attended in person. Machar's statement couched the political battle underway as a fight for the very legacy of the liberation movement. He claimed "anti-Garang elements" had encircled President Kiir, and that Kiir had abandoned the founding principles of the late SPLA leader. While the SPLM opposition wing didn't openly call for Kiir's ousting, they referenced corruption and human rights abuses, accusing him of dictatorial tendencies that were driving the country into "chaos and disorder." The message to the president was clear: we will not sit here quietly as you wrest all control from the party and the state for yourself.

Shortly following the press conference, Machar arrived at the embassy's residential compound for a previously scheduled meeting with Special Envoy Booth, in town for the investment conference that had concluded the previous day. James was already on his way to the airport for a well-deserved vacation back home for the Christmas holiday, so I got to staff the meeting. As the junior political officer, I usually only assisted the ambassador for meetings with NGOs and religious groups, opportunities for US leadership to hear from regular people. This was an exciting time to be in the room with the big kids, talking politics. Everyone in the country, and a lot of people in Washington, were watching the moves of this man, and I got to hear from him firsthand.

Machar walked into the ambassador's residence with swagger, his trademark gap-tooth grin extending from ear to ear. He was feeling confident that he and his coalition had pulled off their press conference without interference. He believed he now had the upper hand. Special Envoy Booth and Ambassador Page impressed upon Machar the importance of exercising restraint and working to avoid instability or violence. Machar said he was willing to commit to showing and preaching restraint, but he urged us to give Kiir the same message. I scribbled notes furiously, trying to capture every word. Unlike the vast majority of the meetings I attended, Washington was going to care about the report on this one.

Machar's words struck the right tone as he responded to our anxieties, but when I glanced up at him, his face sent a different message. His wasn't a sober face of concern, and it contrasted starkly with Special Envoy Booth's furrowed brow. I realized Machar was just going through the motions with his American friends. His day's work was already done, and it was a win. Not unlike Kiir, Machar seemed more concerned about his chance at power than the plight of his country's citizens.

As the meeting wrapped up, Ambassador Page asked for a few minutes without staff, so I walked out to the veranda and joined Lam Chuol, Machar's close aide. In truth, I hobbled, my right foot strapped securely into a stabilizer boot.

"So, what happened to the foot?" Lam asked casually. I gave him the abbreviated version of how I'd broken my foot two weeks prior at the inaugural US Marine Corps ball in South Sudan, a diplomatic version of prom where we got dolled up the world over to celebrate the Marine Corps' birthday. "Juba isn't conducive to high heels. And I shouldn't drink with Marines," I said with a shrug. It was a sentiment he could appreciate. Lam laughed, revealing deep dimples with his big grin.

My previous interactions with Lam had involved little more than coordinating meetings for our principals, but he was pleasant and easy to talk to. From what I knew of him, he seemed to represent the more hopeful side of South Sudan. His family fled the civil war when he was a boy, and after years in refugee camps in the region, they resettled in the United States in the mid-1990s. Lam became a US citizen only days after the September 11 attacks, finished college, and joined the Marines himself. After serving in Iraq, Lam returned to Nebraska and became active in the South Sudanese community there. Like many refugees, he was drawn back to his native country after the civil war ended, abandoning a comfortable life abroad to help his homeland. But Nebraska seemed to have rubbed off on him; he displayed attributes of a typical midwestern farm boy—good natured, affable, and polite. I found it hard to imagine this genteel individual as a ruthless gatekeeper for one of the most controversial political figures in South Sudan, though I wasn't surprised Machar had chosen him to be his liaison with Western diplomats.

I shifted the conversation from my injury and asked Lam how he thought the press conference went. He, too, expressed optimism, but his was more reserved than that of his boss. Lam's sense was that they were finally making headway in the political battle, but he understood they were fighting uphill. Kiir still held the power, and they didn't know what he might do.

Two days later, the evening news quietly announced that the National Liberation Council—a meeting of SPLM political leaders to be held to adopt several organizational documents, including the party constitution, code of conduct, and manifesto—was postponed yet again, as Kiir had to travel to South Africa for Nelson Mandela's memorial service. *Ironic, using the funeral of the continent's greatest democratic leader as another excuse for sidelining democratic action in your own country,* I thought. This marked at least the fourth time Kiir had bumped this critical political meeting. The repeated delays had been grounds for criticism by many of those hoping to use democratic tools to push back against Kiir's tightening clutch on power.

On Friday the thirteenth, the diplomatic corps exchanged a flurry of emails and phone calls.

"Our contacts at the Secretariat say the NLC is convening tomorrow."

"Tomorrow? Who's going? Are you going? What about invitations?"

"I heard you can use the invitations distributed for last Monday's meeting for tomorrow. They're still valid."

"But the last time, the meeting was canceled late the night before. Is it really going to happen?"

James's absence offered a great opportunity for me to step up into the high-profile political issues of the day—a big moment for a junior diplomat like me. My exhaustion was getting the better of me, though. I was working sixteen-hour days consistently, just trying to keep urgent matters at bay. In recent weeks, my already marginal social life had screeched to a halt, and unable to run or climb with a broken foot, I had no outlet for stress. I was tired—we all were—but I had to believe relief was just around the corner. If we could only get to the quiet of the holiday lull, even those of us not on vacation should have time to recharge. But we weren't there yet, and it was depressing that I couldn't muster any excitement about getting to attend such a critical political event as the National Liberation Council meeting.

"Is it bad that I'm hoping it's postponed again so I can have a little bit of a Saturday for a change?" I asked a colleague.

"Officially, yes! This is a necessary part of the uninterrupted development of democracy in South Sudan. Unofficially, well . . ." He shrugged.

Despite rumors that the NLC meeting would be postponed one more time to provide a final opportunity for dialogue between Kiir and the disgruntled SPLM members led by Machar, the show would go on.

Early Saturday morning, I woke up to a message that embassy leadership had decided not to attend. Security had sent a car ahead early to check out the venue and found it guarded by dozens of armed men and trucks mounted with heavy machine guns—uninviting, to say the least. I took my Saturday of reprieve to catch up on other work as we waited for news and hoped calm would prevail.

Pagan Amum, the ousted SPLM secretary-general who had joined Machar for his prior press conference, was warned by police not to attend, but Machar decided to go anyway to try to keep things civil. He was joined by Madam Rebecca Nyandeng de Mabior, a Dinka and the widow of the late Dr. John Garang, South Sudan's founding father. Madam Rebecca, now a prominent politician in her own right, had joined Machar for his press conference too, and her alliance with him against Kiir was politically powerful.

The European Union sent one representative, who gave a report to the rest of the Western diplomatic corps. President Kiir gave the keynote speech, in which he followed a tribute to the late Nelson Mandela and John Garang with harsh criticism of his challengers. He asserted that his political shake-up in the cabinet earlier in the year was in response to the public's demand to end corruption and mismanagement, and reiterated that as the party chairman, he wouldn't tolerate indiscipline. Kiir then said, in a manner that even hopeful diplomats found unconvincing, that the SPLM was a party of free speech and everyone had the right to compete for any position.

The delegates were meant to review the party documents—the manifesto and constitution—that afternoon. On its face, this seemed a routine activity. But, as both Kiir and his opponents recognized, these were the documents that would shape leadership accession, the concentration of party power, and the opportunity to compete for it. This wasn't just political party leadership. Control over the party meant control over the country, and control over the country meant control over its resources, including oil reserves, which might not be high quality but provided plenty of opportunity for looting. It was not only power up for grabs but money, too.

Kiir's language and demeanor in the morning made clear his position. The opening for political competition, or any challenge to his authority for that matter, was closing rapidly. Skeptical that the chairman would allow a fair debate on these controversial and consequential documents, opposition leaders opted not to give the session legitimacy and walked out. At the conclusion of the second day of the meeting on December 15, those still present passed the documents with no significant changes or discussion. But the SPLM as an organization, and the government it represented, was already broken.

A War Begins

December 15, 2013

IT WAS SUNDAY EVENING, SEVERAL HOURS AFTER THE NLC meeting had concluded, and I was sitting in my metal container home when my embassy-issued Nokia cell vibrated loudly on the scratched-up embassy-issued coffee table. By now, most of the embassy's A team had already left town for the holidays—prime vacation choice being one of the benefits of seniority. The rest of us were left to hold down the fort until the new year. The residential compound was quiet, and I was watching *A Charlie Brown Christmas* on my laptop, trying to muster up some holiday cheer. We'd all been waiting to see what the fallout might be from the tense political weekend, but the night had been quiet so far.

I answered my cell, and it was Gordon from Oxfam, not someone I expected to hear from at this hour. Though average height for a South Sudanese man, Gordon dwarfed me significantly, but his studious and soft-spoken nature made him less physically intimidating than some of his compatriots. He'd been reserved but thoughtful when we'd previously discussed humanitarian concerns; now he sounded urgent and alarmed. "When can we meet? Tensions are rising."

He, too, was worried about the repercussions of the political drama of the weekend. My Monday was packed with internal team meetings and consular appointments with American citizens. I asked Gordon if Tuesday would work. "That will be too late." We agreed to meet for an early breakfast the next morning at the Rainbow Hotel, a small guesthouse one block north of the embassy. I thought little of it.

An hour later, Gordon called again. Fighting had broken out near Juba University, he said, just over a mile from our compound. He expected it to spread. From that moment on, the calls rolled in.

POP POP POP! Gunfire reverberated through the phone, louder than what I could hear in the distance outside. I was talking to Lora, whom I'd met when her boyfriend, an American dual national, had been arrested a few months earlier. Her apartment was near the fighting, and rounds hit the walls of her building as we spoke. "Get low! Stay away from the windows!" I shouted into the phone. I'm the US Embassy's consular officer, and in South Sudan people expected that to mean something. In reality, I was helpless to do anything except advise friends and contacts to take cover. I followed my own advice and turned off the lights in my flimsy prefabricated shipping container inside the relative safety of our residential compound.

I texted Ambassador Page. Surely she was aware of the situation in town, but most of our compound still looked dark, everyone asleep. I heard nothing back.

Gordon called again at half past midnight. "You must speak with Riek." While I'd met Machar, it was only in my capacity as notetaker for Ambassador Page. Speaking with him now was quite above my pay grade.

I texted Ambassador Page again. "Fighting in town. RM needs to speak with you urgently." No response.

Gordon called back at 1:52 a.m., clearly frustrated. "Why haven't you called him? He is waiting for your call." Why didn't Machar simply call Ambassador Page himself? Perhaps he thought our phone lines were less likely to be compromised. "I've asked the ambassador to call him. He should hear from her soon," I told Gordon. What I couldn't explain to him was that as a junior officer, I was literally at the bottom of our small mission's short food chain. There were protocols to observe. It was two in the morning. My boss was on vacation. Texting the ambassador directly in the middle of the night already felt out of line.

My phone rang again ten minutes later, and this time I heard a woman's voice on the line. She spoke slowly and deliberately, with long pauses, as though the weight of her voice could temper the clock and buy more time before the country simply unraveled.

"Elizabeth, this is Angelina. I have Dr. Riek on the line for you." Protocols were apparently out the window at this point.

"Elizabeth." Before I could even muster a response, Machar's wife had handed the phone to him. He sounded calm, though his voice was less confident than usual. "I need to reach Ambassador Susan." I cut him off, "We'll call you right back."

I strapped the stabilizing boot onto my broken foot, grabbed a flashlight, notebook, and pen and limped down a few stairs to the sidewalk, then hobbled through the dark to the ambassador's residence. As I made my way toward the center of our compound, Juba had gone quiet but for sporadic gunfire in the distance and the hum of our generator off in a corner. The night seemed darker than usual somehow. With a power grid that reached less than 1 percent of the population, South Sudan could be the darkest country in the world. It felt like that tonight.

When I reached the ambassador's house, I knocked quietly. With two layers of hierarchy between us, I hadn't had much direct interaction with her professionally; at most we had shared a few minutes in her vehicle on the way to and from the occasional meeting when I accompanied her to take notes. Standing on the veranda, I briefly wondered if I should have changed into something more professional. I had only a moment to second-guess myself before she opened the door.

"Machar wants to speak with you," I said quietly, trying to be as unobtrusive as someone could be when standing at your door with bad news in the middle of the night.

Ambassador Page was on another call, Blackberry to her ear. She nodded me inside, so I walked past her, took a seat at the formal dining-room table—part of the State Department's standard-issue Drexel Heritage Queen Anne collection—and exhaled. A matching china cabinet stood on the other side of the room. In contrast to the formality of the furniture were piles of paper, books, a purse—things anyone would drop on a table when coming through the door. This was the first time I thought of the place as the ambassador's private home, though it wouldn't be for much longer. During that night, her residence would transform into mission control for all embassy operations.

I connected the ambassador with Riek at about 2:45 a.m. Over the next half hour or so, most of the core embassy personnel responsible for managing a crisis—the emergency action committee—gathered around the ambassador's dining-room table to compare what we'd heard and plan our next steps in the uncertainty of an unfolding crisis. At this stage, information was still sketchy, trickling in in dribs and drabs. We were in the dark, struggling to separate truth from rumor. The ambassador and Bob, our security chief, agreed to keep the embassy closed and the residence on lockdown until 10 a.m., by which point we hoped to have more information. With little else we could do at that moment, someone mentioned everyone ought to get some sleep before morning, so we adjourned and agreed to meet up again at 7 a.m.

The city was dark as I limped back to my container. I had one more task before I could lie down. Since we'd changed our security protocols, we owed it to the American people in the area to let them know. The "no double standard" rule required it. I called the Operations Center, or "Ops," the State Department's twenty-four-hour communications and crisis-management center back in Washington. The jingle was burned into my memory during Foreign Service orientation three years back: "When a crisis hits, and you don't know what to do, call 647-1512." I was our consular officer, and we needed Washington's clearance to send a security message to American citizens here.

"State Ops, this is Cynthia." "Hi, Cynthia. This is Lizzy from Juba. I need to clear a security message." Within minutes, at approximately 5 a.m., I sent out a hastily drafted and cleared security message by email to registered American citizens in South Sudan.

The U.S. Embassy has received reports from multiple reliable sources of ongoing security incidents and sporadic gunfire in multiple locations across Juba beginning at approximately 10:30 p.m. on December 15 and continuing until approximately 2:30 a.m. on December 16. The U.S. Embassy has not been able to confirm that gunfire and insecurity have fully ceased. Pending further clarity on the security situation, there will be no movement of Embassy personnel prior to 10:00 a.m. on December 16. The Embassy recommends that all U.S. citizens exercise extra caution at all times. The U.S. Embassy will continue to closely monitor the security environment in South Sudan, with particular attention to Juba city and its immediate surroundings, and will advise U.S. citizens further if the security situation changes.

We also posted it to Facebook and Twitter. It was the best we could do at the moment.

I laid down for about forty minutes, my body tired, but my mind racing. *How many Americans are in Juba? Who are the targets of the fighting? How long will this crisis last?*

I was already back at the computer at 6:30 a.m., coffee in hand in my small metal living room, when gunfire and heavy artillery picked up again in the distance. Our contacts reported explosions in different parts of town. If some residents of the city had slept through the skirmishes last night, they were certainly awake now. The duty phone, our after-hours emergency line for American citizens, was getting steady traffic. News of fighting in Juba was likely to make it back home to the States at some point. I didn't want my friends and family to worry, but there was no time for long calls. As a preemptive measure, I posted on Facebook that I was safe and in a secure compound. It would have to do for now.

Our duty phone system—standard in most embassies—was fairly new and simple, consisting of a separate emergency cell phone with a dedicated number that American citizens could call after-hours for emergencies. We required everyone in our small embassy community to take turns manning the phone on nights and weekends. My predecessor, Oliver, had set up and opened our consular services the prior year—a remarkable feat achieved with few resources—but our system was still bare-bones. Only after two months in my post did I realize that the emergency line listed on the embassy's website was incorrect and was actually the cell number for our South Sudanese administrative assistant. I only checked after finding it odd how quiet the duty phone was. No one on duty seemed to be getting any calls. "Have you been getting random calls from Americans at night?" I'd asked our assistant, Jadri, sometime in September. "Yes! All the time, I do not know who these people are. I just tell them the embassy is closed so call when we are open." Who knew how many emergency situations Jadri had simply dismissed.

This weekend, Jason, a USAID colleague with the Office of Foreign Disaster Assistance, had drawn the short stick. While I managed a steady stream of both political and consular calls to my personal cell phone and the consular office cell (Juba had no functional landlines), Jason maintained the duty phone logbook.

6:40am—Alex (Amcit) called saying he is hearing gun shots in his neighborhood (Hai Malakal). He was told to stay indoors.

7:30am—Mohamed (Amcit) called asking about the gun fire that has been going on all around his neighborhood (Hai Sora, near Juba University). Told to stay indoors.

7:32am—Thomas (Amcit) called reporting gun fire. He is living at Eastern Pearl Hotel and was told to stay indoors.

And so on.

I hobbled over to the ambassador's residence for the next meeting at 7 a.m. with my travel mug in hand, taking care this time in the light of day not to trample the small hopeful plot of newly planted grass alongside it. It was the hot season in Juba and dry as a bone. The compound had a scattering of dust-covered trees and a few sparse flower beds along the sidewalks, but otherwise little in the way of greenery. Most of the landscape inside our walls was hard-packed dirt.

As we filed in, creatures of habit, everyone settled into the same seats we had occupied a few hours before, and a few new additions from the security team filled those that were left. Ambassador Page sat at the head of the table opposite the front door, with her deputy, Mike, to her right, and Lori, her office manager, next to him. I sat toward the other end of the table. Across from me were Bob, our ever-calm and deadpan security chief, and both the incoming and outgoing defense attachés. The new guy had arrived only hours before the fighting began and seemed stoked about the timing. The intelligence specialist sat to my right. It was a strategic location for me, since he was always a good source of info.

We all looked haggard but felt less so thanks to adrenaline and lots of coffee. At least none of us were sporting pajamas anymore. Ambassador Page told us that she'd spoken with many high-level officials but had not yet been able to connect with President Kiir. *Well, that's not a good sign.* The United States was Kiir's biggest international defender and supposedly his country's closest partner. If this were a crisis he was trying to contain, one would expect him to reach out immediately, or at the very least take our call.

Ambassador Page had spoken with Machar again and confirmed that he'd left his home but was safe. Otherwise, we hadn't learned much in the past couple of hours. Everyone was restless and distracted. We had no marching orders yet, but staying on top of correspondence and getting ducks in a row was a full-time job for all of us, regardless of our other responsibilities. We adjourned to get back to work, trying to prepare for all possible contingencies.

It wasn't even 8 a.m. when Ajani, our public affairs officer, alerted us to a new, alarming development: the *National Courier*, a widely read local weekly, was reporting that Machar had taken shelter at our embassy. Soon, Twitter was exploding with the rumor. We mobilized to quash it quickly, since it undermined our position of neutrality and raised a real danger of drawing an attack on our compound. We comforted ourselves with the fact that the UN was publicly being accused of the same, but our team remained wary; command and control were not the hallmarks of the SPLA. I'd spent months documenting violent human rights abuses by South Sudan's ragtag military. I wasn't interested in being my own firsthand account.

I was sitting at the desk in my container fielding calls and emails, trying to get a better sense of how many Americans might need assistance if the security situation didn't stabilize, when one of my neighbors poked his head in the doorway. "You gotta see this," he said, and ran back out.

Stabilizer boot on, I limped behind him, following him around the corner and up the stairs of another colleague's second-story container unit on higher ground. With a clear view of Airport Road past the perimeter wall, we watched four tanks loudly lumber down the otherwise empty street, right where I usually crossed on my morning run. This time of morning, the road should have been busy with people and traffic, but instruments of war had taken their place. I'd seen peacekeeping tanks on the move before—in Kosovo a decade ago—but something told me these tanks weren't there to keep the peace. It was such a jarring image, it seemed as likely as not that I was imagining it.

The heavy gunfire in the city had again subsided, but I was hesitant to interpret this as a good sign. Back in my container around 10 a.m., I called Ops to clear another travel advisory to American citizens:

The U.S. Embassy recognizes that there has been a lull in violence in Juba; however, we continue to receive reports of sporadic gunfire in parts of the city, particularly near Juba University. We continue to urge American citizens to exercise caution at this time. If you are in a safe location, the Embassy recommends you remain where you are as travel in Juba is not currently safe. The U.S. Embassy will continue to closely monitor the security environment in South Sudan, with particular attention to Juba city and its im-mediate surroundings, and will advise U.S. citizens further if the security situation changes. We take this opportunity to reaffirm our earlier message that no political or military figures have taken refuge within the U.S. Embassy.

Additionally, all citizens should take note that in response to the violence from this morning and yesterday evening, the government of the Republic of South Sudan has implemented a curfew from 6pm to 6am starting December 16th, 2013 "until further notice." The airport in Juba is currently not operational, and we continue to receive reports that the Nimule border is closed.

American UN officials told us that nearly a thousand civilians were seen rushing across the airport tarmac attempting to escape the Bilpam area of Juba, and many appeared wounded. This only confirmed for me that the government had little control over a key piece of infrastructure, but we never expected the airport perimeter to be particularly secure. More pieces of the puzzle were coming in, but we couldn't quite fit them together just yet.

We continued fielding calls from Americans in distress. Many colleagues were hearing from contacts and friends who were hoping for a lifeline from the US government. We had no offer of help at this stage, as we remained on lockdown ourselves, but we connected with Americans of all stripes across Juba and the country. Some were comforted by a short conversation with an authority figure with an American accent and by the assurance that someone official knew where they were. Others were angry that we weren't sending Marines in armored vehicles to bring them to safety.

I resisted the urge to remind them of our country travel warning, which had long said, in so many words: Don't travel to South Sudan, and if you do, you're on your own. It's dangerous, and we won't come to save you. Luckily, the watered-down new version of the warning hadn't yet been released. Americans traveling around the world often called our bluff, and in this case at least, they were right. To my surprise, we'd go to great lengths and expense over the coming weeks to get as many Americans out of harm's way as we possibly could.

"Hi Lizzy, What's the buzz about Juba issuing a new travel warning?" The cheery email from Suzanne, my mentor and the deputy of Embassy Nairobi's consular section, hit my inbox at 9 a.m. Since Embassy Nairobi handled the routine consular services that we weren't equipped to do in our small shop in Juba, I was always supposed to loop her in. I forwarded her the latest travel warning along with a rambling message apologizing for the delay and asking her to stand by. I expected to have a flurry of questions for her input soon. At this stage, I wasn't even sure what to ask.

Just before 10 a.m., the UN announced that it was taking in displaced persons at both of its locations in Juba: the mission complex adjacent to the airport and the UN House compound in Jebel, the neighborhood hit hardest by the violence. They'd already taken in several hundred seeking refuge. My UN counterparts, whose offices and homes were on these same compounds, told me that in truth they had had little choice. Hundreds of desperate civilians were simply breaking through or climbing over the fences. Opening the gates was the only way the UN could manage, screen, and track who was entering their compound.

By 10:15 a.m., most reports we'd received tied the origins of the fighting to a skirmish within Kiir's Presidential Guard, known as the Tiger Division, although reports differed as to the alleged instigator. Some asserted that forces loyal to Riek Machar attacked a military area called New Site in an attempt to get weapons, and forces loyal to President Kiir then pushed Machar's soldiers to the south. Others claimed Kiir's Dinka forces tried to disarm the Nuer guards in the division. One detail was consistent: the divide was ethnic.

At approximately 10:30 a.m., SPLA spokesperson Colonel Philip Aguer announced by radio that civilians should not be on the streets until given permission, and that any civilians on the streets might be deemed a legitimate target. A bad omen. Public alarm only grew.

The calls to our duty phone continued:

11:50am—Malcom called again to report gunfire all around and a lot of wounded—he's near SPLA HQ. Requested evacuation and was told to stay off the streets and stay inside. He was told that we could not facilitate an evacuation right now. He was reminded that the US Embassy is not providing a safe haven. He was assured that we have his phone number and will get in touch as needed. This was unsatisfactory and duty officer called CONS for further guidance. CONS will get further guidance and call back. CONS confirmed original guidance was correct, but duty officer could not contact the Amcit when trying to return the call.

12:20pm—Peter, AMCIT living near Saba, called to check for information. Duty officer requested he stay put in a safe place and he register on the Embassy website if he has the opportunity (he's not currently registered).

Peter calling again—gave passport number. He is with his brother, Evans, an official with the South Sudan national security service and requesting immediate evacuation. Duty officer requested he stay put in a safe place.

Peter calling again—states he is in danger and not in a safe place. Again requested immediate evacuation. Duty Officer stated that safe evacuation was not possible at this time and that it is best to find a safer location and then remain in place.

Late morning, reports came in of skirmishes in parts of the country farther north, a dangerous sign that other population centers were catching on to the ethnic nature of whatever was underway in Juba. This coincided with reports from high-level contacts that Nuer politicians and others allied with Riek Machar were being arrested.

Entry and exit points from the city were locked down by government security forces. These included the Juba Bridge, the only one spanning the Nile in the city, effectively blocking any escape south toward Uganda. *So this is what trapped feels like*, I thought. In this day and age, was getting the upper hand in battle really so simple?

Physical control of a bridge seemed like an old-fashioned move to me, but damn if it wasn't effective.

Americans located at Terrain Camp, one of the lodges in town housing expat contractors and NGO workers, reported the sounds of rocket-propelled grenades not far outside their compound, as well as a passing tank. Shooting had also started in the vicinity of the two UN compounds. Shortly thereafter, we could again hear gunfire outside our residence.

The hastily written message came from Gordon at 12:37 p.m. My chest grew tight as I read it, and my racing mind stood still.

"Hi, have some info emerged that civilians are being targeted by security forces." Civilians were being identified in the street, he said, by the traditional Nuer scarring across the forehead. And killed.

Not armed. Not fighting. Not in cross fire. Just Nuer.

What we were watching unfold in South Sudan was not a military skirmish or a political clash gone out of control. This was ethnic cleansing. And government forces were executing it in the streets.

AT APPROXIMATELY 1 P.M., President Kiir held a press conference to address the fear and instability that had rocked Juba for the past fifteen hours. We were in the middle of our third emergency action committee meeting when the broadcast began, and we tuned in to watch.

Kiir had swapped his trademark dark suit and black cowboy hat for full military regalia, wearing the green-and-brown-striped uniform of his Presidential Guard Tiger Division. Maybe I just wasn't used to seeing him this way, but Kiir looked slow, unnatural, as he unfolded his reading glasses and delicately placed them on his face below the stiff-billed, tiger-striped cap that sat awkwardly high on his head. The SSTV feed was shaky, zooming in and out; evidently, even the cameraman was unsure what to make of the occasion.

Though his words were stilted, Kiir was unfazed as he read from the papers in front of him. He told the country that the military had foiled an attempted coup by former vice president Riek Machar and declared a dusk-to-dawn curfew in Juba. Pushing forward without offering evidence, Kiir called Machar a "prophet of doom" who was "continuing to pursue his actions of the past," but claimed that he himself would "never allow the transfer of political power through violence." Perhaps Kiir just meant he wouldn't allow a transfer of power, period.

He ended his speech, "Long live the SPLM/SPLA, long live the unity of our people, long live the Republic of South Sudan." The small platform upon which he stood was overflowing with his political allies, who looked serious, if a shade unengaged. They certainly didn't look as shocked as my colleagues and I felt. When asked about the number killed, President Kiir said they hadn't been counted. With no indication of concern, he quipped, "In any war, there are casualties."

In the days and weeks and months to come, as colleagues, analysts, and other watchers of South Sudan tried to piece together what happened on this first day of war, it became clear that this moment was a decisive one. It unleashed in earnest what had already, to some degree, begun.

Until a full and independent investigation of the war's beginning can be conducted, we won't know the truth of how exactly it all played out. But I and others soon surmised that President Salva Kiir's press conference had signaled a green light to Dinka security forces of all stripes to commence an intensive, premeditated ethnic-cleansing campaign across Nuer neighborhoods in Juba.

These revelations represented an inconvenient truth for a US administration that for two and a half years had enthusiastically backed Kiir's government with robust military assistance, despite plentiful evidence long before this war began that the military openly violated human rights and preyed on vulnerable populations with impunity. It would take years for the US government to publicly move away from its vague condemnations of "abuse by both sides" and admit that the government initiated a war by committing the gravest offenses against its people—and that it did so on our watch.

No Safe Haven

December 16, 2013

SHORTLY AFTER KIIR'S PRESS CONFERENCE, THE SOUTH SU-danese government called for a diplomatic briefing. We decided that sending the ambassador would be too risky, so Mike, the deputy chief of mission, and a security team piled into armored vehicles and made their way out of our semi-secured compound to the presidential compound, J1. I wondered how Mike felt about being sent as the fodder.

Foreign Minister Barnaba Marial Benjamin reiterated the baseless story of Machar's coup and assured diplomats that the government was in full control. He urged those present to alert the government should any political leaders seek shelter in their facilities, and he said civilians should be asked to return home as things went back to normal. Nothing new learned, the small convoy departed J1. As they turned onto Airport Road to make their way back to the residence, the road was awash with people: South Sudanese moving en masse toward the UN compound at Tomping for refuge. Kids, mothers, and some men all labored on foot against the oncoming traffic, suitcases or bags of belongings in hand or perched on their heads. As the convoy steered slowly through the masses, the team realized—as had the people passing by—that there was no turning back: war had begun. The government's stubborn lies would make sure of that.

By midafternoon, we were still in information-gathering mode. I was fielding calls and emails in my container on the residential compound and keeping a log of incoming information. Requests to shelter at the embassy were increasing, voices imbued with a fresh urgency. Our response, unfortunately, was not as simple as one would think. Currently, we weren't even at the embassy; only a handful of Marines were there. The city had only two escape routes—one road heading south to the Ugandan border and one airport—and both were blocked indefinitely. If we took people in and provided shelter, we had no idea how long they'd need to stick around. And on a small compound with limited life support and security, we couldn't even guarantee the protection of the people housed here already.

I was frustrated at the ambiguity of our position, though thoroughly relieved that the UN's offer of shelter gave us two alternative locations where we could direct people to protection, supplies, and space that we simply didn't have ourselves. The UN's offer of shelter would save tens of thousands of lives, if not more.

But if we opened our doors, we might be able to save even more. I needed to know: What was our policy on offering refuge in the embassy? People's lives were on the line. Surely, we could give them a straight answer.

By now, Washington had set up a twenty-four-hour Task Force composed of dozens of State Department personnel to monitor and respond to the crisis. I called them up: "We're getting requests to take shelter in the embassy. What is our protocol here? What do we do?" The question bounced around on phone and email to this office and that office and back again. I pushed, yet received little in the way of an answer. "It doesn't sound like a good idea," some experienced consular officers replied as they copied more people onto the emails. But it became clear to me we had no policy. I wished someone would just tell me, "You're there. You decide."

By late afternoon, credible reports indicated that at least four former ministers had been arrested for participation in the "coup," a move almost certain to inflame rather than mitigate conflict. We heard that hundreds of wounded had arrived at the hospital, mostly from gunshots, and the morgue had surpassed capacity with an un-known number of dead. The UN's humanitarian wing, the Office for the Coordination of Humanitarian Affairs (OCHA), couldn't even get permission to move urgent humanitarian supplies. It was too risky. The absence of concrete information and prevalence of con-flicting rumors made me uneasy, giving me a new appreciation for undeniable facts and eyewitness accounts. Even local press outfits were on lockdown—except for when they traveled with armed es-corts (provided by the president) to cover the government's press conference. No one had actual news.

As for our international audience, the *Economist* had already re-leased its initial assessment of the situation. Titled "More Accident than Plot," the short piece missed the story entirely. "There are fears that the fighting could spread quickly to other areas of this impover-ished oil-producing nation. But a civil war along purely ethnic lines remains unlikely. Mr. Machar does not have a sufficient support base in the army and has pursued power through largely political means."

The article portrayed many rumors as though they were fact. Those of us based in South Sudan knew better; there were few hard facts here, but whispers and fears of another Rwandan-style genocide were already filling the air.

We heard gunfire pick up again around 9 p.m., but it sounded farther away than it had that morning. As a precaution, we skipped the shift change for the "mission control" post we had set up in the ambassador's house—a spare bedroom where someone would sleep by the phone for the inevitable urgent calls from Washington over-night. With the potential for bullets to stray inside our compound, the fewer people moving around, the better. Lori, our indefatigable office manager, said she had it covered. Otherwise, the gunfire barely registered. The rest of us went about our work wherever we were.

ON DECEMBER 17, the second day of the civil war, I got up early and tried to navigate a flood of emails that came through in the brief time I was asleep. Given the time difference, Washington was in full swing well into the middle of our night, and all of my counterparts there had reached out. Shortly before 6 a.m., sporadic automatic gunfire started up again. We heard it from two directions: the north toward the military base at Bilpam, and southeast toward Ministries Row and some of the large houses of politicians. I was already at the computer with coffee in hand, sifting through Task Force queries one by one to the tune of battle sounds across the city.

Ambassador Page had been on calls with State Department leadership and the White House for hours already, and Washington sent questions overnight that needed answers. Our early-morning emergency action committee attempted to address them, but we had little clarity. When would the airport reopen? What was SPLA leadership saying? Where was the nearest accessible helicopter landing zone? How many military personnel would we need to secure the US facilities?

Some of the questions we faced required judgment calls that were difficult to make with such sketchy information. We had to consider all contingencies. If we had to evacuate everyone quickly, these walls wouldn't hold for long. What sensitive material would we have to secure at the embassy? How long could we expect the local guard force to stay put? Should we even ask them to?

Our security chief, Bob, reviewed the embassy's emergency action plan (EAP) with the team, hundreds of pages of trip wires and red lines and contacts and contingencies designed to guide our response in a series of potential crisis situations. Regularly updating this plan at each embassy was a thankless task that many people took for granted. I'd taken it for granted myself until this past September, when, as our consular representative, I participated in a two-day emergency action exercise to discuss how we might address hypothetical crisis situations in Juba.

The September exercise began with a trainer from Washington offering a scenario: "There are several reports of shootings in town on Monday morning, and the SPLA or police seem to be involved. What do you do?" Most of the country team—section leaders from the State Department, USAID, and the military—sat around a long table in our prefabricated trailer conference room and looked at each other quizzically. Juba was an unstable place where security forces took what they wanted with impunity, AK-47s were one of the few things that could be bought on the cheap (appearing alongside vegetables at the open-air market in town), and stray gunfire was as common a sound at night as chirping crickets.

Someone chimed in quietly from a corner, "Uh, that's every day in Juba." We proceeded to discuss what constitutes a crisis in a place that is constantly on edge.

At the end of the exercise, I returned to the consular closet and sank into my chair. "If we have a crisis here and Americans are in danger, we're fucked and, more importantly, so are they," I told Gio, who politely ignored my poor language, as usual.

"So, we do what we must do to get prepared," he assured me calmly. "Americans are lucky to have someone working as hard as you are for them. We will be ready." His confidence in me was flattering but not particularly persuasive.

The two of us spent the next six weeks trying to get up to speed. Gio pored over our electronic and paper files to update our American citizen registry and improve our sense of who was where. He even emailed and called all the contacts provided to make sure our information was accurate. We held an American citizens town-hall meeting at the residential compound in November to introduce ourselves, discuss the security situation and precautions to take, and give Americans a better understanding of the resources available to them in a crisis and the importance of staying in touch.

I had deep gratitude for the two-day exercise and our subsequent efforts as I sat in the emergency action committee meeting and listened to Bob read through our designated responsibilities in the EAP. *This might not go smoothly, but at least the consular section is prepared. Well, much more so than we were in August, at least.*

One thing became clear as Bob reviewed the crisis trip wires one by one: we had crossed several, and the situation was not stabilizing.

The committee agreed it was time to request "ordered departure," meaning evacuation of all nonessential personnel. A few dozen would go; our small Marine detachment and all security staff would stay, along with the ambassador and a handful of others—including me. We didn't yet know where the evacuation would take place because the airport was closed. Evacuating by land to the north was a nonstarter. Even if rebels weren't a concern, the Sudd, a massive swamp stretching across nearly 15 percent of the country during rainy season, was prohibitive. Its name was derived from the Arabic word meaning "barrier." The road to the southwest could get us out of town, but unless we wanted to evacuate to a lawless corner of the Congo, it seemed a bad bet. The only reasonable way out of the country by road was to the south, two hundred kilometers by the one main tarmac road in the country, but first we'd have to cross the mighty White Nile, and the only bridge was still blocked by local security forces. Security of the road beyond was also entirely unclear. So we planned for different contingencies and waited for the situation to change.

After the meeting I hurried back to my container, where three enthusiastic USAID colleagues joined me to set up our mini consular operations center. Everyone had at least one phone and their personal laptops to track incoming information on the whereabouts and status of American citizens and other incoming reports, and we were all carrying radios since all other forms of communication were sporadic and unreliable.

At some point midmorning, only about an hour or so after we'd set up shop, Megan, a close friend from the UN Development Program, called my cell. We'd talked a few times in the past twenty-four hours. The first couple of calls were mild. Megan was a seasoned resident of Juba, after all.

"Hey, Lizzy, just checking in. Are you all okay over there? Yeah, the fighting sounded pretty intense, not far from us here."

"Hey Lizzy, I know you're really busy, sorry to call. I just wanted to check what the embassy is recommending for Americans. Do you have plans yet for evacuation? I'm trying to decide if I should plan on evacuating with the embassy or the UN. And anything I can do to help? Just let me know!" Megan was an optimist, and helping was her natural state.

This time, though, she sounded different, very nervous. I'd been fielding dozens of calls from panicked Americans and had little to offer, but this was Megan. It wasn't the same. Parroting the general guidance—stay in a safe place, if you're not in a safe place, get to one—felt like I was failing her.

Megan's compound was only a few blocks from ours, just off a stretch of Ministries Row that was home to the large compounds of several major political players, including Machar's only a few doors down. Not a strategic place to be, under the circumstances.

She was huddled on the floor of her tukul as we spoke. "There's fighting just outside now. It's so close, Lizzy. It's so loud!" I could hear rapid fire and loud explosions in the background. I wanted to reach through the phone and bring her here, tell her it would be okay. But I didn't know that it would be. As we were speaking, tank cannons were blasting the wall of Machar's compound, and it was being over-run by armed men. The gate was blown open and, with it, half the front wall. Machar wasn't there, but dozens of people had sought protection there, and many were cut down by machine-gun fire, women and children among them. Neither Megan nor I were aware of what exactly was going down, but the thundering sounds of war seemed to be closing in.

Then I heard more heavy gunfire, but not over the phone. It erupted closer to us than we'd heard previously. Much closer—on the same block. I asked Megan to let me know if things changed. I had to go, I said, and promised to let her know as soon as we were able to move again. It felt so inadequate.

And then I heard more gunfire from a different direction. On two sides of our compound, firefights were underway with heavy machine guns just on the other side of our palpably insufficient perimeter walls. Now I had a better sense of how Megan felt, my sympathy turning to empathy. Bob announced "Duck and cover" over the radio, and our makeshift consular team got low and scrambled to the tiny container bathroom, where we huddled on the ground, the furthest we could get from the direction of the gunfire. Only days before, I'd decorated my residential unit for the holidays with some ornaments on a limp plant, a stocking brought from home, and chintzy decorations I found at the local Lebanese-run supermarket, including a wildly overpriced flashing "Merry Christmas" sign. This sign now blinked at us from the porch outside, a bizarre counterpoint to the gunshots that punched through the air.

Bob followed up with another urgent announcement, "All personnel evacuate to the nearest safe haven." To me, this move was counterintuitive. With a neighborhood firefight still raging hot and heavy just beyond the compound walls, sheltering in place seemed a more logical choice, particularly given our location at the back of the compound. "Upstate, Upstate," I called back, using Bob's call sign, fumbling through radio protocols I wasn't yet used to. "This is Jackson plus three. Uh," I hesitated. I didn't want to sound weak or scared, but I felt it was a legitimate question under the circumstances. "We're on the back row, is it safe to run from here?"

"Sit tight, we'll send someone to you."

At Embassy Juba, all staff were issued radios and given the opportunity (or burden?) to choose their own call signs. I'd chosen "Jackson," the name of my home town; occasionally I'd regretted not picking something more interesting, but now that we were in the thick of a crisis, it was hard to take "Creampuff" and "Muffin" seriously. "James Bond" had gotten some laughs, but he would soon be on our first evacuation flight out.

We crawled out of the bathroom and kept our eyes on the door of my unit, preparing for our run to the safe haven. I reached for our phones, a pen, and a pad of paper; I was sure I'd need it. Then I looked at my foot—the stabilizer boot. Was I really going to sprint across the compound with this thing on? My foot wasn't quite healed—but no matter, I'd be faster without it. I took it off and slipped my running shoes on for the first time in weeks.

One of the assistant security officers showed up at the door a few minutes later. A quiet, mild-mannered lawyer, he had changed careers only a few years ago, no doubt seeking more excitement. His path to diplomatic security wasn't the usual, and one could tell. His flak jacket looked a size too large, as did his helmet, which was cocked to one side. The gun he was toting didn't look like a natural fit. But his expression suggested he'd been waiting for this moment and was ready to play the part he'd been trained for. I was not particularly reassured, but it was time to move.

We had two safe havens on the residential compound: one toward the north end and one toward the south, no more than a couple hundred meters from my unit. Like most of the other buildings on the compound, the safe havens were just a few shipping containers strung together, albeit more reinforced and fully stocked with a couple days' worth of food and water, protective gear, and a reliable satellite phone line to connect us to Washington. I uncomfortably recalled a conversation with Major Mike, one of our military liaisons in the embassy. "The last place I would want to end up if this compound is overrun is crammed in that metal container with all the other high-value targets on campus. They could cook you alive in there if they wanted to," he'd said. I felt my heart in my throat and told myself that our high-quality security team had thought through the various scenarios and deemed this to be the most appropriate location.

We fell in line behind the officer, keeping our profile as low as possible while still moving quickly. We passed my drooping Christmas plant on the porch, then took a right outside my door and another right across the gravel in between the units to move farther away from the back wall and any stray bullets that might rip through. Once we had retreated farther inside the compound, we all sprinted for the safe haven door and barreled inside. The foot felt all right.

Inside, most people were sitting on the floor—maybe two dozen total. A couple of people looked near tears, some were making jokes, and others were just searching for something to do. People were in shock. I thought it all felt real before, but being inside took the reality of the conflict to another level for me. By calling all staff to the safe havens, our security team was acknowledging that our island in the center of Juba was vulnerable. We were vulnerable. It was a jarring realization, a punch to the gut. I noticed I was breathing rapidly, and it wasn't from the sprint.

Alicia, the acting USAID mission director, took charge. A good leader understands that the best way to keep people calm in a crisis is to give them something to do. In her mild Long Island accent, she gave tasks to those who looked most nervous. "You, start checking off names for accountability. You, radio the other safe haven and compare lists. You, review the local staff list and find out who we haven't connected with yet." It worked. Their nervous energy was directed elsewhere, and productively at that.

Ambassador Page entered, escorted by her security team and in full protective gear. She looked a little flustered, but it might have just been the weight of the helmet and ballistic vest throwing her off-center. Mentally, she was ahead of the game. I was watching an experienced diplomat at work, that much was clear. "Have we informed Ops?" she asked immediately. The ambassador understood well that relentlessly informing Washington of every development was the only way to convince the mothership that we were on top of the situation. We called it "feeding the Beast." The Beast was on alert for the slightest misstep, at which point post (those in the field) would be deemed unable to handle their affairs, and their input shoved to the side—because Washington knew best. Ambassador Page was determined not to give up control of her mission. And she was right not to; Washington didn't understand the situation and it didn't understand the players like Page did. The Beast had no idea what was at stake with each diplomatic move.

I'd been our primary interlocutor with Ops since the crisis began— only about thirty hours ago now, but it seemed like a lifetime. I rang them up on the satellite phone. "This is Lizzy from Juba. We have evacuated to the safe havens due to sustained firefights just outside the residential compound. We have full accountability. This number is the only way to reach us for now." Then I handed the phone to Ambassador Page, who asked to connect with Special Envoy Booth and other State Department leadership. She'd been busy talking to representatives on both sides and her diplomatic counterparts. The writing was on the wall. A "drawdown" of staff was needed, reducing our numbers to emergency staff only. It was time to firm up evacuation plans.

We then heard the security team consulting over the radio. "Upstate, Upstate, this is Shaolin." It was the assistant security officer, radioing Bob. He had chosen an ancient form of kung fu for his call sign. I wasn't sure if I was impressed or alarmed.

"There is a group of armed men on the wall." "ON THE WALL??" Bob shouted back. Our chief security officer was as even-keeled as they come. His tone never shifted a note higher or lower, and his dry sense of humor was almost imperceptible to the untrained ear. He smirked rarely and betrayed few other emotions—until now, when his voice jumped an octave. The assistant security officer quickly clarified: "BY the wall, on the other side of the wall, not on the wall! Sorry!"

We all had a laugh at the misstatement and Bob's uncharacteristic outburst of emotion in response, but as I glanced around at my colleagues seated on the floor and leaning against the metal walls, I could tell what we were all quietly thinking: that could happen. Unfriendly, unruly, heavily armed forces could get in. The deadly attack on our compound in Benghazi was only a year ago, after all. We worked in dangerous places. But knowing that theoretically felt very different from facing it in real time. Under the circumstances, being barricaded in a safe haven fit our security protocols, but for me it only reinforced a feeling of helplessness. Adrenaline urges you toward fight or flight, and "sit tight" felt unnatural. I got antsy as time passed. I envied our security and military colleagues who were outside, usefully monitoring the situation. I needed to do something, so I listened in on the ambassador's phone calls and took note of any tasks or questions I heard. I kept looking for guidance and direction anywhere I could find it.

From inside the safe haven, we could watch the camera feed at the periphery of the compound. We all huddled around it. All I could see were people running, right past our front gate, heading uphill toward the road to the airport carrying children, bags, whatever they could. Even through the poor video feed, their faces betrayed terror. *So this is what war looks like*, I thought.

After a couple of hours, the gunfights died down or moved on, and our security team deemed it okay to leave the safe havens. Top-floor containers were abandoned as a precaution against stray fire, and staff doubled up with buddies in the safest locations. Everyone was told to finalize their "go bag" in preparation for a quick departure if needed. I returned to my ground-floor home-turned-operations-center, ready to respond to dozens of emails that had come in during our time on lockdown, but my nerves felt head-to-toe electric, like I was blanketed in high energy from an overdose of caffeine. It was uncomfortable, but it wasn't all fear. It was a sense of urgency I could channel productively, if I could keep my mind from wandering toward how vulnerable I felt.

In the afternoon, the ambassador called for an all-hands meeting poolside to update staff on the current situation and plans for the drawdown. Despite its poor condition, the pool remained a popular gathering spot, given the dearth of other recreational opportunities in Juba. Since we were all still marooned on the residential compound, a more appropriate meeting space wasn't available.

All nonessential personnel were told to bring their go bag for a dry run of the departure to the airport that would take place the following day, assuming the airport was open again. Armored vehicles, all numbered, were lined up across the field used for softball each Friday afternoon. All departing personnel were assigned a seat in a vehicle. At the meeting, the staff was reminded of what to bring: passports, cash, credit cards, medical records, anything of high value, but no one would be allowed a bag larger than a carry-on. Space was at a premium, and we wanted to evacuate as many people as we could—not only our staff but private American citizens and other diplomats as well. Deputy Chief of Mission Mike explained that military personnel would likely be living in the residences for the duration of the crisis, so "lock up anything you don't want bothered or eaten." He advised those departing to take some time to organize their homes so that someone else could easily pack up in their absence. "It's possible some of you won't be returning to post," Mike said. The somber mood was an odd contrast to the cheap Christmas decor adorning the wooden columns and hanging above the bar behind Mike as he relayed the news.

Several USAID colleagues came to find me after the meeting. About a half dozen of them had been instrumental parts of our makeshift consular squad. They all needed to organize their residences and prepare for their own departures, but they wanted to do whatever possible to help me before evacuations the next day. The idea of doing this without them after they departed hit me. I was still a junior diplomat, referred to as an entry-level officer before tenure. Relatively speaking, I was quite inexperienced. I'd been in Juba for five months—nearly half of my one-year assignment, but a short time for such a complex place. I was our only consular officer, though, so emergency assistance to US citizens in South Sudan was my responsibility. Rong, our junior economic officer and backup consular officer, had gone on leave a few weeks ago only to quit the Foreign Service and never return; Juba seemed to have that effect on people. (He graciously donated his remaining alcohol supply to me as an apology.) With James on vacation, I was also our only political officer. This got me not one but two seats on the emergency action committee and a secure spot among the essential personnel who would stay behind while the rest of the embassy evacuated.

Being busy was a blessing and helped me keep my doubts at bay. But, every few hours, I couldn't help it. What the hell was I doing in this position? Of course I wanted to stay—most of my colleagues wanted to stay and help, and several pleaded their case to do so—but I was scared. Not of violence or death directly—even in such close proximity, the danger to us still felt distant and abstract most of the time. What I feared most was letting people down. Making poor decisions. Failing, at a time when failing could cost lives. Everyone else on the list to stay had experience—some extensive—in active war zones or crisis response. In fact, a large percentage of the staff who were leaving had such experience. But not me.

Washington was aware it had an inexperienced part-time consular officer taking charge in a wartime evacuation likely to involve hundreds of American citizens. It was a full mission effort, with support from the entire remaining team at the embassy and significant dedicated resources in Washington, so I certainly wasn't alone. But the consular lead in any evacuation is a meaty position with heavy responsibility. I knew people were wondering if I was up for it.

Washington had considered alternatives. They could hand the reins to our economic chief, whose career specialty was consular services. He had far more experience than I did, so they could trade him out for me on the stay list. They could also send in an experienced senior consular officer to take my place. This was seriously considered. In the end, the Consular Affairs office seemed keen to give me the opportunity to rise to the occasion, if I wanted it. Before the evacuations began the next day, I had a few short conversations with the office back in Washington and exchanged emails with the Entry Level Officer Division. They all wanted to know if I was okay. They assured me I had support back in Washington, whatever I needed. Did I want to stay? I didn't have to if I didn't want to. I spent ample time worrying if I'd prove up to the task, but I never actually considered leaving. In the end, I always knew I would stay and help for as long as I could.

As soon as plans were finalized for the evacuation and Washington gave us the go-ahead to make it public, we needed to inform Americans. We were changing our own security posture, so the "no double standard" rule required it, and Washington wanted to organize additional assets so we could assist private American citizens to leave too. While we could quickly send out messages by email and through the press, many people had no access to the internet at the moment. Our nascent consular section hadn't secured a system to rapidly share messages with American citizens by text, so this meant phone calls. Hundreds of them. My USAID colleagues set out to distill multiple call logs and lists from the duty phone and floods of emails into a single list of Americans with contact information, cross-referencing with the list of registered Americans and taking care to thin out duplicates or dead numbers wherever possible.

But we still had to wait for Washington's okay to start the calls. Ajani, our public affairs officer—known by his online nom de guerre Dreadlock Diplomacy and to us by his call sign Facebook—had been rocking social media all day in a surprisingly effective effort to share information. We learned that some Americans here were getting updates by phone from their relatives in the United States, who could track developments online. But we still didn't have the answer to the most obvious question on everyone's mind: When could we get them to safety?

By late afternoon, we'd negotiated the plans with Washington and had cleared the language for the public notification about the embassy staff drawdown and evacuation plans for the next morning. Ajani emailed it to the Task Force to post it online. Once it was live, he could share it with radio stations and other local media outlets, and he was eager to do so ASAP.

We expected it to go up imminently. When we didn't hear back from the Task Force, we simply refreshed the embassy website, expecting to see it online. But nothing.

We pinged Washington almost hourly into the night, asking when they would make public the message on evacuating the next day. Whether due to oversight or an abundance of caution, since the city streets remained dangerous, no one gave the okay. People had to plan to get to the airport, and we expected many would simply walk, for lack of other options. This would take time in the morning, and we didn't know how much time we would have.

"I do apologize for being a bother. Just checked the Travel.gov website and our own. Still haven't seen it. Do we have a realistic estimate for when the message goes live? If we don't get it out before the hour, I sincerely doubt most of the AmCits will have access to the info before violence resumes in the morning," Ajani pleaded in a very polite but urgent email.

We didn't get approval. The culprit appeared to be oversight. We'd have to manage it in the morning. We hoped that would be soon enough.

Meanwhile, across the city, in the midst of terrible acts of violence, there were also extraordinary acts of bravery, neighbors risking their own safety to help others. Chol was living with his uncle's family, far more exposed than we were inside our compound, and they had all hunkered down as soon as the violence broke out. Government soldiers had moved into the neighborhood that day, and Chol's aunt, a member of the National Legislative Assembly, received a call from a colleague telling her that soldiers had surrounded the home of the assembly speaker, a Nuer. The speaker was not home at the time, but about twenty women and children had taken shelter there. Chol's aunt knew they were in danger. For the first time since the violence began, Chol left his uncle's home with his cousin and aunt, and they rushed by foot down the street to the speaker's home. A handful of soldiers stood on all sides of the house. They told Chol's aunt that they'd seen someone run into the house with a gun and were waiting for backup, urging her to return home and leave them to their business. His aunt realized that greater danger would come when the sun set, if the women and children were still there. Over the soldiers' objection, she entered the house, and they formed a human chain with the women and children to walk them from the speaker's house to Chol's uncle's home together. By the time the speaker showed up with a convoy to ferry the group to safety, the soldiers had given up and departed. Other vulnerable groups who had taken shelter in the homes of targeted politicians were not so lucky.

Before the day was out, the always sinister minister of information, Michael Makuei Lueth, announced by radio that the airport had reopened, the government was in control, and people should return to work and normal life tomorrow. He gleefully confirmed the arrest of several former ministers who'd been ousted along with Riek Machar earlier in the year. Madam Rebecca was under house arrest. Notably, this group of accused "conspirators" was not all Nuer. It became increasingly difficult, however, for Kiir's government to convincingly claim that the violence was not ethnically motivated, or even that it was not being committed by government security forces. Realizing this, leadership turned to a different explanation. Ministers and deputy ministers assured diplomats of all stripes that the ongoing targeted violence was being committed by "criminal elements" who "will be apprehended." For good measure, Kiir had this message delivered by some of his non-Dinka supporters. But these messages came alongside reports that thousands of irregular Dinka reinforcements had arrived in Juba from up-country to finish what the Tiger Division had begun.

As darkness fell on Juba and the second day of the crisis came to a close, people continued to flood into the UN camps in the city by the thousands, along with hundreds filing into bases in Bor and Pibor farther north. The hospital was beyond max capacity, and bodies were simply left outside the overflowing morgue. Even the government's official body count acknowledged a few hundred dead. One of the politicians arrested for treason was American, and already we had two reports of American citizens killed. This was unsurprising, given the level of violence and the large number of dual nationals in the city. Under normal circumstances, either of these occurrences would become all-consuming for a consular officer, but with no movement possible and evacuation planning in full swing, I merely reported them to Washington and added them to my ever-growing list of "critical actions for follow-up." Fighting had also spread to other parts of the country.

The special envoy's office was working with National Security Council staff in the White House to brainstorm creative ways to diplomatically press for peace. Kiir attended mass regularly and portrayed himself as a devout Catholic, so someone suggested getting the pope involved. Washington quickly sent an action request to our embassy in the Vatican to urge the Catholic Church leadership to reach out. Could Kiir's Catholic guilt prevail? It felt like we were grasping at straws.

Most international partners remained focused on "urging calm" and reminding the South Sudanese government that it was responsible for protecting its civilians. *Forget protection,* I thought. *How about the government just stops killing them?*

12

Drawdown

December 18, 2013

BY EARLY MORNING, WE FINALLY HAD APPROVAL TO RE-
lease the security message about evacuations. We didn't know what
time the first plane would go, and we also didn't know how much
time we'd need to clear and load passengers. I was doing my best to
follow what guidelines I could. Most of my colleagues were preparing for their own departures, while I was frantically trying to find a
working printer on the residential compound to print off a couple
hundred promissory notes.

Our emergency evacuations aren't free, in theory. All passengers
are required to fill out a two-page form in which they agree to reim-
burse us for the "reasonable cost" at some point in the future. The
policy was intended to encourage Americans to get out of harm's way
using commercial airlines or other options before situations become
so risky that the only option left is a US military flight. We'd hand the
forms out; it was the most we could do at this stage, leaving our colleagues on the receiving end of the flights to collect.

Other guidelines proved more unrealistic under the circumstances:

*If a crisis evacuation recipient does not have a passport, an EPDP
[Emergency Photo Digitized Passport] limited for return/transit to
the United States will be issued.*

I briefly considered bringing blank passport books and the laminator to the airport, but with no mobile consular system, portable printer, or internet connection, that wouldn't do much good. I'd have to figure out later how to manage Americans without passports.

I also printed off our rough list of Americans in South Sudan and handed different pages of it to different people who'd volunteered to make calls. Washington was already asking for a manifest of the flight passengers. The best we could do was try urgently to inform as many Americans as possible that evacuation flights were on.

I'd asked Washington repeatedly for more clarity regarding passenger priority. With no answers forthcoming, the rule follower in me turned to our regulations. The Foreign Affairs Manual says US citizens are the priority along with their immediate family members, followed by legal permanent residents. But the manual doesn't define immediate family members. Parents? In-laws who live with you? Grandparents who are primary caregivers for children? Adult children? Cousins? No one from Washington clarified it further.

The term "family" is applied differently around the world, and South Sudan had an expansive definition. I anticipated some Americans would show up with brothers, sisters, girlfriends, boyfriends, a slew of kids (likely not all theirs), cousins, and in-laws. Some families would hand their children over to American friends in a desperate attempt to get them to safety. We wanted to help as many people as we could, but we needed some parameters and had to ensure we could accommodate all American citizens first. I mentally prepared myself for the challenge and created more specific rules for us to use for admission; I knew it would be easier to make these rules now, when ambiguous cases weren't staring me in the face. Priority for an American's family members would go to spouses and children only—no brothers, sisters, or parents of adult children who couldn't independently show American residence status of some sort. We'd be as flexible as possible with American legal permanent residents, but they'd need travel documents from another country, since a US green card wouldn't get them in anywhere else. And based on reciprocity agreements with other close allies—the UK, Germany, Canada—we would accommodate their citizens as well on a space-available basis. Other diplomatic missions were exploring evacuation options, but ours would be the first planes in and out. No one was certain how long a window we'd have or how long this crisis would continue, so many other embassies were seeking our help.

I sought solace in the fact that we could help a finite number of people that day, and that turning away one person meant assisting another. I'd set and applied parameters that were transparent, consistent, and as fair as I could make them. I was prepared for a lot, but not for the heartbreak of what we'd face.

Clem, our defense attaché and liaison with authorities at the airport, confirmed we had clearance for landing two C-130 aircraft midday. We could still hear sporadic gunfire in the city, but the road to the airport was clear.

I was rushing back to my container with a pile of poorly printed promissory notes and ran into one of my USAID colleagues making calls to Americans. "They want to know where to go at the airport. What do I tell them?" Others were getting the same question; the airport was tiny but in chaos today, predictably. I hadn't really thought this part through. We weren't set up there yet—and how would we set up? I couldn't even picture it. I radioed out to Chris, one of the three security and military personnel who'd volunteered to be part of the airport team and who was already on-site. "Bravo Two Four, Bravo Two Four. This is Jackson."

"Jackson, send your traffic," Chris replied.

"Where are we going to set up there? How do people find us? Some are already arriving."

"Uh, tell 'em to look for three white guys in yellow vests," he answered.

"Okay, guess that'll work." And that's what we told them.

The head of the ambassador's close protection detail, Ruiz, was ready to drive me and Ajani to the airport to join the three white guys in yellow vests. I climbed into the back of the armored vehicle, struggling to open the heavy reinforced door with a pile of documents in my hands. Against my better judgment, I'd left the stabilizer boot behind. My foot felt okay, and I thought the boot would be a distraction. (This was a mistake I would only make once.)

I was looking down at piles of paper on my lap when I heard Ruiz call our departure on the radio. I looked up. We were out the gate and roaring up the dirt road, shortly turning onto Airport Road, the main drag that led, logically, to the airport. I hadn't set foot outside the residential compound since the crisis began about sixty hours ago.

Juba's streets were empty. It felt eerie and too quiet, like an empty movie set. Even inside the armored car walls, I felt exposed. Only then did it dawn on me what we were really doing that day. We were sending people to safety, admitting that it wasn't safe here. We were reducing our own footprint to essential emergency staff in a country where we'd spent hundreds of millions of dollars in support in recent years. Were we recognizing the inevitable, or were we just giving up? Did we have a choice? No doubt, our drawdown would be considered a slap in the face by many—the Americans turning their collective back on the country we had carried to independence—and we knew other embassies would likely follow our lead. In South Sudan, they usually did.

As we drove through what would usually be a busy part of town, it didn't feel like the Juba I knew. The Juba where I'd start my mornings with a run through the quiet streets, buy bananas on the side of the road, walk to the Ethiopian restaurant around the corner, shop at the Phoenician grocery store, or meet friends or contacts at the nearby Rainbow Hotel for a coffee or mediocre glass of lukewarm white wine. The city felt foreign, hostile. I realized we had been kidding ourselves by thinking it wasn't so before. We had ignored so many signs. Sure, the people of the country appreciated our presence and support and our efforts at helping them build a more democratic and developed state. At least I thought so. But the government and leadership of the country? The security forces they directed? They were not who we thought they were. Were they ever?

Juba would never feel the same again.

We arrived at the airport's dirt and broken-asphalt parking lot. Thousands of people were nervously milling about—some with luggage, most without. I looked over my shoulder, and the road was thick with more people heading this way. While some commercial flights were scheduled, they were selling tickets on-site for cash only, at more than three times the usual rate. With banks closed, securing $1,500 in cash for a single ticket was not a viable option for many desperate people.

Our three white guys in yellow vests had directed hundreds of Americans and others seeking assistance to the northwest corner of the parking lot, opposite the dilapidated terminal building. One of the guys tossed me my own yellow police vest. I had no idea where the vests had come from, and mine was so large I used duct tape to secure it in the back. We looked like a ragtag bunch, but this was as official as we were going to get. It was midmorning already and the sun was creeping high, along with the temperature.

"So, what's the plan?" I asked. Everyone looked at me. "You tell us, boss," I heard one of the yellow-vest guys say. I turned around and looked at the crowd. Amid the South Sudanese families, I saw a scattering of expats I knew, people I'd worked with or run with or dined with in the past months. My chest tightened a bit as I realized the weight of the task ahead of us. And I was in charge.

One of the guys pulled me aside and said, "Hey, we're here to back you up. You need bodies to direct things, we're bodies to direct things. You need help getting people in line, you let us know. You need a break, we'll make the space. But you're the boss. We're here to help." I took a deep breath and turned my attention to what needed to be done.

I scanned the crowd of people who were literally looking for a ticket out, and they looked tired, scared, and alarmed. Some were sick; some were pregnant. Most were dual nationals, and the South Sudanese were the most vulnerable, we knew. I'd always felt particularly short in Juba, and today, surrounded by all these people, was no different. I felt small—not just physically, but in the universe.

With all the last-minute preparation, we had forgotten something crucial: we had no desk or table to work from. We were just standing there in the parking lot amid hundreds of people seeking our help, distinguished only by our yellow vests. The guys had spotted a rusted, broken-down sedan near our corner of the parking lot. It looked like it had been there for years. We quickly co-opted it as our desk, and I shouted into the crowd, "American citizens, on this side. Legal permanent residents, over there. All other nationals, that way."

We directed traffic to different sides of the car, but it wasn't going well. By shifting locations, we'd angered people who had arrived early, hovering near the yellow-vested white guys for the longest. People began yelling and pushing, and we were making no progress. It was hot and oppressive inside what seemed to be growing into a mob. The crowd was towering around me and closing in.

I pushed through the mass of people and made my way to the edge of the parking lot, ducking under a drooping barrier fence into a patch of weeds to give myself some space. I shouted out as loudly as I could for everyone to quiet. I wished I had a bullhorn. My guys in vests did a more effective job of hushing the crowd as they followed me to the fence line. "WHO WANTS TO GET ON A PLANE TODAY?" I shouted, already getting hoarse. The crowd responded with "YEAHS" and nods. "We should be able to get most of you out, but only if we stay calm. But no one gets on a plane unless you cooperate, and no one who is aggressive gets on a plane at all!" Big men furrowed their brows, women with babies cheered, and expats looked a bit alarmed at the direction things were taking. We reorganized the crowd again into groups of American citizens and their families, permanent residents, and others. Lines had not worked thus far. To great disappointment, I shouted out over the crowd which family members would be ticketed. It wouldn't stop anyone from trying to litigate exceptions along the way.

It was late morning now, and I heard over the radio that one of our C-130s had just landed. It parked at the other end of the runway, the back cargo door dropped open, and forty-five US Army soldiers from the East African Response Force piled out to form a security perimeter around the plane. The force was based in Djibouti and was established shortly after the attack on our facility in Benghazi to enable rapid response within a difficult region. This was their first crisis deployment, and their presence really brought the feeling of a war zone home.

Shortly thereafter, I heard the callout on the radio that the convoy with our departing colleagues was en route from the residential compound to the airport with police escorts. Since boarding would happen at the other end of the runway, and the convoy would reach the runway from a military gate down the road, I wouldn't see them before they went. I had rushed out so quickly that morning, I hadn't even said goodbye to the three dozen colleagues I might not see in Juba again.

But now was not the time to reflect. With the first C-130 on the ground and the second one landing, we needed to identify who in this crowd would be joining our staff and other diplomats on these two planes. We didn't have much time, and I was told that out of the crowd of several hundred in front of me, today we had space for about fifty Americans on the first planes, and another 150 on a charter flight arriving shortly thereafter.

A convoy of vehicles had just pulled up on the dirt road behind me, ready to take our passengers to the planes. Byron, the consular officer from Djibouti, jumped out of the first vehicle. Reinforcements had arrived! He had come in with the soldiers and had the look of one himself. Clad in clean khaki, olive drab, and a can-do attitude, the only thing that gave me pause was his fair skin and reddish-blond hair. *This guy is going to fry in this sun.* He also looked well rested, a trait in short supply here. He sprinted over to me with a stack of promissory notes he had brought with him, along with a palpable sense of order and discipline likely gained during his army days. Byron understood how to function in a crisis zone, and I knew immediately that he'd be indispensable.

We realized that many of the hopeful passengers didn't have passports, more than we were expecting. Documents were either expired or left at home when departing in a hurry, as houses were crushed by tanks or burned to the ground. It felt terrible, but we asked those without documents to step to the side for now.

We'd focus first on those who had documents to travel. Even with prioritization rules in place, I had to start somewhere, and I was looking at a crowd, not a line, of people. I did what I assume most people would in the same situation. I pointed to the pregnant women, some adults with kids, and the elderly and directed them one by one to a colleague who would check their passports and add their names to the manifest. As they began to file off, a tall dual national muscled his way to the front and said, "But I was here first. I was here before these people!" I looked at him with dismay; he had just physically pushed aside a pregnant woman. I don't care if this is a war—you don't push a pregnant woman. He was closing in on my personal space now too, and my nose hit him about mid-chest as he tried to use his size for intimidation. But it didn't have his intended effect.

I looked to the crowd and asked, "Who here thinks this man should board a flight out of here before this woman?" The question was met with jeers and boos. Looking up almost vertically to meet his gaze, it was hard to stare him down, but I had the day's most valuable currency and wanted to make sure he knew it.

"You want on my plane?" He just stared at me. "Then back off."

His look of anger shifted ever so slightly toward one of resignation with a slight hint of embarrassment, and he faded back into the crowd—to the extent a nearly seven-foot-tall man can ever do that.

As if my little demonstration had flipped a switch, the crowd became much more amenable. The families and women and expats were all with me. The aggressive men realized they had to comply. I knew everyone here was emerging from a terrifying situation, but today I had particularly little patience for shows of force against the weaker.

It was a tense scene, but things started to move, and before we knew it, the first batch of passengers was in the armored convoy headed toward the far end of the runway. And then the second. We still had a crowd, but people seemed to feel better as they witnessed the progress.

At midday, the sun and the heat were punishing. I could feel the burn on my skin, though perhaps the thick layers of dust would protect against some of it. We should've brought water, I realized. And tables. And chairs. Some kind of work space so we weren't using the backs of waiting passengers to write down names and passport numbers on our makeshift flight manifest. We radioed back to mission control, our small task force set up in the ambassador's home, and asked for help. Shortly thereafter, two folding tables with chairs arrived, along with a crate of water. We were in business.

We'd shipped off the first couple of groups to the C-130s down the runway, and we were lining up the rest in front of our much-improved office space. A South Sudanese man with a US passport walked up to me and asked if we expected to be doing additional flights tomorrow. "We have space today, and we have no idea what will happen tomorrow. Depends on the security situation and the need. If you can leave today, I would do it," I urged him.

"I know," he said quietly. "I'm just, I'm looking for my brothers. They're Americans. I don't know if they're still alive, but I have to look for them. I thought maybe I'd find them here," he said, scanning the crowd behind me nervously.

I read the name on the passport and looked up. There was a resemblance as well. Could this be Lam Chuol's brother? I felt heat rush to my face but tried not to let it show. I stared back down at his passport and feverishly blinked back tears.

It was just over a week ago when I'd seen Lam, Riek Machar's close aide, last, when he was at the residence for Machar's meeting with the special envoy. I'd heard from several contacts that he had been killed on the first day of the crisis, along with his other brother. The stories I'd heard differed. Some said he was dragged out of a hotel and executed in the street, others said he was in his car at a checkpoint. It was hard to believe, but to the extent that we knew much of anything at that point, I was fairly certain the news of his death was true. We'd even reported it to Washington.

"Are you sure you don't want to go today? It isn't safe here," I told the man. I was still looking down, pretending to study the words and dates on the passport.

"I'm sure," he said. "I can't just leave them. Not yet."

"Do what you need to do, but be careful. We'll probably have a flight tomorrow," I said quietly.

Then I looked up in his eyes and I knew he must know it, but maybe he wasn't ready to accept it yet. I waited until he turned away, then quickly walked behind our parked armored vehicle out of view of the crowd. Leaning my head against the back of the truck, I sobbed.

Should I have told him that his brothers were dead, that everyone knew it and he needed to get to safety, for his family's sake at least? Probably. He didn't come back again, so I wouldn't know if he got out of Juba in the end. I wished I'd insisted he get on that plane.

But time was at a premium, and there were others we could help. So I wiped my face with the corner of my oversize yellow vest, pulled my baseball cap down a bit further over my eyes, took some deep breaths, walked back to the crowd, and got back to work.

Byron and I started to address the passengers without passports. Embassy Nairobi was on the receiving end of our flights that day, and they had several staff at the airport, ready to greet our passengers and assist with entry and other emergency needs. We got them on the phone, and they logged in to our consular systems so they could help verify the citizenship of the passengers standing in front of us. It was up to me and Byron to conduct roadside interviews to decide, as best we could, whether people without documents were who they said they were. It was an imperfect system, but it was the best we could do for now. What I would do for an internet connection, even a Black-berry, so Nairobi could email us passengers' photos. Such a simple fix was out of reach.

In a few cases, Byron and I divided up couples to conduct crude visa-style interviews in the parking lot. While Nairobi could com-pare passport numbers against names and dates of birth, we knew it would be easy for South Sudanese citizens with friends in the United States to give us details that would match someone's records, but not their own. Occasionally (thankfully, not often) a couple's story just didn't hold up—usually someone claiming to be the spouse of the American, hoping for a quick way out of the country. I told myself that we only had so many seats, and as long as we filled every seat, we were helping as many people as we could. Every time I turned someone away, though, it was hard.

We were not filling the plane with bodies and numbers; we were filling the plane with people. And we were *not* filling it with other people, people I could see in front of me, who were telling me that their relatives had already been killed, that their homes had been destroyed, that their friends and children were missing, that they feared being killed in the streets if they didn't get out now. Their tragedies and fears were not a laundry list of atrocities in numbers too great to comprehend. Their traumas were individual and immensely painful. I could see them on their faces, like scars.

You can only help so many people, I kept telling myself, but I didn't really believe it. If I were better at my job, more organized, more prepared, could I be doing this better, helping more people, helping those most in danger? More importantly, if I were a better political officer, could I have done something sooner to make Washington intervene to prevent this crisis before it began? I'd felt fairly confident that I'd asked the right questions: Were we doing enough to promote accountability? To condemn impunity? Why were we letting Kiir off the hook as he kept amassing control? I asked the right questions, but I also accepted inadequate answers. I assumed those above me knew better about what we were doing and why. What more should I have done? What could we have done to stop this?

THE TENSE ATMOSPHERE in the parking lot started to give way to a sense that we were all in this together. People had seen us ship off dozens to safety, and they were starting to give us the benefit of the doubt. They were also looking out for us. Throughout the day, people standing or sitting on the asphalt in our long lines waiting for a "ticket"—a simple printed number on a piece of paper—offered me and the team bags of trail mix, sunscreen, water. They knew it was a long day for all of us and seemed to appreciate that we were doing our best. In the middle of a city facing unconscionable violence and inhumanity, the small acts of kindness restored some hope.

We felt like we were making progress, but it was never enough to satiate the demand for constant updates from headquarters in DC. Every so often, I'd get a radio call from the residence, asking if I had a complete flight manifest yet to share with Ops. They wanted numbers, names, passport data, birthdates. We joked that they'd be demanding sock color next. Evacuation details seemed like the singular focus of Washington that day, but we knew other conversations were ongoing about diplomatic efforts too. While we were focused on bodies and tickets and numbers, the special envoy's office and the National Security Council staff at the White House were trying to determine how to stop whatever was going on. But what that was still wasn't entirely clear. Media reports were presenting the violence mostly in the passive voice, as some kind of generic, inevitable ethnic conflict. Fighting "broke out," and civilians "were killed." It's Africa; it happens. It was the kind of accounting that leaves no one in particular responsible. The scene at the airport and the stories coming in told a different story, though. I wondered if Washington understood that.

Ajani and I were sitting at our folding table checking documents and taking names when a thickset man in an orange golf shirt and sunglasses walked up. "I hear you're in charge? I'm with the charter company. You have the manifest for the flight?" It seemed everyone wanted the manifest, but at least this guy had a reason to need it.

His accent was hard to place. Could be South African, Zimbabwean, or just a British guy on the continent too long.

"The manifest is . . . coming," I said, looking down at the three different scribbled lists I had going.

"We need the manifest to clear the flight. Should be done soon so we can share with the tower." His words had a staccato of urgency, but he didn't press too hard. I imagined he knew how these things tended to go.

"I hear ya. We're working as fast as we can," was all I could offer.

Soon after, we'd identified our passengers for our third and final flight of the day and had distributed tickets to all the Americans who'd been waiting since morning. By this time, it seemed the open onslaught of violence that began Monday and Tuesday had abated somewhat, so with safer streets, even more Americans were emerging looking for a way out. It was getting late, though, and authorities at the airport had warned us that the airport would close at 5 p.m. sharp to accommodate the city's 6 p.m. curfew. It looked like evacuations would continue into the next day.

Two planes had departed, but getting the third and last out before the airport closed would be more of a challenge. The first two had bypassed immigration entirely and loaded the passengers through a military gate farther down the runway. Now, despite the chaos, South Sudanese authorities were not as keen to let such things slide. The small terminal building was overwhelmed with people, so Clem convinced the airport authorities to let us use the VIP lounge and its dedicated security check; few VIPs were risking the airport today.

Throughout the day, I'd felt the lurking presence of the NSS at the airport. Their officers paced about in military uniform, toting AK-47s, looking angry, and almost invariably wearing dark shades. They could have been extras in any recent film about war on the continent. As I led passengers to the VIP entrance, an NSS officer, looking particularly miffed, took up post at the security check to examine passports as people entered. He was not an immigration official; he just wanted to know who was getting on our plane. Several people in line looked uncomfortable as they approached him. This made me uneasy as well.

I stepped up next to the angry NSS man and explained that I was the consular officer and could attest that these were all Americans or their family members, and that we'd taken responsibility for them. He just stared past me. He didn't flinch much at the women and children passing through and just looked suspiciously at the expats, but he puffed up at the first South Sudanese man to reach the front of the line. "Why are you leaving your country? This is your home!" the NSS officer demanded. Then he turned to me and said, "You can evacuate Americans, but you cannot take out South Sudanese."

"See that blue passport?" I pushed back. "This is an American citizen. We have the right to help our citizens."

"He is trying to sneak out of his country! This man is South Sudanese."

"I see a blue passport," I replied, as calmly as I could. "You see him as your countryman. I see him as mine. These are all American citizens." I took a deep breath, gently plucking the man's passport out of the NSS officer's hands as I spoke. "You must do your job, but I must do mine." I stared into his dark glasses and tried to keep his attention as I quickly handed the passport back to the passenger and pushed him past the officer. The NSS man grew tired of the discussion, and he let this one go.

Time was short, and we were barely through the first batch of passengers for the third flight. I hoped it would get easier.

We struggled again as we got to a group of passengers without travel documents. At this point, I needed to convince the NSS officer and the immigration authorities as well. One family was toting a slew of kids, and I could only guess how many were actually American citizens or even related to the parents. The kids might not have been, to be honest; they were young, and the parents claimed they just hadn't applied for their US passports yet. The father was able to show something I could cling to—photos of the kids in his wallet—and Nairobi could confirm that someone with the names and birthdates of the parents used to have US passports. We decided to give them the benefit of the doubt.

I explained to the immigration officers, "They had to flee their home urgently, and it's my fault really. I just didn't have time to print off an emergency passport at the embassy. But I'm the US consular officer here, and I have confirmed their identities in our consular systems, and I assure you, I take full responsibility for them. Our embassy in Nairobi will be doing the same on the other side and will meet them with the necessary travel papers for entry." I couldn't imagine I looked official, sweating and sunburned in khaki shorts and an ill-fitting yellow police vest, but I did my best to sound so. I only had to convince these guys that it made more sense to buy what I was selling than it did to try to fight me on it.

I shifted the conversation. "See this line? We have fifty more to go, and there will be more like this. I give you my assurances, but we need to get them through in time to get on that plane before the airport closes at five o'clock. We all want to make it home by curfew, right?" The NSS officer looked unhappy but increasingly disinterested, and the immigration officers bought it. The line started to move through again.

I called over a couple of our guys and asked what we could do to lubricate the process. One of our yellow-vest guys had an idea. He ran off to a small shop just outside the airport barrier and returned in ten minutes with a bag of cold Cokes. Coke diplomacy was brilliant, particularly on a hot, dusty day.

"Hey, guys, I know it's hot out here and it's been a long day. Soda?" He handed out a couple to the immigration officers loosely monitoring the luggage check and metal detector, and of course to our angry NSS friend at the door. The beverages thawed relations for a bit. The pace of our line picked up.

It occurred to me that even the NSS officers must be stressed. A large percentage of the security forces didn't know what was going on in their country, and many of them were young. Everyone saw enemies everywhere. It was hard to muster compassion for the angry guy in dark shades with a large gun, but I tried.

Getting 150 passengers through security, even with our own dedicated line, took much longer than anticipated. By late afternoon, I needed to move to the tarmac to work with the charter company to get boarding started, so I enlisted one of our own dark-shaded military guys—our new defense attaché—to mind the security line. He stood stiffly with arms folded, mimicking the dead NSS stare effectively. Ajani and Byron were nearby in case any civilian officials needed to give the all-important vague assurances that we were totally on top of this.

It was just before 5 p.m., and the airport was starting to clear out ahead of closing. Ours was the last plane of the day. Clem was getting hard looks from airport officials who knew our plane should've departed already, but he worked to keep them calm, assuring them we'd be done any moment. Once the last plane departs, the airport crew would have to shut things down before they rushed home ahead of the 6 p.m. curfew, so every minute we delayed put them at risk. I feared that any moment the control tower would tell us they were shutting down and the plane would have to go tomorrow. This would put much more than the airport staff at risk. I wouldn't even know what to advise our 150 passengers: Sleep in the parking lot? Try to rush home, if you still have one? It just wasn't safe. And what about the charter crew? Tomorrow wasn't an option for this group. We had to get the plane out tonight.

As Ajani pushed the last batch of passengers through the security checkpoint, Byron and I worked with the charter crew on the tarmac to match the passengers with names and numbers on the manifest as they boarded the plane. We were moving quickly, but the clock was ticking. 5:10. 5:20. Finally, everyone was on. Ajani snapped photos of the final manifest pages so we had a copy to satisfy Nairobi and Washington, who had wanted it finalized and in triplicate hours ago, and a charter crew member rushed the scribbled pages across the tarmac to the tower on foot. In minutes, he was back on the plane, the door closed, and they were taxiing up the runway. Most of our crew headed back to the vehicles. Clem and I stayed behind to wait for wheels up. We'd notify the team at the residential compound, who were standing by to inform Washington, when the bird was in the air. We waved at the plane as it moved down the runway and breathed a sigh of relief as it lifted.

"Dugout, Dugout, this is Jackson," I called out to Lori, who was manning communications at the ambassador's house.

"Wheels up, 17:40," I said with a smile on my face.

I stuck the radio back on my hip and looked out at the tarmac, empty but for a few small parked planes in the distance. The atmosphere was calm and quiet, and the sun had begun to drop in the cloudless blue sky, giving the horizon the beginnings of a tranquil pink glow. It felt so peaceful compared to the rest of the day. This particular moment, it didn't feel like war.

But, pushing up against curfew, we had little time to reflect. The terminal doors were locked, and the rest of the crew was already loaded in two armored vehicles. They called us on the radio, asking us to hurry.

We got into the last vehicle in the parking lot. As we drove down Airport Road, we were met only by the long shadows of the buildings that lined it. The streets were empty. The team inside the car was hot, dirty, tired, and sweaty, but we were happy. We all felt a great sense of satisfaction with the day. We had been able to evacuate nearly three hundred people to safety.

As I looked out at the empty streets, I remembered they were deserted because of fear and danger. My sense of satisfaction was tempered by the reminder that we had turned a lot of people down too. I had turned a lot of people down.

I could still see the faces of some of the people I turned away. Some feared they were targeted specifically, based on political or family connections. Others simply feared remaining as Nuer. I told myself again that as long as we filled every seat we had out of the country, we had done the best we could.

But I knew some people were at much greater risk than others, and I knew that was not the basis on which I had filled our flights. I took it for granted that I should follow the rules and prioritize American citizens. But how great was the risk to many of the expatriates we put on our planes? To those who lived in more secure compounds and weren't the targets of the government's ethnic cleansing operation? We understood so little about the war at this stage that it wasn't really a fair question, but in my conflicted state I asked it to myself. I recalled stories and reports of other wartime evacuations: Saigon, Beirut, Mogadishu. We Westerners played in these spaces, sought out economic opportunities and security gains, but when the going got tough, we got going.

Would I look back on this moment with pride or shame? I simply didn't know. I knew we saved some lives, but could we have saved more? And what about the decisions I had made that day? Did they cost lives?

Maybe, and it haunts me.

WE PULLED INTO the residential compound and were greeted like victors returning from battle. We'd left our poor colleagues in Nairobi a proper mess to sort out on their end, including undocumented children and a few people they couldn't confirm to be Americans after all. Somehow, they got them all out of the airport eventually, but I assured Suzanne, who was helming the operation there, that we'd try to make the next round a cleaner bunch. That would be tomorrow, though. For now, we'd try to enjoy a job mostly well done.

I walked directly into the evening emergency action committee meeting that'd just begun and was met with a round of high fives and smiles. I knew not everyone in our leadership thought it was a good idea to leave me in charge of the evacuations, but maybe now I'd earned my stripes. I was still shaken by some of the decisions of the day, but on balance it was a good moment.

Only now, with the pressure starting to lift, did I realize that my broken foot was throbbing and swollen. Not surprising, as I'd been on it for over twelve hours and it simply hadn't healed yet. All day, wiser colleagues had implored me to sit down, take a break, but time seemed too precious, and I felt responsible for every piece of our mission. I was determined not to be a weak link.

I propped my now very sore foot up on a chair and gave a quick briefing of the day's events, most of which the entire team had followed by radio in real time. We discussed other developments. Ambassador Page had met with President Kiir that afternoon. Special Envoy Booth was considering a visit. Juba had been largely calm and quiet, but fighting in Bor, about two hundred kilometers north of Juba, was heating up. *Today's evacuations weren't the end*, I realized. *They were just the beginning.*

Someone suggested I go shower and put the boot back on my foot, and I complied. Limping back to my little metal cottage, I realized just how much had changed in our compound since I had left that morning. Our community had largely been dominated by a USAID crowd of humanitarians and development professionals; they outnumbered State Department officials three-to-one, at least. But now almost all of them were gone, and soldiers had taken their place—a stark contrast. Our new army neighbors had made themselves known quickly. As part of their security protocols, the East African Response Force created an internal security perimeter of large rolls of barbed wire and other obstacles. Metal stars littered sidewalks near the laundry facility. Dining tables had been piled up in walkways between units to block exit routes. Upturned chairs littered open spaces between buildings. Sandbagged shooting positions were set up in the gazebo. Heavily armed gentlemen in military fatigues paced up and down the interior wall by the pool, part of our new twenty-four-hour patrol.

Unfortunately, my unit was located outside the new internal perimeter. Not terribly reassuring. As I tried to climb delicately over a large roll of barbed wire to get back to my home in the fading light, I sliced the ankle above my good foot. Hopefully we wouldn't have to sprint to the safe haven again tonight.

13

Diplomacy Is
the Long Game

WHILE WE WERE BUSY WITH EVACUATIONS AT THE AIRPORT, Ambassador Page was forging ahead with urgent diplomatic action, connecting with South Sudan's political leaders to urge restraint and call for peace, while working with the special envoy, the White House, and others to weave together an action plan. Which diplomatic partners had the right relationships with which targets of influence? Who in the US government should reach out to whom and with what message? What carrots or sticks could persuade action or restraint? Time was of the essence, but diplomacy isn't a last-minute fix. How effective diplomacy would be in a crisis depended on the foundations, knowledge, and influence built over years. As described by former statesmen like George Shultz and George Kennan, diplomacy is like gardening: a methodical and constant process that is critical to America's foreign policy successes.

It was a different scale, but we were utilizing many of the same tools at the airport, on a lower, but critical, level. The close relationship between the United States and South Sudan was often tested, but our access at the airport and the favors we were granted were built on a long history and were facilitated by the close working relationships Clem and others had forged in the country. We negotiated solutions based on shared interests, like getting everyone—our evacuees and the airport staff—out of the airport ahead of curfew. Even Coke diplomacy involved identifying our counterparts' interests at the time.

Diplomacy isn't magic fairy dust you sprinkle on international crises when they erupt. It's a skill and a day job, and it's something we Americans have been practicing professionally for a while, with varying degrees of success. The heyday of American diplomacy began with the end of World War II and our instrumental role in birthing the preeminent multilateral institution: the United Nations. A period of isolationism following the First World War had proven wholly ineffective, and poor diplomatic relations were a contributing factor to the second. By 1945, US leaders, in particular Secretary of State George Marshall, were determined not to repeat the mistakes of the past and launched an unprecedented period of international cooperation and diplomatic engagement that we continue to benefit from today. Our leadership role in this movement began to wane sometime shortly after the end of the Cold War, and we began again to turn inward, losing patience for slow, deliberate solutions. Multilateralism (multicountry alliances and action) began to see a revival under President Obama. Even as his administration doubled down on certain military solutions, it also welcomed a return to traditional diplomatic approaches, with the high-profile multilateral Paris Agreement on climate, the Iran nuclear deal, and the bilateral Cuba breakthrough. (This comeback would be short-lived, however, and quickly unraveled by Donald Trump.)

You're possibly familiar (at least at a cocktail-party-chat level) with the greatest hits of our period of robust internationalism and brave global leadership.* In the aftermath of World War II, it was the Marshall Plan—a $12 billion economic aid initiative—that rebuilt

---

* For a deep dive into how the United States has played a key diplomatic role in the cases discussed here and in several other examples, I recommend *Foreign Policy Breakthroughs: Cases in Successful Diplomacy*, edited by Robert Hutchings and Jeremi Suri (New York: Oxford University Press, 2015). The case-study authors walk through what made these breakthroughs possible and what diplomatic lessons we can learn from them.

Europe from the rubble, kick-starting the postwar economic recovery and, with it, our strongest and most important alliances for decades to come. The Marshall Plan was not just a generous development initiative but also the foundation of our soft-power fight against the spread of communism, bringing Europe soundly into our sphere of influence at the outset of the Cold War. Leveraging our relative economic strength to dramatically boost allies was not the obvious move for a country an ocean away that had already expended significant resources in the fight, but it provided a level of shared long-term security and stability that war alone never would.

The United States then spearheaded a multilateral effort to curb nuclear weapons, a rather bold move since we had dropped the only nuclear bombs ever used in warfare less than a decade earlier. This was a recognition that holding nuclear weapons was not sufficient to insulate us from the threat they posed. The framework for limiting the proliferation of nuclear weapons was many years in the making. President Dwight D. Eisenhower first proposed to the UN General Assembly the establishment of an international organization to manage the spread of nuclear technology and limit the proliferation of nuclear weapons in 1953. This initiative led to the creation of the International Atomic Energy Agency in 1957, and eventually to the adoption in 1968 of the Treaty on the Non-Proliferation of Nuclear Weapons, painstakingly negotiated by the Eighteen-Nation Committee on Disarmament, a diverse group of countries, including both nuclear haves and have-nots, to maximize the influence of overlapping interests and ensure broad buy-in. The treaty resulted from six years of negotiations and four hundred meetings of multinational bodies—a true exercise in patience and a view toward the long game. Its results haven't been perfect, but today the world faces fewer than ten states that hold nuclear weapons—far fewer than anyone would have expected fifty years ago. We have seen no further use of nuclear weapons since our own in 1945.*

---

* Hutchings and Suri, *Foreign Policy Breakthroughs*, 94.

The Camp David Accords provide another example of American diplomatic leadership making the world a more peaceful place. The initiative, led directly by President Jimmy Carter, failed to secure a comprehensive peace between Israel and the Arab states but resulted in a meaningful and long-standing bilateral peace between Egypt and Israel, which had fought several wars since Israel's independence. Twelve days of negotiations followed fourteen months of diplomatic groundwork, which led to the Egypt-Israel peace treaty. President Carter's determination, personal leadership, and diplomacy were critical to the initiative's success, but openings created by leadership changes, and strategic diplomatic moves, by Egypt and Israel also paved the way. A key lesson for effective diplomacy: it worked this time because timing was right and political will for a solution finally existed on both sides.

A peaceful German reunification in the wake of the rapid collapse of the Soviet Union was also an achievement made possible by careful and strategic diplomacy, and the United States played the leading role. The Berlin Wall fell on November 10, 1989, but reunification would not be sealed until October the following year, and it was in no way the inevitable outcome. The British and French didn't even support the idea at first.* Through careful and exhaustive negotiation, the United States would take the lead in securing a collective Western position on Germany's unification and membership in NATO, and would thereafter broker a deal to convince the Soviet Union to accept the outcome. US diplomats navigated each party's interests to find a way to get everyone to agree to the solution that the United States deemed most beneficial.

These situations are all depicted at the forty-thousand-foot view, but innumerable accounts can walk you through the nitty-gritty of diplomacy that got us to an acceptable and durable negotiated solution in each case. The underlying lesson is what each of these events have in common: a long-game approach, careful consideration of overlapping interests, and extensive outreach through durable relationships

---

* Hutchings and Suri, *Foreign Policy Breakthroughs*, 196–198.

built and managed over time and treated with respect. They also share patience, wisdom, and some measure of luck. At times, we face intractable problems, where conflicts are not yet ripe to provide an opening for diplomatic solutions. But, as my father has always told me, the harder one works, the luckier one gets. None of these outcomes could have been reached through military means alone.

But these are a handful of notable exceptions, you say. These are the moments when leadership at the highest levels decided an international predicament demanded the utmost attention and delicate management. Beyond these anomalies, what role does diplomacy really play, especially now?

Far more than you think, is the answer. Diplomacy laid the groundwork for all of the greatest hits described above. Long before the ministers, special envoys, or presidents got involved, dozens of working diplomats painted the picture, showed the trends, profiled the key players, and built relationships and trust with counterparts who would help make big successes possible later. That's the day-to-day work of diplomacy.

Diplomacy is quiet and unassuming. It isn't a strategic bomb drop or a single sharpshooter. Even the greatest diplomatic achievements (like those discussed above) are built on years of relationship building and preparation and patience and study. A thousand small diplomatic efforts make one great diplomatic achievement possible, and a thousand small diplomatic efforts mitigate a thousand small conflicts you didn't even know were a threat to our national prosperity, security, and well-being.

Every day, diplomacy delivers in critical moments of life, death, and tragedy. Every day, diplomats navigate complex legal, economic, and emotional challenges on your behalf. The most successful of these you often don't hear about, because successful diplomacy keeps potential points of bilateral friction out of the front-page news. And yet, no one thinks to thank diplomats for their service, because few even know what their service means. These battles, and victories, tend to go unsung. That's a shame, because they sure are interesting. And while these efforts are important in and of themselves, to

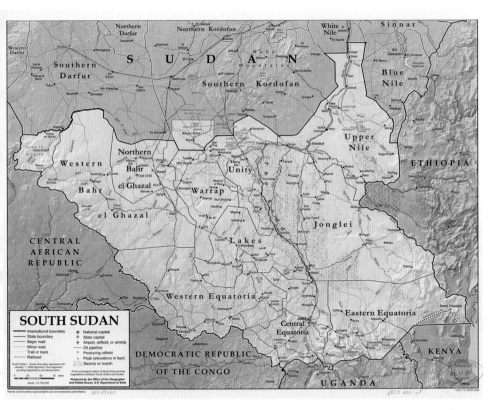

Map of South Sudan at its founding in 2011. Photo credit: United States Department of State. Office of the Geographer. South Sudan (Washington, DC: Office of the Geographer and Global Issues, US Dept. of State, 2011). Map. www.loc.gov/item/2011594751/.

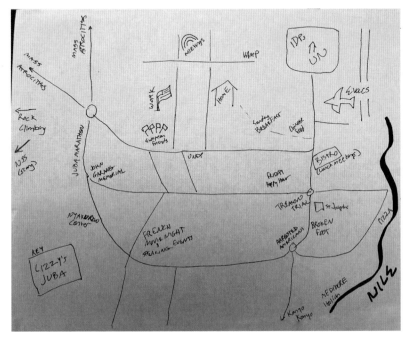

Author's depiction of Juba, drawn for a friend's farewell, June 2014.

An SPLA soldier observes destruction after an armed Lou Nuer attack on Likuangole, Pibor county, in Jonglei state, December 30, 2011. Photo credit: Themba Linden.

A neighborhood in Juba as seen from the air, September 2013. Photo by author.

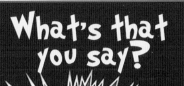

What's that you say?

A cocktail party on the RC?
Shut the front door!
With festive holiday treats
and so much more.

Join the kids
from the back of the bus
for holiday music & movies
by the fire with us.

So where is this party
for the Christmas holiday?
Well, unless you have clearance,
I can't really say.

But if you go Midtown Unit 8B at 6:30 pm
it will be clear where to meet.
Don't worry about dinner
there will be plenty to eat!

The author's porch decorated for the holidays, December 2013. Photo by author.

Invitation to a compound holiday party that never happened—part of a series of festivities planned for those staying in Juba for the holidays, December 2013.

The Citizen — Opinion — 7

What other news outlets say about the crushed coup attempt

Kiir Says Ex-VP Machar Planned Attack, Declares Curfew in Juba

ST

South Sudan President, Salva Kiir has accused former vice-president Riek Machar of alleged involvement in Sunday's attack on a military headquarters in the country's capital, Juba.

Speaking at a brief press conference, Kiir who dressed in full military attire said "a group of soldiers allied to the former vice-president Dr Riek Machar and his group" attacked the army headquarters near Juba University. Sporadic gunfire, which started on Sunday evening, rocked Juba and continued this morning, sending residents into panic as soldiers were fully deployed on streets.

"These attacks continued until this morning", the President, flanked by his deputy, James Wani Igga told the press in Juba. "I can however tell you that my government is now in full control of the situation," added Kiir, also commander in chief of the na-

tional army (SPLA).

CURFEW IN JUBA

Meanwhile, the South Sudanese leader has announced a dust-to-dawn curfew in Juba, saying justice would prevail on those behind the attack.

"The curfew will start from 6 p.m. to 6 a.m. local time in Juba," Kiir told reporters.

HUNDREDS CAMP AT UN-MISS

Hundreds of civilians, the United Nations said, have sought refuge in their compound adjacent to the country's airport and at their base in Jebel Kujur area. Most of them are women and children.

"While UNMISS is not a humanitarian operator, and our mandate

is to protect civilians, basic water supplies and medical treatment are being provided. We hope the security situation to enable the civilians to return very soon to their residential areas," it said in a statement.

To that end, UNMISS calls on all parties to show continued calm and restraint, it added and dismissed any suggestion that it was harbouring any key political or military figures linked to the incident.

US ADVISES CITIZENS

Meanwhile, the United States embassy in Juba advised its citizens in the country to exercise extra caution at all times.

"The U.S. Embassy will continue to closely monitor the security environment in South Sudan, with particular attention to Juba city and its immediate surroundings, and will advise U.S. citizens further if the security situation changes." It said for a statement extended to Sudan Tribune.

US Embassy, Juba Denies Riek's Refuge in its Premises

Staff Reporter

An official in the US Embassy in Juba has refuted widespread rumours that Dr. Riek Machar Teny, former Vice President of South Sudan has sought refuge in its premises after the coup he was said by the Government to have masterminded has been crushed.

Riek was said to have sought refuge in the embassy when he realized that the coup was unsuccessful and he had to evade arrest and trial. With the embassy declaring that he is not with them the politician's whereabouts remain unknown.

China's Reform Brings Opportunities to South Sudan's Development

seven straight years and its residents' income increased 71 times, China has definitely captured world attention with all the remarkable achievements it has made. Nonetheless, China's per capita GDP only ranks 86th in the world indicating huge dis-

China's development will bring. As the youngest nation in the world, South Sudan shares the historical missions of maintaining peace, growing economy and fighting for the well-being of the people. With its abundant resources and unique en-

Vice President James Wani Igga and other cabinet ministers offered a clear blueprint for future development of South Sudan by diversifying the economy and emphasizing on priority areas such as agriculture, mining, petroleum and infrastructure.

A local newspaper the day after violence engulfed Juba at the outset of the war, December 2013.

The consular team in the consular closet, October 2013. Photo courtesy of the author.

The author shares a flight manifest with a C-130 crew member as evacuees wait to board the aircraft, December 2013. Photo credit: Ajani Husbands.

The author with a South Sudanese American evacuee, December 2013.
Photo credit: Ajani Husbands.

The author in front of C-130 aircraft used to evacuate Americans from Juba, December 2013.
Photo credit: Ajani Husbands.

A gazebo on the US government residential compound, sandbagged to prepare for use as a defensive position. Photo by author.

Refugee camp for South Sudanese, northern Uganda. Photo by author.

Northern Uganda, a few miles from the South Sudanese border at Nimule, where South Sudanese refugees were arriving in droves, February 2014. Photo by author.

Secretary of State John Kerry meeting with civil society representatives, May 2014. Photo by author.

Rebel leader Riek Machar, January 2014. Photo credit: Reuters / Goran Tomasevic—stock.adobe.com.

President Barack Obama and First Lady Michelle Obama greet president of South Sudan Salva Kiir during a US-Africa Leaders Summit dinner, August 2014. Photo credit: Official White House Photo by Amanda Lucidon, www.flickr.com/photos/statephotos /14837359811.

Author boarding C-130 to evacuate from Juba, January 2014.
Photo credit: Ajani Husbands.

everyday Americans who travel and do business abroad, they are also often the foundation of our relationships in these countries, with political leaders, government bureaucrats, and the public. When the secretary of state calls a foreign minister or head of state to arrange for the release of an American prisoner or the signing of a bilateral agreement, that moment is made possible by innumerable moments behind the scenes, over weeks and months and years. Every day, diplomats make those moments happen.

I can't tell you the stories of the diplomats who were in the room or wrote the background briefings or pitched the ideas or built the relationships that led to the Marshall Plan or nuclear nonproliferation, but I can share a few examples of the consequential everyday work that diplomats do.

Chris hadn't been in Lagos long when Dana Air Flight 992 crashed on its descent following engine failure, killing all 153 people onboard and six on the ground. The dead included several Americans, the pilot among them. A Nigerian employee of the consular section went directly to the airport upon hearing the news to find the flight manifest and determine if any Americans were on the flight. He found it in the trash can. The Dana Air crew had fled the scene. Chris and a colleague ran all 153 names through the Passport Information Electronic Records System (PIERS) database to identify the Americans onboard. Chris then went down to the morgue, wreaking of jet fuel in the heat, after government contacts told him they might have found a few of the Americans. They wheeled out twenty or thirty bodies for him to look at, and he did a three-way comparison with the body, the photo from the passport record, and any photo IDs found in pockets. Then it was time to inform the families back home, a task all consular officers are familiar with. "Two of them hung up on the phone with me. They thought I was a scammer." Chris worked closely with government officials, desperate to unload decaying bodies in the heat, to convince them not to cremate any of the bodies until they were able to recover some for return to the families. Chris's close contacts with the airport director, the attorney general's office, and others facilitated this difficult emergency work every step of the way.

Meghan was a newly minted mid-level diplomat when she headed to Madrid as the environment, science, technology, and health officer and found herself at the center of our attempts to resolve a fifty-year-old conflict that had impeded the US bilateral relationship with Spain after we accidentally dropped nuclear bombs on their coastline.

In 1966, a US Air Force B-52 bomber collided with a refueling aircraft at thirty-one thousand feet above the Mediterranean Sea, dropping four nuclear warheads. Three of them hit land near the small fishing village of Palomares and the fourth was found in the ocean after a search lasting more than two months. Two of the warheads that hit land caught fire, leaching highly toxic plutonium across about two hundred hectares of land primarily used for agriculture. Our understanding of nuclear science at the time was less advanced than it is today, but even by past standards, our initial cleanup effort was haphazard at best. When Spain retested the site in the 1990s, it was still contaminated with radiation well beyond acceptable levels under Spanish law, causing serious economic issues that impeded the area's development.

By 2014, when Meghan arrived at post, the pace of talks had picked up ahead of the fiftieth anniversary of the disaster, with Spanish leadership raising the issue regularly in recent years in exchanges with Vice President Joe Biden, Secretary Hillary Clinton, and later Secretary John Kerry. It had become evident that the Palomares situation risked impacting other areas of bilateral cooperation, such as the two US military bases in Spain. While the issue had the attention of the front office—the ambassador and his deputy chief of mission—Meghan became the point person, navigating day-to-day progress with Santiago Gómez-Acebo, the deputy director of the North America desk at the Spanish Foreign Ministry, as the two sides explored concrete methods for resolution, eventually concluding that the two thousand tons of contaminated soil would need to be trucked out and relocated to a secure location in the United States. As the one who best understood the interests and needs of her Spanish counterparts as well as the technical details, Meghan played a key role in ensuring the conversations within the

US government still fit inside the parameters of what was physically and politically possible.

In the months that followed, State's treaty office and Department of Energy lawyers both got involved in hammering out drafts of an agreement, and Meghan would be the go-between, shuffling the drafts, responses, questions, and issues between the Spaniards and the many US government offices involved, using her deep understanding of the concerns on both sides to help guide the process to an acceptable point of agreement, including the correct technical translations. In the end, many of the details were negotiated between Meghan and Santiago on their governments' behalf. When Secretary of State John Kerry came to Spain in October 2015 and signed the agreement, Meghan was holding the paper. Ultimately, the Spanish government reneged on plans to sign a further binding treaty, which at the time was not politically appealing due to a pending election, but the United States had worked tirelessly for a good-faith solution and held up its end of the deal. The fifty-year thorn had been removed, strengthening our bilateral relationship and making it just a little easier the next time we might have a favor to ask.

Anya worked for three years in Kyiv in the economics section covering major international cyberattacks targeting Ukraine, including the BlackEnergy malware attack by a Russian cybercrime group on Ukraine's electricity infrastructure in 2015. Anya argued successfully for the State Department to play the primary role in our cyber engagements with Ukraine, and she organized the first US-Ukraine cyber dialogue in Kyiv. Why was this initiative important? Because Russia has and will again employ the same cyber tactics against us. By building better relationships with the Ukrainians on cyber issues, the United States got access to more information than we had before, which allowed us to strengthen our own systems and better anticipate and thwart future attacks. Cyber expertise is critical, but so are the relationships our diplomats build, through which we share that expertise with our partners and they share theirs in return.

I could go on with examples all day, but the gist is that diplomacy isn't a quick fix and doesn't take a straight path. Diplomacy is the long game we play as we build relationships, study cultures, learn local politics, discern interests and alliances, honor commitments, set precedents, practice influence, and lead by example. It requires time, investment, and an honest assessment of the target audience, the relationship, and the goals. Success in war is measured in bombs dropped, combatants killed, and territory held. Hard power is visible. Most diplomatic progress is far harder to quantify and often difficult to see. But without it, the greatest foreign policy feats of the twentieth century could not have been achieved.

So what happened in South Sudan? Our working-level relationships helped tremendously as we navigated evacuations, and Ambassador Page's influence was critical in ensuring the airport was open and accessible for our flights. But we had squandered influence over South Sudan's affairs by long failing to hold our "friends" to account. South Sudan's leaders had learned impunity over time, while we had learned less than we realized. Washington chose not to learn what we didn't want to know. We misread the warning signs. We hesitated at short-term costs to the detriment of long-term goals. We hoped for something better than what we saw, and so failed to use the tools we had available when they could have made a difference.

Could we have prevented war in 2013? Likely not. But we could have prevented our complicity, and mitigated the scale of suffering, by championing our values and condemning human rights violations and anti-democratic actions. We could have put our money where our mouth is, ending funding to corrupt and abusive arms of the government and security forces far sooner. We could have been honest, with the South Sudanese and with ourselves. Dishonest relationships simply don't carry the same benefits.

As the great poet and author Maya Angelou has said, "If someone shows you who they are, believe them." We chose not to. By repeatedly ignoring the truth, we undercut our own diplomatic influence.

14

Destruction

December 19–25, 2013

THE ALARM JARRED ME OUT OF BED AT 5 A.M. THE CRISIS was entering its fourth day. We had an emergency action committee meeting at the ambassador's residence at 7 a.m., and after that I would head to the airport, where I'd again be without email access for an unknown period of time. I had two precious hours to try to get on top of Washington's demands and urgent queries from contacts and Americans that came in overnight. I knew the day would be filled with more. I was hungry, perhaps for the first time in days. I couldn't really recall what I'd eaten since the crisis started. I opened the fridge and scanned the cupboard, but my compact kitchen was fairly bare. I relied on coffee and a spoonful of peanut butter to get me moving.

We'd asked the Task Force in Washington to consolidate into a single document any reports they'd received of kidnapped, injured, dead, or detained Americans, allowing me to gloss over some of the correspondence for now so I could focus on what was relevant for today's evacuation flight. But Washington remained demanding. Our team was sending back a steady stream of updates: on fighting in different areas of the country, American citizens stranded in different locations, conditions at the growing camps inside the UN facilities, evacuation planning of other diplomatic missions in Juba, and the status of activity—normal and otherwise—in the streets. In return, Washington sent us mostly questions.

The minutes ticked by quickly, and soon it was time for the emergency action committee meeting, so I pulled on my khaki shorts, T-shirt, and baseball cap and grabbed my yellow vest, papers, and a couple of clipboards to keep lists organized. I strapped my stabilizer boot onto one foot—leaving it behind yesterday had clearly been a mistake—and slipped my yellow running shoe onto the other before heading out the door.

Gathered again at the ambassador's dining table, we discussed the upcoming evacuation flight for American citizens and the reports that Bor, about ninety-four miles north of Juba, had fallen to rebel control under Peter Gadet, commander of the SPLA's Eighth Division. Gadet's relationship with the SPLA had been on-again, off-again since 2006, and as a Nuer his recent defection was not much of a surprise. According to some reports, he'd joined forces with the Murle rebels (yes, this was an alliance of those who had been killing each other only months before) to march south toward Juba. Juba itself seemed to be stabilizing, certainly compared to events a couple of days ago. The streets during the day were relatively quiet, so our attention turned to the north and to the question of whether rebels would attack the capital city. It hadn't begun as a coup, but now it was a full-fledged insurgency.

Separately, I mentioned that we'd heard from an American citizen with gunshot wounds who was stranded at the Juba Teaching Hospital. The American was shot in both feet by the SPLA as he tried to escape a checkpoint. His driver and another passenger were killed. The American was trying to find his way to safety but unable to walk. "I'll be at the airport for the evacuation flight today, but would it be possible, now that the streets are quieter, for anyone to visit him and check on the injuries?" Jim, our med officer (call sign Alaska), very quietly suggested he'd be willing to see him. Bob wasn't thrilled about the idea of his subjects entering into the fray in town, but he agreed to send a security team with Jim to visit the injured American.

Jim's small medical office was located on the residential compound. I didn't think he'd left the compound much in the months he'd been here, so I wondered how he felt about doing so now.

Jim was so quiet and unassuming that it was easy to forget he was in the room. He was a skilled RN with extensive experience in tropical medicine and all the other ills that go with this territory, but unless you had medical needs, you tended to overlook his presence, save those rare occasions when he showed up at the bar with one of his delicious homemade pizzas to share. During the crisis, however, Jim would become indispensable. After we'd evacuated all nonessential personnel, he asked if he could help. "I'm not that busy, just here if people need medical care," he'd said almost apologetically, so I gave him the duty phone. Based on his shyness, I never would have expected this role to suit him, but Jim would become the empathetic voice of comfort that Americans in distress needed. In the weeks ahead, we would receive dozens of thank-you messages for the kindness and support he had offered by phone to American citizens all across the country.

The management officer from USAID (who managed facilities and operations for the embassy overall) mentioned that most local staff were still being asked to stay home, given the continued concerns about security in the city, but managers could assure them their pay would continue as normal. Some drivers might be asked to come in when it was deemed safe enough. Some staff, he mentioned, had left Juba for their home towns and were difficult to contact at this point. I asked if we knew whether all the embassy's Nuer staff were in safe locations and whether we were taking any precautions for their safety when they returned to work, and he gave me a puzzled look. "Well, we don't know which ones are Nuer. It isn't like we can include that on a job application." And it was true. US law wouldn't allow it, but in a situation like this, it was critical information. Moving around the city if you're Nuer under current circumstances was far more dangerous than if you weren't. One of the security officers mentioned that a Nuer local guard had already taken refuge in the

UN camp with his family, and I learned that one of our agency's Nuer drivers had simply moved into our compound. At least some direct managers weren't taking it lightly.

After the meeting, I asked one of our assistant security officers if he could take me quickly to the embassy before we headed to the airport. An American UN officer flying out today had recently applied for a replacement passport, which we had received by mail a week prior. I was sure she was regretting not coming in when we first notified her of its arrival, but I was hopeful I could get it to her at the airport. I had a handful of other passports waiting for pickup that were probably best to have on hand.

. This was my first trip to the embassy since the crisis began. My first stop was my desk in the chancery by the political office. When James left for the holidays, he gave me a list of contacts to reach out to should anything develop on the political front. I hadn't had much time to think about it as I focused on American citizens but figured it was worth a look now. At some point, I hoped I'd have an opportunity to follow up on the political side of my job, including tracking the human rights developments.

I sat down at my desk and pulled the paper off the wall where I'd pinned it up for reference. As I ran my finger down the list of names, I realized it wasn't much use after all. *He's dead, he's arrested, he's arrested, he's missing, he fled to Uganda, he's missing . . .* I didn't have time to be shocked, so I filed it away to consider the implications at another time. And I did. That night, as I tried to sleep, I saw the list in my head. *He's dead, he's arrested, he's arrested, he's missing, he fled to Uganda, he's missing . . .*

The only person on the list I might reach was a government minister rumored to have sought refuge at the UN's growing makeshift camp for those fleeing the violence. UNMISS and humanitarian personnel had begun calling them PoC sites, meaning "protection of civilians," perhaps because it sounded less permanent, but essentially they were internal refugee camps—internally displaced person (IDP) camps in the humanitarian lingo—slowly formalizing inside the walls of UN facilities across the country. These places were every bit as dire as they sounded. It was shocking to realize that a well-respected minister, who less than a week ago had lived in a plush compound on Ministries Row, was now holing up inside one of them.

My next stop was the consular closet. I grabbed the four new US passports I had to distribute, along with a dozen South Sudanese official passports that were awaiting visas for travel to the United States. The Americans weren't the only ones trying to leave the country after all. I also emptied all the sensitive and controlled items from the safe into a large beach bag and backpack I had brought: three different types of embassy seals, a few hundred passport books, and a few hundred visa and passport foils. Nearly everything would need to be destroyed in case we ended up having to close down the embassy and evacuate on short notice. This would involve my hammering the seals until they were unrecognizable and burning batches of everything else in a fifty-gallon drum. I chucked in all the files of applications as well—no sense leaving behind the personal information of Americans in case this place got overrun. I threw the bags into the back of the armored SUV, and we quickly headed back to the residential compound.

Byron and Ajani were ready to go once I was back at the residence, so I hobbled quickly to my unit to drop off the two bags of sensitive materials, pausing only momentarily to consider protocols. The Consular Affairs office had instructed me to reduce holdings of controlled items, and retrieving them from the embassy was the first step. I had no safe on this compound, though, so I locked my unit for perhaps the first time ever and considered that the best I could do under the circumstances.

We arrived at the airport parking lot, and our setup already looked far more professional than it had the day prior, though the airport remained chaotic and crowded. It seemed like anyone who could scrounge up the cash for a one-way ticket out was trying to buy their way to safety. The three white guys in yellow vests had already set up the tables and had Americans and other citizens in organized lines waiting for our arrival. Ajani and Byron took a seat and started checking documents and filling out the first draft of the manifest.

Ajani was multitasking, monitoring social media from a Blackberry. Ajani's use of social media, through Facebook and Twitter, to rapidly inform Americans of security developments and evacuation plans, and to respond to urgent queries in real time, would become a case study of the State Department's most effective use of public diplomacy in a crisis to date.

I radioed Clem to find out the status of the flight. Clem was our liaison with the tower and the rest of the airport. "Well, the good news is the plane is here, and the crew is ready to go once you're ready to load passengers. The bad news is that the only runway is blocked by a plane that just crashed. No one was hurt, but it's blocking departures." The nose gear of a charter flight for the Japanese Embassy had collapsed on landing, and Clem and another military colleague were working with airport authorities to help clear it from the runway.

"Any idea when it'll be moved?" I asked hopefully.

"Eh, unclear. They aren't exactly equipped for contingencies here."

Departures might be stalled, but our plane still needed to be a priority once they resumed, and we had 130 passengers to organize. I returned to the line to check on progress. We had worked through a lot of kinks in our system yesterday, so prioritization and ticketing was going much smoother today. We looked to have about one hundred Americans seeking travel and nearly the same number of others. The British government had a C-17 military aircraft expected to depart that afternoon, so we redirected British citizens to their own embassy staff across the parking lot. Their C-17 had been the only aircraft to navigate around the crash, using half the runway and a combat landing.

By early afternoon, the blocked runway problem hadn't yet been resolved, but we had our passengers ticketed and were beginning to move them through security, again in the borrowed VIP section. We'd had to tell dozens of non-US citizens that we didn't have room for them today, and a handful of Americans opted not to travel since we couldn't accommodate their extended families or friends. The ticketing process again involved difficult decisions and hard conversations, but our team was getting more comfortable with it.

The day was hot and the air flat and still. Sweat was dripping down my face and neck and occasionally onto the scribbled partial manifest on the clipboard in my hand. The waiting passengers had no shade. One woman sat on a suitcase, visibly ill. I handed her some water and she said she had malaria. It was a statement more than a complaint, but she was keen to get out of the sun. I handed her a spare hat I'd brought; it was all I had to offer. Moms draped children and babies in scarves and traditional cloth *kikois* to protect them from the sun. We started moving groups of twenty at a time from our staging area in the northwest corner of the parking lot to the VIP security entrance. Even with the boot, I found it hard to stand still, so I enthusiastically led this exercise. I heard passengers muttering about the heat and the long wait as I walked by, but the boot seemed to be serving a purpose. I looked fairly pathetic hobbling back and forth, and most people assumed it was a war injury, so no one felt they could complain to me. I'd take the unearned sympathy if it helped us stay orderly.

While we were beginning the security checks to get the passengers to the tarmac, news came in that the airport authorities had managed to tow the crashed plane just far enough off the runway to make it usable. Departures were moving again, and a sense of urgency swelled across the airport as everyone realized we only had a couple of hours before the airport would close ahead of curfew. The immigration officer checking passports at the VIP entrance moved through the motions rapidly, and he seemed content to take our word on those who were boarding without documentation, as long as he got to leave the airport on time. I'd been standing by the entrance keeping an eye on the NSS minder and pushing our passengers through the line. A mom showed up with three children to shepherd, so I carried her baby through security and the lounge to the outside waiting area next to the tarmac. On the other side, I ran into one of the charter crew, who had some questions about the scribbles on the manifest.

Byron and I then finished boarding our 130 passengers. The door closed, and we backed away toward the waiting area barrier to watch the plane's taxi and takeoff.

"Dugout, Dugout, this is Jackson. Wheels up 16:42." It was a cathartic call.

We piled into the vehicles and headed back through the lightly trafficked streets of Juba. Curfew wasn't far off. Clem mentioned that the situation in Bor was still uncertain, with rebels in control and flights grounded, so three US contractors working on a criminal investigative training program were stranded there, isolated in their compound. The embassy was working with UNMISS to see if military peacekeepers could at least move the contractors to the relative security of the UN compound. And it was relative. UNMISS compounds across the country were looking more and more vulnerable to attack. That same day, an UNMISS compound in Akobo, in the northeast near the Ethiopian border, was invaded and three Indian UN peacekeepers were killed. What little remained of our sense of security by virtue of being diplomatic personnel was fading fast.

HUMANS ARE ADAPTABLE creatures. By the third day of evacuations and fifth day of the crisis, it was the new normal. I woke up at 5 a.m., cup of coffee, spoon of peanut butter, rapid response to emails received overnight. At 7 a.m., meeting at the ambassador's residence. Then to the airport. Line them up, check documents, issue seats, clear security, keep an eye on sketchy NSS officer and close watch on dual-national men vulnerable to detention. Cross-check manifest, board passengers, wheels-up, inform mission control and the Task Force in Washington.

The process became efficient, but no flight or day was quite the same. The evacuations would drag on for far longer than we would have guessed in those first days, as people made their way to Juba from distant parts of the country as fighting spread. People came to the city by car, boat, and foot, however they could manage. Every time we thought the need was dissipating, another wave of desperate people would arrive. The subsequent flights were mostly much smaller, one or two charter flights a day rather than multiple C-130s, but Washington seemed willing to spare no expense as long as some

Americans were involved. We might only have a handful of citizens to evacuate, but we'd fill the remaining seats with anyone in need. Getting people out of South Sudan, it turns out, was a much simpler prospect than winning the peace. The planes would keep coming for three weeks, nearly every day. In the end, we took 1,100 people to safety on nineteen flights. It wasn't the numbers that stood out, however. It was the stories, 1,100 of them.

"I don't have my passport. They burned down my home. I was lucky to get out alive."

"I have no luggage. It isn't safe to go back to my neighborhood. I was across town when the violence started. These clothes are all I have. I haven't been home since."

"I want to go, but I'm looking for my father. I hoped to find him here. They killed my neighbors and my brother. I managed to run away. But my father wasn't there. I can't leave until I find him."

"Will there be a flight tomorrow? I want to go, but I'm waiting for my sister and her children who are coming down from Bor. They're fleeing fighting there and plan to make their way here by foot. I haven't heard from them since yesterday though. Her cell battery was dying, and they were hiding in the bush."

I didn't hear everyone's story, but I didn't need to. I could read them in the tired, anxious, desperate faces. Even as they smiled receiving a ticket, passing security, or boarding the plane, so many eyes conveyed a deep, unmistakable sadness for what they had seen and what they were leaving behind.

Those eyes were a constant reminder that there was other work to be done. The evacuations had been all-consuming, but as we got the hang of it, and the demand slowed down, we were able to make it a part-time activity. The consular part of my job—taking care of American citizens—was under control. Now I had some time to pursue my other portfolio: human rights reporting. I'd been hearing stories, but I wanted to get to the bottom of what was really happening out there and to make sure Washington knew. Ambassador Page was deeply involved in political developments, with Kiir and Machar at a stalemate, but we had no other reporting officer left at post. Even the press seemed to have only partial secondhand information. Someone had to document what we were hearing and seeing. Someone had to take the time to corroborate it, to compile it, to assess the violence: what was happening, to whom, by whom, and what it meant. Someone had to write it up coherently so the embassy could officially report it to Washington. If I didn't do it, who would?

On the third day of evacuations, I convinced Bob, reluctantly, to let me go to the IDP camp at the UNMISS compound near the airport. This was where the two sides of my job could meet. Human rights victims were fleeing to the camp, and we'd heard that at least a half-dozen American citizens were stranded inside too—Nuer dual nationals afraid to make even the short walk from the camp to the airport. We'd encouraged them to come for previous flights, noting that the streets were largely calm and reports of targeted attacks had fallen sharply, though we continued to hear rumors of death squads roaming at night and lurking outside the camps. A South Sudanese friend conceded that attacks in Juba had mostly stopped but suggested that was merely because there were no more Nuer left in the streets to kill. Nuer had largely been eradicated from town, one way or another. An American UN officer had been liaising with the group inside the camp. "They aren't leaving here unless you take them," she told me. "And the situation inside here is not going to improve. If you can drive them that short distance and make sure they get on the plane, that's the only way this is going to happen." We were going to great lengths to help Americans—this seemed a manageable task to me, and it was an opportunity for me to see the inside of this new camp for myself. I knew I could learn a lot.

Byron and I had teed up other passengers for the day's flight by midday, so I headed over to the IDP camp in an armored vehicle with a couple of our security officers. We stopped briefly at the UNMISS Tomping compound gate to show our diplomatic IDs, and then followed a dirt road past the tukul, trailer office blocks, and staff residences. We arrived in a low-lying area toward the far back of the compound, where an unassuming makeshift registration area had been set up, manned by a couple of humanitarians who took little notice of us as they spoke to what I assumed were new arrivals. The American UN officer met us there and told us she had organized a van to help transport the American IDPs back to the airport once I reviewed their documents and gave them the okay to join the flight. This wasn't part of her job, but in the face of so much suffering, she was looking for any opportunity she could to provide concrete help.

I followed her through an open gate into what was officially the "protection of civilians" area. My security team followed close behind. I knew the officers felt we were exposed, away from the vehicle and moving into masses of people who were under severe stress. The area was dry, dusty, and looked like a cross between a disorganized yard sale and a dumpster that extended as far as the eye could see, and it was teeming with people. In only a few days, the camp had exceeded ten thousand. Nothing about it appeared planned: haphazard tents of all types and sizes, mattresses along the pathway, folding chairs, office chairs, plastic chairs, perhaps some picked off from the UN facilities or maybe brought from home. A crowd of men had taken shelter from the sun under an abandoned truck trailer that had probably been sitting here when the makeshift tent city grew up around it.

We found Samuel, the American who had been the UN officer's primary contact and the only one with a functioning cell phone. He shook my hand enthusiastically and expressed his gratitude for the US Embassy coming to his aid. He told us he'd gather the others and bring them out to the van. One of the security guys told me it was time to head back to the vehicle. While I knew the numbers, seeing it firsthand—a makeshift camp of ten thousand desperately thrown together—brought the scale of this crisis home even more. I wanted to move farther into the camp, talk to the people, find out what happened to them, what were their plans, and what brought them here. But I knew we had a flight to run, and our responsibility today was to get these Americans on it. I'd have to return.

Samuel came back with nine others, all miraculously with passports in hand. Two, however, seemed hesitant. They had friends they hadn't found and extended family they couldn't bring with them. I urged them to go while they could, but I could see they were con-flicted. No one carried with them any more than a plastic grocery bag of belongings. Leave with almost nothing and no one, or stay behind and see what happened. It was a brutal decision. In the end, the two gentlemen decided to stay. The UN officer promised to check up on them and let me know how they fared, but leaving them still felt terrible.

At the airport, I asked one of the Americans from the camp if he thought the ones left behind were safe there. "That camp isn't safe. There isn't enough food or shelter. Sanitation is terrible. People will only take that for so long. It's very unstable, and SPLA wait just out-side the gates for an opportunity, so you can't go out safely either. And who would want to go out after what we've seen. Is anyone being punished for the killings? No. So why should we believe the govern-ment when they say it's safe now?" He told me to go back to the camp if I really want to know what had been happening in Juba. "You have ten thousand witnesses. And they have nothing to do but tell you their stories."

Eight of the Americans from the camp joined fifty other Amer-icans and fifty-eight others on our charter flight early that evening. They'd all left a lot behind, but at least they'd be out of squalid condi-tions that night and should sleep a little better, met at the other end by my consular colleagues in Nairobi, who would help them connect with family, find a place to stay, or reach their final destination. I won-dered, though, as I'm sure they did, about those they'd left behind.

The next morning after the emergency action committee meet-ing, I met up with Byron to head to the airport to put a few dozen evacuees on a C-130 that came in to resupply the troops protecting our compound. People fleeing Jonglei state had started to arrive in Juba but weren't looking to stay long. At the airport parking lot, we had our tables set up as a check-in desk, and a crowd of people were there, hopeful for escape.

We had several elderly and sick passengers that day, and more than a couple needed help getting through security and onto the plane. An old man with glasses and a concerned look told me his daughter was supposed to meet him at the airport in Nairobi, but he wasn't sure she'd be there and was worried he wouldn't know what to do. "My colleagues are meeting the plane at the other end. They'll help you get where you need to be," I assured him. And I knew it was true. The Nairobi and Kampala teams had been extremely welcoming and helpful with all passengers, helping them find places to stay, contact family members, or organize onward travel. I was very proud of the work we were all doing for Americans and others here.

We went through the usual drill and ended up with about eighty passengers, got them through security, and lined them up on the tarmac outside the VIP lounge. It was a long line of people and luggage, and the scene seemed more dramatic and foreboding as they awaited to board the large gray C-130 instead of a simple white commercial aircraft. I stood back behind the plane and to the side, out of the trajectory of the loud and powerful fan of the engine, awaiting instruction. One of our soldiers approached me to check the manifest. We ran through the numbers, and I advised him of the special cases, shouting over the engine.

The soldier looked down the line of passengers and commented that it was well organized. He took the manifest, thanked me, and began to walk away. Then he turned back and shouted, "What service are you with, anyway?"

"State Department! I'm the consular officer!" I shouted back.

"Really? Huh," he replied, cocking his helmeted head. Apparently, I was not the only one with a new sense of respect for consular work.

Not long after we lined up our passengers on the tarmac, we learned that the three V-22 Osprey helicopters the US government had sent to Bor to evacuate stranded American citizens had taken on small-arms fire as they approached the airfield and had to abort the landing. Later reports indicated 119 rounds hit the three helicopters, seriously injuring four of the Navy SEALs on board. One would lose his leg. The Air Force Special Operations Command crews managed to fly the damaged helicopters all the way to Entebbe, Uganda, five hundred miles south and the nearest safe landing space with sufficient medical care. Peter Gadet later apologized for the "misunderstanding." I never got the full story, but there was apparently a hiccup somewhere along the communication chain between our embassy, the UN force commander in Bor, and rebel leadership, so they weren't expecting military aircraft in the air.

The day after the aborted US evacuation attempt, the UN stepped up its own efforts to evacuate staff and others out of Bor, leaving behind a military and protection staff clearly insufficient to ensure the safety of the fourteen thousand IDPs who had taken refuge there. The US government would be joining forces with the UN, offering three more military helicopters, this time staffed with some of the embassy's security and military personnel as well. The situation inside the UNMISS camp in Bor continued to deteriorate, so everyone wanted to take advantage of a window of calm and the rebels' willingness to facilitate safe passage following the recent debacle. The rebels weren't doing themselves any favors by agitating friends of the South Sudanese people. The urgency of the evacuation intensified as rumors swirled that the government planned to send SPLA troops en masse up to Bor to engage the rebels, which many feared would leave Juba undefended. Kiir's enemies weren't all concentrated in Jonglei state, after all. The government assured us that the SPLA would stand down on its own operations in the area as well, clearing a window for humanitarian efforts.

Meanwhile, in Juba, diplomatic efforts to hurry peace plodded along. Ministers descended on the capital city from all the neighboring countries, along with the African Union commissioner for peace and security and the UN's special envoy to the African Union, attempting to smooth things over between President Kiir and his opponents. But Kiir backtracked on his promises to let the ministers meet with the political detainees arrested during the first day of the conflict, who were at the center of the power struggle over peace negotiations. Meanwhile, what began with targeted killings in Juba had erupted into rebellion across the country. Neither side at this point appeared interested in a quiet resolution.

We had a single charter flight out of Juba that seventh day of the crisis, so I headed back to the airport in the early afternoon. It wasn't the usual crowd milling about the parking lot. Tired, ragged-looking Chinese laborers made up a surprising percentage of the people there. Dozens and dozens. "That can't be a good sign," I noted.

"What do you mean?" asked a colleague.

"It means the oil fields up north are really in trouble."

Within a few days, the Chinese National Petroleum Corporation had shut down oil production in Unity state and evacuated seven hundred Chinese staff. Even the tough were getting going.

We coordinated with the UN teams and our own folks making sorties to Bor to ensure most of the Americans who had been stranded there made it to Juba in time to catch our flight out to Nairobi. The plane was wheels up around 5 p.m., but I stuck around for the helicopters carrying our embassy colleagues. These were the last evacuation aircraft out of Bor for the day, and they carried a couple dozen Kenyan and Ugandan UN workers from the base. One of my security colleagues, John, texted me from the helicopter and asked if I could reach out to the UN to help get the workers space in the UNMISS compound in Juba for the night, since it was so late. It proved harder than we expected. The UN bureaucrats I could reach were hesitant to take anyone else into the overflowing IDP camp. "But these are your employees. These aren't random people," I implored them. They conceded, and John and I took the UN workers directly across the tarmac to the airport gate of the UNMISS compound. They were clearly terrified but relieved to have escaped Bor. We doubled back to the helicopters quickly to pick up the rest of the crew. It was too late for the aircraft to refuel and depart, so the teams who flew in would be staying with us for the night. We all crammed into a couple of vehicles and hightailed it through the remaining open gate and off to Airport Road. The day's light was only a sliver above the horizon by then, and we were well past curfew.

I was sitting in the very back on the lap of a soldier I had just met, with someone's rifle across my legs. Nerves were high. The soldier was tense. I don't remember his name, but I remember the angry look on his face. I learned that he was a medic and part of the unit that had been in the aborted evacuation mission the day before. I asked him, "You alright? Sorry, it's not comfortable in here."

"I just don't understand what we're doing here. Why one of my guys lost his leg for this shit."

I wasn't sure I understood either anymore.

Back at the residence, we moved quickly from the vehicles to the emergency action committee meeting, which had been on hold awaiting our return. I asked John about what he saw in Bor. "Well, from the air, I saw a few hundred UPDF [Ugandan People's Defense Force] in defensive positions around the airport there and a tank just off the runway." Uganda had swooped in to provide reinforcements to Kiir. If it hadn't, all of this would have been going very differently. Juba was safer in the meantime, but the Ugandan presence made a long-term war far more possible than it would otherwise have been.

John continued, "The mood up in Bor is hairy. The ROK [Republic of Korea peacekeeping] forces are scared as shit. They didn't want rebels anywhere around there to see them anywhere near US military uniforms, that's for sure. We couldn't leave fast enough. Though none of them want to be there. They're just sitting ducks, waiting to be attacked. Some locals are leaving the camps, thinking it might make more sense to take their chances in the bush."

On day eight of the crisis, we had no evacuation flights scheduled. US special envoy for Sudan and South Sudan Donald Booth was arriving for a few hours of meetings, including with President Kiir and the political detainees accused of the imaginary coup, and VIP visits needed staff and resources. His office promised it wouldn't affect the mission, but we held off on flights anyway as a precaution.

Juba was slowly getting back to some version of normal, but I still hadn't been anywhere but the embassy, the airport, and the UNMISS compound since the fighting began. I talked Bob into letting me take an armored vehicle and a well-armed security escort to drive around town. I wasn't sure what we'd find. I understood from Gio and Chol, who had both crossed town, that the "cleanup" of bodies was mostly completed. Chol had witnessed some of it directly. He'd called me a few days ago to tell me he'd seen six large trucks piled high with corpses heading north in the direction of the military headquarters at Bilpam, with military escorts. They hadn't even tried to be stealthy about it. I'd hear about the convoy of dead bodies from several other contacts who'd witnessed it. I knew the neighborhoods that were reportedly hardest hit, and I'd heard rumors about a police station where a massacre took place. A friend at the UN's Office for the Coordination of Humanitarian Affairs was one of the first expats to get out in town to assess the situation. He drew me a primitive map so I could find the station. Addresses and street signs weren't common in the city, so directions usually went something like "Turn left at the mango tree; it's just past the green shack selling phone credit."

My security escort and I headed out shortly after the morning's emergency action committee meeting. Much of the information I had to guide me came from friends in the Atrocities Crowd. As I would have expected from these seasoned South Sudan watchers, they had found ways to get out and about sooner than I did, and they were tracking incidents in Juba and beyond with a well-developed and far-reaching set of trusted contacts.

My escort was a quiet guy, one of the temporary-duty security officers brought in as emergency reinforcements right after the crisis began. I didn't really know him, but he was keen for a more interesting assignment than just waiting around for shit to hit the fan, and I needed a security detail.

We turned left out of the embassy and then right onto Airport Road, opposite our usual direction in recent days. Airport Road becomes the Juba-Mundri Road as it heads northwest and out of the city. In the center of town, in our neighborhood, the pace of life had almost returned to normal—except for a heavier security presence in the streets. We saw some traffic, and even a few people walking about. As we worked our way northwest, the activity thinned out. We were moving into predominantly Nuer areas. The city wasn't segregated, but many neighborhoods had a strong ethnic lean. We picked a couple of Nuer neighborhoods in the general area where we'd heard the most reports of violence. These were humble neighborhoods: dirt roads, simple houses, some surrounded by walls of hard-packed dirt or concrete, other lots designated with simple reed fences. Rows of small shop fronts lined the main streets, with residential areas stretching out along rough pedestrian trails, pocketed with pits and gaps left over from the last rainy season.

I'd been in a lot of African neighborhoods in a lot of African cities and towns in the past few years. As a tourist and a consultant for several years before I joined the Foreign Service, I traveled in many rural and urban places on the continent. Africa is an extremely diverse place, but some commonalities and familiarities you expect to see. These familiar signs were now missing. All signs of life were gone.

We rolled slowly up the rough dirt roads, looked up the residential paths, gazed into compounds and shop fronts in Gudele, Mangateen, Muniki, and Mia Saba—bustling neighborhoods only days ago.

No smiling children playing on shop steps, no moms with babies strapped to their backs or loads balanced on their heads, no men sitting on plastic chairs under scrappy shade trees trading stories. No chickens, no dogs. No commerce. Nothing. No one. Anywhere.

People had left here in a hurry.

The streets were eerie, so empty I couldn't recognize neighborhoods at all. Signs of destruction and violence had replaced the signs of life. Tukuls burned, gates busted, doors torn off hinges, shop stalls shattered into broken bits of wood. Homes and stores appeared looted, except for the handful with heavy security doors.

It looked like a movie set suddenly abandoned halfway through takedown. There were no visible bodies, but the stench of death hung in the still air. I took notes and a few photos, but pictures didn't capture the unnatural sense it evoked. Everything about it felt wrong.

Leaving the Gudele neighborhood, we headed back toward Airport Road. We had one more stop to make. We neared the Gudele-Mia Saba Road and saw the Lou Clinic on the right. It was my landmark to start looking for the turnoff on the left, by a large mango tree. It was a small dirt road, easy to miss. We turned cautiously. From the main road, you couldn't see them. The view was blocked by the tree and a wall, but then suddenly they were in front of us: an unfriendly crowd. Eight uniformed SPLA officers quickly surrounded our vehicle, weapons raised, one pointing directly in the windshield and another at the driver's-side window. They were yelling angrily and some were gesturing wildly for us to leave. We both raised our hands in a gesture of compliance, and my escort started slowly backing out. The officers stayed close to the car, blocking the view as best they could, but I could see the police station behind them, next to another mango tree. I couldn't make out many details of the building, but I saw a room with an open door on the left side and what appeared to be the cell area to the right, with barred windows facing us, opening directly to the outside. It looked just as described. Perhaps twenty more uniformed men were milling about it, all alarmed at our presence.

Our vehicle backed into a turn, and the officers peeled off to let my escort pull forward. Nerves were high, and it was such a brief encounter, it took me a moment to realize what I had seen. I looked back as we pulled into the main road just to confirm. All the officers were wearing surgical masks. I guess the cleanup wasn't yet complete.

ON THE TENTH day of the crisis, I got up early. It was Christmas. We had one small charter flight that morning for a handful of Americans who had finally made it to Juba and gotten their ticket out. I'd promised Byron I'd do my best to make sure he got home for Christmas after helping us through the most chaotic time of the evacuations, so he had caught a flight out on Christmas Eve and would be with his family in Djibouti today, which made me happy. He told me later that he had a spoonful of peanut butter that morning in my honor.

As I hurried out of my container to meet Clem, who was the only help I needed for today's small charter, I grabbed a Santa hat lying next to my droopy Christmas plant. It had been a heavy period, so maybe I could bring a bit of levity to the airport today.

The hat brought some smiles from the passengers, the charter crew, and the airport staff working the holiday. It was sunny with bright blue skies above. As Clem and I sat just off the tarmac waiting for wheels up, we made up our own version of "The Twelve Days of Christmas" to mark some of the more memorable moments over the past ten days.

> *On the twelfth day of evacuation, the Task Force gave to me:*
> *Twelve short-fuse taskings*
> *Eleven detainees*
> *Ten SPLA defectors*
> *Nine evac flights*
> *Eight fighting positions*
> *Seven tweets from Ajani*
> *Six bags for shredding*
> *Five LPRs [Legal Permanent Residents]*
> *Four undocumented infants*
> *Three Eritreans*
> *Two C-130s*
> *And an angry NSS guy!*

Sunshine and humor invigorated me. For a moment, I felt content. For a moment, I forgot that a war was still raging around us.

15

A New Year

December 26, 2013–January 3, 2014

THE HEAVY PRESENCE OF UGANDAN FORCES IN THE COUNTRY had become even more clear. They were monitoring and patrolling the road between Juba and the Ugandan border in the south, and several hundred appeared to be guarding the airport. The Ugandan government claimed this was all to assist with the safe evacuation of its citizens, but it became evident that the Ugandans had decided propping up Kiir's hold on the country was the simplest way to reinforce stability north of its border. Given the ragtag nature of the fracturing SPLA, this was likely the only reason Kiir prevailed.

A South Sudanese spokesperson announced that forces loyal to the government had retaken Bor from the rebels. A humanitarian friend at the base in Bor told me the troops leading the march into town were in fact the far more effective Ugandan forces. "I saw them myself. They weren't even hiding it," he said. Fighting continued in the area, though the government, thanks to the Ugandans, controlled the airport there and had the upper hand.

Fighting had also been raging in Malakal, the capital of Upper Nile state and South Sudan's second largest city, four hundred miles due north of Juba. The UNMISS compound there was housing twelve thousand civilians seeking refuge, and it was squarely in the middle of the heavy fighting now underway. Even inside the makeshift

IDP camp, UNMISS peacekeepers were starting to separate citizens by tribe because violence had broken out. Tensions were high everywhere in Malakal. Shells had rained down on the base hospital. During a lull in the fighting, IDPs reported that they saw some SPLA troops remove their uniforms to seek shelter inside the camp. Government forces were north of the town and expected to make a push to retake it imminently.

At least a dozen American citizens had sought refuge inside the UNMISS camp. Seven were missionaries running a small orphanage in the area. The others were dual nationals. We were fielding calls from them and their families in the United States. Jim, our med officer, and Lori, the ambassador's office manager, spoke with the stranded ones by phone, and the Task Force in Washington was in touch with their families in the United States.

At least that was something we could offer. The situation in the base was dire, the Americans told us, and terrifying. They still had some water but had run out of food. UNMISS was unable to safely resupply. We wanted to get them out to safety, but the situation was too dangerous so far.

I FOUND A few hours to return to the IDP camp in the UNMISS base in Tomping near the Juba airport. David, one of the American citizens who had decided to stay behind, had offered to introduce me to survivors. I met him at the entrance of the camp, and we walked in, with three US security personnel trailing close behind me. I was again surprised we weren't stopped from entering or required to sign in, show identification, or offer some explanation or purpose for being here. I saw people—maybe staff, maybe IDPs, it's hard to say— walking freely in and out. The usual security protocols were still not in place.

We walked down a wide dirt path lined with makeshift tents, mattresses, and tarps strung up on whatever could be found, with household goods, pots and pans, and clothing strewn about as though a thousand households had exploded inside a dirt lot. The mess stretched as far as I could see. It felt awkward to look at the people as we passed, seeing them in this squalor, a disaster tourist ogling at their suffering. Some of the children were mildly curious at the white woman walking through their camp, flanked by intimidating and serious men, but most of the eyes I saw looked empty, as though they had seen too much and just given up.

David walked me up to a group of adults, men and women, old and young, sitting in a circle on hard-packed dirt, just in front of a low-slung blue tarp that provided meek shelter to a few threadbare mattresses. Several of the men and women sat in mismatched plastic chairs or on stools they'd pulled together, and others sat on the ground or on upturned buckets. A man in the center of the circle got up and offered me his plastic chair. They knew who I was and they wanted to receive me. It was a solemn occasion, and they had set up as formal a reception area as possible under the circumstances. These were chosen representatives of their communities, and they hoped that telling their stories to a Western diplomat would mean something would be done, that peace would return and they could go back to their homes and lives.

I introduced myself, shaking the hands of everyone in the circle before I sat. Tradition can be an important cultural glue when all else is lost, and greetings were key in South Sudan. In waiting rooms in ministry buildings or private offices, every person who entered shook the hand of everyone already present. It was rude not to extend a hand. No matter how dire things got, there was no need to be impolite. The group had already decided among themselves how to proceed. Most spoke in slow, labored English, and David translated for others.

Once I sat, two women from the Gudele neighborhood began. They told me that several families had gathered into a couple of private homes for protection after the violence began the night of December 15. They felt safe, they said, because they thought civilians who stayed indoors would be spared the violence of a conflict that seemed at first to be only a military scuffle. Juba was a violent place, after all. On the afternoon of December 16, however, Dinka soldiers from the SPLA they believed to be part of the Presidential Guard began going house to house, searching, they said, for "Nuer men" and taking them away. The women did not know where, but they knew the men did not return.

One man from the Mia Saba neighborhood told a similar story. He and his neighbors also believed the fighting was strictly military, so they went about their business on December 16. After a few hours, uniformed men began going door to door. He and twenty-nine other men were collected from their homes forcefully and taken to an NSS facility nearby, where twenty-five of them (those suspected to be aligned with the opposition) were immediately shot and killed. The remaining five were taken to NSS headquarters near Jebel Kujur to be questioned but later released; he was not sure why they were so lucky.

A university student told me he was at his uncle's home when it was surrounded by Dinka officers at 3 p.m. on the sixteenth. The soldiers demanded the occupants come out, but they locked the doors and refused. The soldiers began shooting into the house, rounds easily permeating the packed-earth walls. This drove everyone out to the street, where the soldiers lined them up and checked their ID cards. The student said the soldiers were looking for obviously Nuer names. Then the officers shot nine people on the spot. Eight of them died there. The student ran away as the bullets fell, escaping to the house of an Equatorian neighbor, where he hid until the following night, when he walked across town in darkness to the UNMISS Tomping base. He had slept just outside the fence until the morning when he was allowed to enter.

Another man said he was dragged from his home near the Nile River and taken with more than two hundred other men to a location farther downriver, where soldiers began tying up and blindfolding the men. It was a confusing and chaotic scene when they began lining them up, and this man broke away and ran. He was unsure how he managed not to be shot as bullets rang out while he sprinted away in fear. He made it to the riverbank and leapt into the muddy Nile. He floated downstream a ways until he could pull into a carved-out bank that provided some cover. He then heard extensive shooting.

Moments later, dozens of bodies floated past him. He remained hidden in the water for three days, he said, before he emerged, waterlogged but alive. Like so many others, he walked to the UNMISS compound as the only known refuge.

An elderly man chimed in that tanks had come to his neighborhood of Lologo early on December 16 and plowed through fifteen occupied homes with no warning, killing many people inside. He and his family fled to the UNMISS compound.

He asked me, when the violence is perpetrated by men of the government, in government uniforms with government resources, what authorities are there to protect you? So he, and all the others, had walked, by the dozens, then the hundreds, then the thousands to the UNMISS compound. They had nowhere else safe to go.

It felt awkward to write notes as these witnesses and victims told their horrors. I tried to recall some of the general pointers we were given in the consular training classes about how to interact with victims. As a consular officer, you expect to occasionally inform families that a relative has died abroad or assist an American victim of crime overseas, but I would never have anticipated anything on this scale. Over and over, the stories pummeled me like waves.

I jotted down key words and phrases in my notebook, mostly without even glancing down. I wanted to be sure to remember details, but I wanted to respect their telling too. I knew that individual stories, stories that people could see and feel and imagine, would have far greater impact than unimaginable numbers and faceless statistics about strangers. I'd fill my notebook with more details as soon as I left, when the memory was still fresh—though I'd learn that wasn't really necessary. These stories would stay with me for a long time.

This wasn't part of my consular job. These weren't American citizen-welfare cases. I was here only seeking the truth about what had happened in this city. No one had told me to come here, and I wasn't even sure what end it would serve. But the other, separate part of my job, the part that had been pushed aside while I focused on helping Americans, was to report on the human rights situation. As a demonstration of how little the United States prioritized this portfolio generally, it was routinely assigned to junior officers. But if it ever mattered anywhere, it seemed this situation would qualify.

I didn't think anyone was expecting me to learn much beyond additional details of the horror stories already floating around the diplomatic community. I wasn't a journalist looking for the emotional hook, but I knew this place had a history of impunity, of atrocities being overlooked. I didn't intend to overlook them. I'd long suspected that this history was part of South Sudan's original sin, part of what drove the current conflict and the conflicts that had come before.

I recalled that the crimes in Jonglei state were hard for me to understand because I couldn't picture them. If I could make others picture these crimes, would we treat them differently? What might we do that we wouldn't otherwise?

I looked in the victims' eyes as they told their stories. I was grateful they were willing to speak with me, and I wanted to help them retain, or regain, as much dignity in the process as I could. This camp, after all, was a hard place to find dignity, and I had nothing more to offer.

We concluded with this group. I offered handshakes and gratitude, but even to me, my words and gestures felt shallow, unbefitting of the magnitude of what they had offered me. David took me to see two other groups gathered to share similar stories.

Our last stop was the abandoned truck trailer I'd noticed on my first visit. It sat about four feet off the ground, and a half-dozen men were lying listlessly or propped up on an elbow on dirty mattresses in the shade beneath it. David leaned over and extended his hand to one of the men, who sat up to greet him in Nuer. David introduced me. I shook his hand and took a seat, somewhat awkwardly, on the corner of the mattress under the trailer, notebook open on my lap. The sun was punishing, so I didn't blame the men for retaining their shade.

With simple English and some help from David, this man told me his story. The afternoon of December 16, he heard shooting outside his home. He was aware of the unrest in town and had heard rumors that soldiers were rounding up men, so he sent the women outside to check on what was happening. The women of the house went into the neighborhood to see, and when they returned, they told the men, "Dinka are killing Nuers." He and two other Nuer neighbors were at his home at the time, so they fled on foot to the nearby Gudele police station to take shelter.

When they arrived, they saw three dead bodies in front of the building. They froze at the sight, and before they could flee, SPLA forces standing nearby began shooting at them. The other two men were hit and killed, and the man telling us this story was grabbed, beaten, and thrown into a small cell adjacent to the police station. He estimated 250 other men were crowded in the cell, body to body, in suffocating heat. He could hear what sounded like another crowded cell next door.

At about six that evening, he told me, soldiers forced their rifles through the barred windows on three sides of the cell and began shooting into the mass of compressed men. They continued shooting for several minutes, he said, until nearly everyone was dead. He was shot four times and collapsed under a pile of bodies as other men fell on top of him. He lay there for hours under bodies dripping with blood and bloating in the evening's heat. He dared not speak, breathing as quietly as he could.

After a few hours, the commotion outside had ceased, but still he didn't try to move. He lay there until 4 p.m. the following afternoon, he said, when military police arrived at the scene and shouted into the cell asking if anyone was alive. Only then did he begin hearing other tentative voices. This man and seven others had miraculously survived, lying under the corpses for a terrifying night and day. Four of them had been shot. Bullets had somehow missed the others entirely.

The military police—men of various ethnicities—took the four injured to the hospital and told the others to go to UNMISS for shelter, that it wasn't safe elsewhere in the city. The man explained that he had spent another day at the Juba Teaching Hospital until uniformed soldiers came, hunting down and killing one of the other survivors. At this point, he understood even the hospital wasn't safe, so he limped miles to the relative safety of the UNMISS compound.

The man recounted the story to me calmly, almost without emotion, as though he simply had no more energy to waste. He showed me two of his wounds, pulling up his pant leg to display a gunshot and pulling up his shirt to show me one under his shoulder on his back. His arm was also broken and hung in a sling. I couldn't imagine how he had had the fortitude to survive so long under those dead bodies, and then to drag himself in this condition from the compromised hospital to the UN camp. I was amazed by the resilience all of these victims showed, but I could also see the damage—and it wasn't just physical. There was a heaviness to their weak bodies and an emptiness in their eyes, as though they'd shut off all but the most essential senses, a type of emotional hibernation. But dozens of people that day mustered a little extra to tell me about their experiences.

I felt terrible that I had nothing to offer them but to listen to their stories and bear witness to their suffering. They thought I was important because I was with the US government, and the US government had always helped their country. In telling me, in telling America, they had some hope that someone would intervene to end their suffering. How could America know of this and not do anything? How could it not have the power and influence to do so?

I returned to the UNMISS camp to speak with a few more IDPs the next day, including displaced Nuer government officials who had fled into the camp under threat. I heard more stories and did my best to corroborate details of what I'd heard so far. That afternoon, I went to Logali House to meet with a UN counterpart who worked in Hilde Johnson's office. I wanted to compare notes.

It was my first time visiting this popular hangout since the crisis began, and it was one of the few commercial businesses still functioning. Logali was home to a small boardinghouse as well, housing a handful of expats and locals, so I guessed closing entirely wasn't really an option. I was grateful for a change in venue. It seemed almost normal to be there, almost prewar, though it felt like we were the only customers. We sat in the back garden, and my two security minders took a seat nearby. These were the only two tables occupied; the entire venue was otherwise empty. I walked up the stairs to the bar on the veranda to notify the lone waiter that we were there. He seemed pleasantly surprised, our beer order a novelty that week.

My UN counterpart and I were coming to the same conclusions, but I wondered if his superiors held the same view. The reports we were both hearing were consistent. The perpetrators were Dinka, government security forces and others, and the victims were Nuer, mostly men. The targeting was very intentional and had effectively rid the city of Nuer in only a couple of days.

Back at my container that evening, I compiled and reviewed notes, made phone calls, and started writing. Write and edit, write and edit—citing sources, sharing details, outlining what was confirmed and what was reported, carefully noting what remained unknown. This would be my first in-depth report back to Washington on the atrocities committed.

Many important people were working hard right now to help find a diplomatic solution to restore peace. At the start of the crisis, the diplomatic engagement plan was focused mainly on outreach by Ambassador Page and Special Envoy Booth, with the assistant secretary of state for African affairs tasked with contacting heads of state in the region. But Special Envoy Booth had only taken up the position a few months earlier, so he hadn't had time to build up personal currency with the country's key actors. Even Ambassador Page, with her long-standing relationships in the region, couldn't get Kiir on the phone for a couple of days.

The diplomatic push quickly scaled up, though the Obama White House noticeably lacked the close relationship with Kiir that the George W. Bush administration had fostered. Ever since Kiir's first meeting with President Obama, in 2011, when Kiir brazenly lied to his face regarding arming rebels to fight in Sudan, the president hadn't bothered much with the relationship. While that didn't stop Susan Rice, then ambassador to the United Nations and later national security advisor, from continuing to come to Kiir's defense, it did mean a call from President Obama might not be the most persuasive. With this in mind, the White House looked elsewhere for trusted friends to deliver the message pushing for peace, including former presidents George W. Bush and Jimmy Carter.* By this point, Secretary of State John Kerry had also spoken with Kiir, and Rice had spoken with both Kiir and Machar. The UN Security Council, meanwhile, was discussing UN secretary-general Ban Ki-moon's request for 5,500 additional peacekeeping troops.

I thought all these people would benefit from the information I'd collected, information they needed to incorporate into their plans and strategies and talking points if any resolution they reached with the warring parties could be effective or sustainable. The enmity that enabled such rapid mobilization of ethnic violence—not just by the Dinka in Juba, but in wide-ranging revenge killings by Nuer against Dinka in other parts of the country, which were similarly horrific— was based on historic grievances that had been swept under the carpet with independence. I felt certain that addressing these atrocities needed to be part of the peace if the next peace was to last.

It was after midnight when I finished the draft cable. It ended with a modest call to action:

> Post urges U.S. support for robust human rights investigation teams, as well as forensic experts with mobile labs, to be brought to South Sudan immediately to begin investigating and documenting the most egregious atrocities before all evidence is lost.

It was a call to action that would go unheeded.

UN FLIGHTS OUT of Malakal had been scheduled and canceled and scheduled and canceled as fighting there continued, but the government had regained control of the town, and the situation was starting to stabilize by the end of the year. We'd been waiting to send in our own evacuation flight. It had been a week now of dangerous and declining conditions in the camp, and the calls from Americans

---

* Ty McCormick, "Unmade in the USA," *Foreign Policy*, February 25, 2015, https://foreignpolicy.com/2015/02/25/unmade-in-the-usa-south-sudan-bush -obama/.

stranded there had been getting more urgent. Riek (no relation to the rebel leader), one of the Americans, had become the de facto leader of the group and our main interlocutor. He had located twenty-three Americans stranded with him in the UNMISS compound, which now housed twenty-two thousand people. Much of the town outside the walls had been ransacked and looted, and bodies littered the streets. Jim and Lori had been managing most of the calls out of Malakal, but as Riek had grown more alarmed, they were not sure what else to say. They asked me to speak with him—the equivalent, I suppose, of "we can't really help, but here, speak with the manager."

"You have to get us out. We got a resupply last week, but we're out of food again. People here have been killed by shells falling inside the camp. People are dying. You can't leave us here."

He'd been so calm when I'd spoken to him before, trying to be strong for the group and doing an admirable job. But that sentiment was all gone now. His voice shook with fear and desperation, and I had nothing to offer. The feeling of helplessness was gutting, to both of us.

"I understand" was what we often defaulted to saying, but I knew that I didn't really. I couldn't possibly. I was not in that kind of danger. I was not worried about food and water or an imminent attack on the camp or shells raining from the sky. And I told him so. I could give him honesty at least.

"I can't possibly understand how difficult this is for all of you. I know that." I choked back my own emotions because I knew they wouldn't help. I wanted him to know we had a plan, but until it was in progress, it provided him little comfort. "We are ready to go as soon as it's safe to do so. But you won't be safe on a flight out until it's more stable."

"I'll take my chances. It's better than being here."

As I hung up, I could hear his reluctant resignation to the fact that relief was not yet on the way.

We had a twin turboprop charter plane standing by, ready to go when the situation permitted, but Bob raised strong concerns about sending two embassy personnel—me and one security officer—on a flight in those conditions. We had general agreement that a civilian plane was less likely to encounter trouble or be misconstrued, but Bob didn't like it. In case of emergency, we had little in the way of a backup plan. For now, though, the imperfect plan was on hold anyway.

Special Envoy Booth concluded his third brief visit to Juba with a press conference at the residence, announcing that both sides had agreed to send delegations to Addis Ababa to begin negotiations. This breakthrough was the culmination of a multifaceted, multilateral effort to exert pressure, involving UN leadership, Western diplomats, and the highest representation from countries in the region, including travel to Juba by the Kenyan president and Ethiopian prime minister. The diplomatic set was thrilled but still unsure of the political will for peace, since President Kiir had failed to follow through on prior promises to release at least some of the political detainees he'd accused of a coup. Maybe it was because these external peace efforts had gone on entirely outside my view, but I was not optimistic. All I could see was war raging unabated. I saw no signs that either side might be willing to back down, and no signs that they'd face consequences for their acts if they didn't.

The pendulum of conflict continued its backward-forward motion, as rebel forces again took control of Bor, rekindling concern of a rebel march south toward Juba. The pace of refugees fleeing the country's borders had increased, with more than ten thousand now in camps outside the country. At the evening's emergency action committee meeting, Bob told us to reevaluate our "go bags" and be ready for departure at any time. "Keep your passports on you always, wherever you are." He also warned us about the possibility of traditional celebratory gunfire that evening in honor of New Year's Eve. We were warned to stay inside or under overhead cover. It might not be hostile on that occasion, but what goes up must come down.

I woke up early New Year's Day to news that our evacuation flight to Malakal had been approved. I went with one of our assistant security officers. It was tense, following the attack on our Ospreys during the aborted Bor evacuation, but thankfully uneventful as we cruised at a low altitude north along the Nile. Finding Riek and his fellow Americans there, weary but well, was a joy. We got back to Juba too late in the day to fly them farther out of the country, so they had to stay the night at the UNMISS camp. Despite the poor conditions, it was a welcome change.

On January 2, we were already at the airport with the Americans from Malakal, staging for the flight, when a van pulled up in the parking lot. It was an American dual national with five American children. Four six-year-old quintuplet girls and a boy. I wouldn't have believed it myself if I hadn't seen their passports. We were suddenly over capacity for the Embraer charter. Riek immediately gathered what was going on and pulled me aside. "Let the children go. We are safe enough here now. You will get us out, I know." The camp where he was stranded now was a marginal improvement on Malakal but also squalid and unstable, and yet this man who had only just escaped a week of living in the middle of a battlefield was willing to risk his chance for this family he didn't even know. The small acts of kindness and selflessness that persisted even in war continued to amaze me.

I was conflicted, since this was the first we'd even heard from this family, but I could see in Riek's face that he wouldn't take no for an answer. "I'll get you out of here as soon as I'm able. I promise," I said, and I meant it. I radioed back to the residence to let them know the situation and plead for another flight out that day.

It was a small group of passengers, so we got through security and to the tarmac quickly. I mentioned the conundrum to one of the charter crew as we loaded the plane. "It's early enough. We could do another sortie if you get it cleared." And we did. It was a compelling case, I thought, and Washington agreed. Riek and the last of the Malakal passengers were on their way to safety only a few hours later. I saw them off at the steps of the plane, and it was a teary goodbye on both sides. A few days earlier, I hadn't known if he would survive, and neither had he.

"Thank you," Riek told me with a hug.

"Thank *you*," I replied, and I meant it.

Back at the residence at the evening's meeting, we learned that the rebel forces had again recaptured Bor and were reportedly beginning to slowly move south toward Juba. The White House was considering a further staffing reduction at the embassy, so that we would have no more people on the ground than could be fully evacuated with a single C-130 flight. With all the military we now had as our security, that left space for an even smaller handful of embassy personnel. We were already at the level of essential staff, the number and combination of staff determined ahead of time to be the minimum needed to maintain essential operations, below which the embassy would presumably shut down. The idea of continuing with even fewer personnel seemed unwise, but no one was willing to pull the plug on this experiment in which the United States had invested so heavily, financially and otherwise. We just didn't have the stomach to close our doors.

I talked to Mike, the deputy chief of mission, and Alicia, the acting USAID mission director, about it, and none of us were comfortable with the idea. There was a reason staffing needs, trip wires, and other important criteria were determined in times of calm. In times of crisis, emotions and other irrational factors could impede good decision-making. And South Sudan was an emotional issue for many in Washington. We suspected Susan Rice, now national security advisor, was wielding a heavy hand in this decision. It was Rice, after all, who had given the South Sudanese people assurances on their first independence day that the United States would remain steadfast in its support. Concurring with our mission's closure would be a hard call.

Ambassador Page told us that Washington would share its final decision at 6 a.m. Juba time. We'd reconvene at 7 a.m., but we all were instructed to prepare ourselves to go.

On January 3, the usual crowd took their usual seats around the table. We were anxious, and from the look on Ambassador Page's face, we anticipated bad news. It was our thirty-third emergency action committee meeting, and the room was quiet, still, and heavy. A driven energy usually filled the air around the table, but there was none of that this day.

"We've been instructed to reduce staffing today to below essential levels. If you haven't heard from me already, you'll be departing on a C-130 at 10 a.m. I'll inform President Kiir of this later today." Mike, Ajani, Alicia, Lori, Jim, and I would all be on that flight, along with several of the life-support staff who ran the residence facilities and the artwork and silver from the ambassador's residence (as a precaution, they said). Staying behind would be the ambassador, the IT guy (if you can't communicate to Washington, why be there at all?), the USAID management officer (tracking and managing supplies and life support), and our now-expanded security and military teams. Since I'd be departing, Mike told me to prepare an announcement of the suspension of emergency services to American citizens. Consular Affairs in Washington had lobbied hard for me to stay. An emergency-level mission without emergency consular services seemed nonsensical to them, and they foresaw messy attempts to help Americans in need without the right people around to do it. They'd be proven right, but the list was final. The White House had spoken.

While our numbers would further dwindle, our public messaging was clear:

> We have not suspended diplomatic relations. We continue to provide lifesaving humanitarian services.

Our talking points called on all sides to end the violence and protect civilians, but they also made clear that our commitment to the government remained firm.

> Those who seek to seize power through the use of military force will lose the longstanding support of the United States and the international community.

I had a suitcase and backpack ready to go. I'd warned Gio that this might be coming and asked him to meet me at the residence as soon as possible. I asked him if he wanted to leave too. I was not sure I could get him on this specific flight, but I was sure I could get him out somehow. I had some favors to call in with people who had planes. He declined. "I'd like to take my family to Khartoum, though, where it's safer. I'll return and be ready for work when it's needed," he told me calmly. He had lived in Khartoum before and knew it well. It felt more secure to him, which was ironic to me. "Of course. Do whatever you need to do for your family. I'll reach out in a couple of days once I know what the plan is for me," I told him. I had no idea what that plan was, after all. We didn't even yet know where the C-130 was taking us. It felt like such a betrayal leaving Gio behind, leaving anyone behind.

We didn't find out until just before we left for the airport that our destination was in fact Entebbe, Uganda, the airport just outside the capital Kampala. We had all been expecting Nairobi, including my colleagues there, who were already preparing for our arrival. I had been looking forward to some friendly faces.

I called Chol as well. He had family in Uganda and had wanted to stay there for a while. He was thrilled when he realized that was where we were going. "Get to the residence ASAP. Bring your passport," I told him.

The C-130 landed and soldiers emptied out to secure the perimeter. It was standard procedure but always gave the whole exercise a more dramatic feel. We lined up behind the plane, steeling ourselves against the powerful hot draft from the engine. It was going to be a quick load. We'd gathered a handful of other American citizens to join the flight. Some close contacts—hardened security-industry folk who had chosen not to leave sooner—took our decision to downsize as a sign and joined too. Ambassador Page was there to see us off, and she was teary. This was a hard moment for her. Like the first drawdown, it suggested another stage in this country's demise, this country she had given her professional and personal life to for many years. She had invested probably more than anyone else there that day, but she tried to put on a brave face for the rest of us, telling us she was proud of the work that we'd done.

It had been easy for me to be critical of her positions, particularly those that seemed to give the South Sudanese leadership credit or leeway I didn't think it deserved. I had interpreted this at times as being inconsiderate of the South Sudanese people, sacrificing them for the benefit of those running the country. But moments like this reminded me that the path Ambassador Page had taken was driven only by hope and wanting the best for the country and its people. While I believed I would have done things differently, I didn't have the same history here. That history came with a deeper understanding, but also with baggage and inertia. I asked myself, *At what point did experience in a place like this become a liability?* I wondered if Ambassador Page would ever look back and wish she'd done anything differently. I knew I would.

It all felt so hollow. I felt hollow. One of the soldiers cross-checked our names on the manifest as we climbed up the ramp in the back of the aircraft. *That's my job. I should be on that side of the clipboard, not this one.*

It all went so quickly, I barely had time to realize that I might never return. I might not see my container again. I might not see Juba again outside of war. *I should have taken down the Christmas tree*: one of many odd thoughts that crossed my mind.

The inside of the C-130 was stark, dark, utilitarian. We sat on long benches stretching along the walls of the aircraft and back-to-back in the middle. The civilian passengers were significantly outnumbered by our military colleagues in uniform. The scene looked and felt like the end of something. As the aircraft began to taxi down the runway, I quickly texted several contacts to let them know I was leaving. I sent my personal email, as I didn't know about access to my work address in the near future. As the plane lifted into the air, a panicked text pinged back from the protocol chief at the Ministry of Foreign Affairs. "What does this mean? What do you know? God help us all!"

Refugees

January–February 2014 (Uganda)

THE LAYOUT OF THE ROOM WAS FAMILIAR. I HAD STAYED IN an exact replica on a different floor six years ago, on my first trip to Uganda. The Kampala Serena Hotel. I was a consultant on a USAID project then. It felt like a lifetime ago or a distant dream. This room alone was larger than the entire metal cottage I had left behind in Juba.

I was shell-shocked. I walked into the bathroom, leaned over the sink, and scrubbed my face with warm water. I straightened my back and looked in the mirror. Sunburned, windswept, dusty, with dark circles under bloodshot eyes, my hair clinging to what remained of a haphazard bun that couldn't hold its own in the draft of the C-130 engine. I looked even worse for wear compared to the pristine surroundings of a luxury hotel. My eyes looked as empty and emotionally drained as I felt. And they were familiar. I'd seen these eyes hundreds of times: on the tarmac, in the IDP camp. This was the other side of evacuation.

There had been no end to the essential work that we were doing in Juba. I had fallen into bed each night mentally reviewing the long list of critical actions I'd need to take the following day. The pace never slowed. And then, it slammed to a halt. There was nothing to be done. No emails to answer. No people to call. No deadlines to meet. No decisions to make. No one to help. I had so much more to do there. But now I was here, four hundred miles away.

"So glad you're out! Go sit by the pool. Relax. Read a book. Watch a movie."

The advice from our colleagues at the embassy here in Kampala matched that from friends and family back home and in Washington, all pleased I was no longer in the eye of the storm.

But I couldn't switch gears like that.

A management officer from Embassy Kampala had checked us in for three nights. We had no idea what Washington would decide to do with us now. We were out, so we were no longer a priority. One of the reasons it was such a hard decision to take people out of a country is that Washington's bureaucracy makes it incredibly difficult to get them back in, so I had no illusions of an imminent return or clear direction soon. Every move was deliberate, and we had no input now. All we could do was wait.

I took a long, hot shower, hoping it could bring some life back into my limp body and soul. It didn't, but I felt cleaner than I had in weeks, so that was something. Stepping out, I noticed an envelope had been slipped under the door. In it was a handwritten message from Dr. Duncan, the State Department's regional psychiatrist who happened to be in Kampala for the week. He'd made himself available to those who "need to talk."

"You can call me in room 412 at any time or email me, and we can meet."

I should have. But I wasn't ready to talk to anyone who didn't understand what we had just left.

I SPENT FORTY-EIGHT hours in a daze. The Juba crew had a late lunch at the hotel's garden restaurant, the Lakes. It was the fanciest fare we'd had in a while in a delightful setting, and the weather was perfect, but it was hard to appreciate under the circumstances. None of us were particularly conversational at first. We were all in shock. That evening, we tried Explorer's, another colonial-themed in-house restaurant. We lacked the energy to move further afield, but I sensed the moods of the others were cheerier now as they adjusted to the new normal, made plans for R & R, and embraced the escape. But I couldn't shake my despondence.

I slept for a long time that night, but it was fitful. Come morning, I struggled to drag myself out of bed. I couldn't think of a reason to. When I finally got up, it was much of the same. Meet some of the team at the breakfast buffet, make plans to see them at lunch, see them again at dinner. I read emails, I read the news, I read Facebook. I didn't know what else to do.

Forty-eight hours was all I'd allow myself to sulk, though. It didn't come easily, but by the end of my third day at the Kampala Serena, I looked in the mirror again and told myself it was time to get back to work.

I still had many questions about what had happened in the early days of the crisis. I might not be in South Sudan, and I was entirely without instruction, but Chol reminded me that plenty of South Sudanese were here too. Even before the war, Kampala was a popular hub, and now, many Nuer in particular had fled here for safety. I remembered that my friend Gordon was one of them. I got his local number from Oxfam staff in the United States.

"Yes, let us meet. I have many people who would like to speak with you." Once word got out that I was in town, so did my local number and my email, and I got a steady stream of inquiries and requests to meet. I represented America, after all, and people wanted America to know what was happening in South Sudan, what had happened to them.

Soon, I had several meetings planned. The South Sudanese who had escaped were keen to tell what they'd seen firsthand, although they were still nervous to speak out, claiming they saw NSS and other government informants everywhere. They didn't want to meet out in the open.

One morning, at Gordon's direction, I taxied to a restaurant in the Kabalagala neighborhood, not far from the embassy, though a part of the city I'd not seen before. The restaurant sat on a backstreet and appeared to be a very basic café at most, with only a few plastic tables and chairs outside. The inside appeared dark and empty, as though the minimal furniture merely moved in or out based on modest changes in the weather.

Gordon had connected me to several former government officers, and they brought a few more people, so the group reached nearly a dozen men. I took a seat at the end of two tables strung together in the scrubby courtyard. We appeared to be the only customers, and waitstaff was scarce. I expected this place was chosen for its anonymity. The group included a former police officer, a former National Legislative Assembly worker, a former SPLA military justice officer, a former bank official, and a former state minister from Upper Nile. The men had their own established hierarchy, and as tradition often dictates, the eldest man was the de facto leader. He welcomed me, thanked me for my time, introduced the rest of the group one by one, and then, in an orderly fashion, they made their way around the circle and told me their stories. I listened, I nodded, I asked a few questions, and I subtly scribbled copious notes. This group worked in English, so no translation needed.

"I went by car on December 17 to search different neighborhoods after the fighting. I went to Gudele, Area 107, New Side, Jebel, and Loklogo and saw many bodies, hundreds of bodies, all Nuer. There were many people, many civilians, students, women, and children. There were government officials. All of them, executed," one man said. He had little emotion in his voice but had those same dead eyes. He handed me a piece of paper with a photo printed on it, and in the photo were a few dozen bodies collapsed on the ground, more or less in a couple of rows.

"Who took this photo?" I asked.

"It was me, but the camera is still in UNMISS with my cousin." He claimed he took the photo in Gudele not far from the police station.

The police officer also said he had driven to the Gudele police station that day, but SPLA forces shot up his vehicle as it approached, so they took injured colleagues to the hospital and then fled to the UNMISS camp until he could escape to Uganda.

I ask the men who these Dinka forces were who seemed to fall outside the main SPLA structure. "They are *Dutku Beny*," one man said. It translates, "Protect the boss."

The next man told of fleeing his neighborhood by car with other neighbors after SPLA began attacking the area. The car was stopped as it approached the gate of the UN House (the other UNMISS camp, near the Jebel neighborhood). He saw several people shot and dozens of other Nuer men detained at the checkpoint, where he was also taken. He was kept for several days and moved to a couple of different locations during that time. He was transported in vehicles and held in rooms that he described as covered in blood. He was ultimately housed in an underground cell at a facility he called the "white house" with about three hundred other Nuer men, so crowded that he struggled to breathe. A high-level intelligence official was at the location and told him and others that he knew this group was mostly civilians but that it was not safe to release them at that time. The man being detained asked this individual what had happened to the dozens of Nuer he had seen carted away at different times during his detention. "He told me they were probably no longer alive," he said softly, his eyes looking down at the table. On December 19, he and the other Nuer men who remained in detention with him were released and fled to the UN camp.

The stories continued, and the themes were the same. Dinka officers go door-to-door, Nuer are gathered and killed, and some individuals escape through daring attempts, luck, or intervention by friends across the ethnic divide or someone on the inside who wasn't fully on board with the initiative. The only safe place to escape to was UNMISS or outside the country.

One of the former state government officials told me that the numbers killed were far higher than anyone was saying so far, but that the Nuer communities were naming and counting the dead. Community leaders inside the IDP camps in South Sudan were compiling lists. They did not want their family members to be forgotten, and they did not want a peace agreement to gloss over the loss of life their community had suffered deliberately at the hands of government forces.

Everyone at the table also agreed that they were not safe in Uganda. They saw the NSS's reach deep in the country, noting that friends still inside the agency had warned them to watch their backs.

The men concluded their stories, and the eldest man thanked me for my time and implored me, as America's representative here, to take action to stop the violence and seek justice for those killed. And then silence hung in the air, the mood heavy with the tales of death and fear. I took a deep breath, paused, and thanked them for trusting me with their stories and giving me their time. I assured them I would share the gravity of the situation and the extent of the atrocities with Washington, and that their stories would help leadership back home fully understand what was going on. What that would mean in the end, I didn't know, but I didn't tell them that.

I had a few more meetings over the next few days, with more former officials, civil society leaders, and human rights defenders, all of whom had fled South Sudan under threat—general and specific. They had all lost multiple family members. Many had seen killings firsthand. All remained afraid.

Meanwhile, Washington had decided that the rest of my colleagues in exile in Kampala would relocate to Nairobi to set up a small Juba Support Unit in our embassy there, but Washington had decided that I would stay put. "It's the shortest distance to fly into Juba. M wants you there in case we need to do an evacuation flight on short notice," Mike told me. In the State Department, being known by a single letter is a sign of power, and M was the undersecretary for management, Pat Kennedy. Undersecretary Kennedy was a legend, serving as M under three presidents over ten years, but he was also a legendary micromanager, and he was apparently making these decisions directly. If M wanted me in Kampala, I stayed in Kampala.

Embassy Kampala colleagues and leadership were extremely supportive and welcomed me to work out of their space, but I was working with no direction. I heard little from Embassy Juba, and none of us exiles heard anything from Ambassador Page. I reached out to Mike once he had settled in Nairobi, looking for some indication of how I could help. He was inundated setting up the new support unit and trying to smooth things over with Embassy Nairobi leadership, which was less amenable to its new squatters than Kampala was, so he had his hands full. Mike told me to chip in with consular, try updating the human rights report, and consider taking a vacation.

Mike's suggestions were reasonable, but I had other priorities. I quickly found a desk in Embassy Kampala's political section, keen to get back into the department computer system so I could get back to reporting.

I drafted a long cable. It was my second cable documenting testimonials of the atrocities, but it was more detailed and extensive, with more firsthand witness accounts. I reiterated the call to action from the last one:

> *Independent human rights investigations are needed. Current efforts by UNMISS and NGOs to document and investigate human rights violations in Juba and elsewhere are very limited.*

Most cables are released in the ether and you just hope anyone reads them. You hope the work you do matters at all, under any circumstances, in this job. You rarely know if it does. We were all small cogs in a massive foreign policy wheel that covered the globe but was centered in Washington.

But this cable was widely read. I heard from dozens of people across the State Department and other agencies who were following developments in South Sudan. The director of the special envoy's office wrote, telling me my cable was one in a million. It appeared that it really brought home the horrors of what was going on. It was forwarded around the department and to the White House: "Read this, it reinforces our question of how much this continues and how to stop it." People far more important than I was were reading it. I thought it mattered.

A deputy assistant secretary wanted to speak by phone. She was well known in the department and influential. This was a good sign. Of course I'd be available.

I told myself this reporting would help change policy, lead the United States to use our leverage to begin independent investigations, force us to call out our friends for what they were doing. It would inform US leadership as they pressed both sides for peace negotiations. In a recent public statement, National Security Advisor Susan Rice had made clear her continued partiality toward the government. "Mr. Machar, in particular, must commit to a cessation of hostilities without precondition," she had said, and a prior White House statement offered no more than a lukewarm reprimand of "all sides." To me, these statements didn't represent a fulsome understanding of how we got to where we were or how we could resolve it. If they really understood what was happening, our leaders would have to approach this differently, I thought.

It was evening in Kampala, the light fading in the hotel gardens, and I settled down with my laptop at a table on the patio waiting for the deputy assistant secretary to call my cell. I was hoping that she'd ask me my thoughts on next steps, that we'd talk about what her bureau might be able to offer in the way of investigative support and pressure. I was hoping this call would be an opportunity for progress toward my modest recommendations in the cable, toward an honest approach to the conflict at hand.

She rang, and we exchanged brief introductions, talked about mutual friends at UNMISS, and then got to the point of the call. I tried to manage my expectations, but I was hopeful she would give me the direction I'd been looking for. "Elizabeth, we haven't met, but I'd heard about you before reading your cable. I just want to applaud you for the incredibly important work you're doing."

"So what comes next? What can we do about this now? Can we coordinate with our mission in New York to push for UN action? Or maybe we have resources we can use at State?" I asked her in rapid fire.

She waited a beat and then muddled through a timid and apologetic statement of how these things were difficult. She said something about the White House and our complicated history with the country and, and, and . . .

And then, sounding resigned but doing her best to be encouraging, she concluded: "At least you're there to bear witness."

The sun was gone now, dipped well below the horizon, and I stared out into the darkness of the garden where the patio ended. Her words hung in the emptiness in front of me.

"Elizabeth," she said. "That does matter. One day that record is going to matter." *But not today.*

LATER THAT WEEK, I met a former state minister living in exile in Kampala. One of the activists I'd met with earlier had put him in touch. I'd spoken to four dozen refugees by this point and feared that empathy fatigue was starting to hamper my effectiveness. I worried I was beginning to just go through the motions. I wanted to cancel the meeting because it felt futile and I was tired. But I had little else to occupy my time to justify doing so.

The minister met me at the Serena, joined by one of his advisors from the ministry, also in exile. We sat at the same patio table by the gardens where my hopes had been dashed a few nights before. "At least you're there to bear witness." The deputy assistant secretary's words still hung heavily in my mind.

The setting was indeed serene. It was a sunny afternoon. The gardens were lush, a healthy green dotted with flowering bushes and trees, roses and dahlias, blooming aloe and birds of paradise. I thought of the hotel's sordid history. Before it was the Serena, these grounds housed the Nile Mansions Hotel, where the brutal, cruel dictator Idi Amin held events and parties while his security service housed a torture chamber in the basement of the hotel's convention center. This place, I thought, could serve either as a symbol of rebirth and hope or a reminder that the innate cruelty of man lies just beneath the surface of the beautiful things we see.

The minister was reserved, quiet, and very formal. He introduced himself and his colleague and proceeded to tell me his experience of the conflict in a very matter-of-fact tone. He told of his family being targeted, of many relatives dying in the first days of the fighting, of his son being shot and killed at a checkpoint. He told me how he sought refuge at UNMISS before being snuck out of the country by car. Then he spoke of his other son who had been safe, studying in Southeast Asia at a university, far from the conflict. I couldn't blame so many of the government officials for using their positions of privilege and good pay to seek greener pastures for their children.

A few days ago, however, he'd received word that his son had lost his life falling from a window of the high-rise apartment where he'd lived. The minister was certain he'd been targeted, that NSS officers had tracked him there and murdered him. He did not believe it was an accident or a suicide.

It seemed far-fetched to me, that the South Sudanese government, with so many enemies so close to home and limited resources with which to pursue them, would travel so far to slaughter someone's son, no matter how politically connected. It was one thing to believe the government was sending NSS officers to its allied neighbor to the south, but beyond the region seemed unlikely. I suspected it was just a terrible accident at a particularly terrible time. I never learned the truth of the matter or further evidence one way or another, but even so, this man had lost both his sons to unnatural and violent deaths in short order, along with many other relatives and his home. Yet there he sat in front of me, pulled together in a suit, a proud man intent on retaining his dignity despite the horrors he was facing. Like so many others, he had come to tell me about this incident because I represented the United States, and he wanted us to know what was happening. He thought that telling us meant it would matter, meant that someone with influence and power could avenge the wrongs against them and make things right.

I was humbled, watching this man carry himself with such grace, even as he shared the details of this living nightmare with a stranger. But my mind kept returning to the futility of it. I had nothing to offer but my ear, my waning empathy, and my outrage at all the suffering. My sadness for this man and his losses turned to anger and frustration at my country's impotence in the face of it all. I felt the blood rush to my face, my lip start to quiver, and my eyes well with tears. I blinked them back, but it was futile. I looked directly at him, wanting to give him the respect at least of listening, but I couldn't stop the tears as they rolled down my cheeks. I'd made it weeks without crying in front of anyone. I was but an observer, my sorrow secondary. I had no right to cry, particularly in front of victims who showed such composure.

The minister tried to ignore it, to speak past it, but he couldn't. It was a distraction. Very abruptly, he finished his story, thanked me for my time, and he and his colleague were gone before I could even reply.

I was embarrassed at my breakdown in protocol and professionalism. I scolded myself for this behavior, but I had to admit that the secondhand trauma was taking its toll. The sense of helplessness was particularly hard to bear.

That night, I received an email from the minister. He offered me heartfelt thanks. He was honored a US diplomat had shed a tear for his sons. It gave him hope that South Sudan was not lost, for my great country, he believed, would not let that be so. He knew now that America had not forgotten them, that America would not let these injustices go unanswered.

I did not tell him that I no longer had such hope. That night, I cried again, in my room alone—a long, heavy, unstoppable flood of frustration.

UNLIKE THE REFUGEES I spoke to, I felt safer in Uganda than I had before. I traveled freely, riding in "soft-skin" vehicles, walking and even jogging now in leafy neighborhoods near the hotel. I no longer sensed government officers lurking in the shadows or feared the acts of security forces ready to strike with impunity.

My UN and NGO counterparts still in South Sudan, however, were increasingly at risk. The government's harassment of them continued unimpeded, along with a systematic assault in the press against both the UN and the United States. Government representatives, attempting to steer anger toward a different foe, referred to us all as "colonial powers," and much of the Dinka population still supporting Kiir was buying it. Even Hilde Johnson's seemingly boundless tolerance for the government began to find its limits, but she continued to look elsewhere for offenders, taking any steps she could to prevent the UN from earning the government's ire.

From Kampala, I reached out by phone and email to my counterparts still in the country, particularly the political and human rights officers at the UN, to keep my finger on the pulse of what was happening as best I could. Former confidants, however, found it harder to speak with me. "They're trying to find out who's leaking information to the US," a human rights officer told me, imploring me to protect my sources of information.

"Leaking?" I replied, astonished. "But we're on the same team. We're the biggest contributor to the UNMISS mission. How is it 'leaking' to share information with us?"

"I know," she said. "But that assumes we're all on the same page here in UNMISS. And we aren't."

UNMISS had long been a conflicted organization. Its very foundation was a shaky contradiction. The organization's mandate, established with independence in July 2011, charged UNMISS with consolidating peace and security, monitoring and investigating human rights abuses against citizens, and advising and assisting the government. What do you do when the human rights abuses you're investigating are committed by the government you're charged with supporting? What do you do when that same government is the main threat to the peace and security you're supposed to promote? The organization's commitments were at odds, and this put UNMISS leadership and many of its staff at odds too.

Facing no real consequences for demonizing the UN, the government grew bolder, attacking UN personnel and property across the country, commandeering humanitarian vehicles and food, impeding aid delivery, and organizing protests against the organization and its leadership. For Kiir's administration, undermining the UN had no downside. It proved a useful common enemy to focus on, and the government had no interest in assistance that might reach the rebels or investigations that would reveal its crimes. UN secretary-general Ban Ki-moon publicly condemned the actions, declaring that offenders would be held accountable, but it was yet another empty threat.

Kiir's administration actively sought opportunities for conflict with the UN. Minister of Information Michael Makuei Lueth, one of Kiir's most vocal and aggressive hard-liners, traveled to Bor on January 19, just after government forces had retaken the town. He showed up at the gates of the UNMISS compound flanked by eighty armed SPLA soldiers and state press journalists, demanding to know if the people inside were pro- or anti-government. This clearly wasn't a peace mission. Ken, the head of UNMISS's Jonglei state office, tried his best to accommodate the high-level official, but he wouldn't answer Makuei's question or allow his armed forces entry to the IDP camp, where twelve thousand displaced civilians were in the UN's care. He'd watched the day before as approximately five thousand SPLA and allied forces had marched past the compound in a victory lap of sorts. They were camped now only a few miles away, and Ken feared that if he failed to make a stand now, he could face them next.

Makuei was indignant, but Ken stood firm, placing himself between the minister and the camp and commanding the gate be shut behind him. For this brave move, which undoubtedly prevented violence, Ken was rewarded with hand-wringing from Hilde Johnson for angering Makuei. Within a couple of days, Ken was given forty-five minutes' notice to pack his bags and board a flight to Juba. Thereafter, the UN would unceremoniously send him out of the country, along with another UN official the government had baselessly accused of supporting the rebels. The UN claimed it was for their own security, and the government was once again rewarded for its bad behavior.

I tried to raise alarm with Washington and the embassy, but Washington could only focus on one issue at a time, and this one was quickly overshadowed. To great fanfare, the government and rebels signed a cessation of hostilities agreement on January 23. It wouldn't stick, of course, but it bought both sides goodwill, generously topping up our shallowing reservoirs of tolerance for any number of bad acts.

I SPENT TWO months in exile, first in Kampala, then in Washington, DC—a pilgrimage I made on my own initiative to shake loose the approval to send me back into South Sudan. By now, Juba was firmly under government control with no looming threats, and dozens of NGO staff and other diplomatic workers had returned already. I'd exhausted the information I could glean from my location in Kampala and was ready to get back. Unsurprisingly, I found that bureaucratic oversight appeared to be the culprit. M had approved the return of five staff, me among them, but others in Washington remained almost singularly focused on peace talks in Addis Ababa. We fell through the cracks.

To me, the talks seemed futile. Neither side had shown any interest in restraint or peace following the short-lived cessation of hostilities agreement, which they obviously had no intention of respecting. We saw few other indications that the two sides had any plans to put down their arms. But Addis was where the special envoy's office was focused. What was happening elsewhere was of minimal concern. If the action wasn't in Juba, why would they really care who was there?

I couldn't be sure I played a part, but I got the email directing me to make travel plans to Juba the day after I told the deputy director of the special envoy's office that I planned to curtail my assignment and take a new position somewhere I could actually be. It was a bluff, but I was keen to avoid spending more time spinning my wheels in Uganda. Whatever the trigger, I was thrilled with the news. I scheduled a quick stop in Kampala to pick up emergency consular supplies—as much as I could fit under the seat in front of me on the plane, and I was on a short flight to Juba the following morning.

Trial and Error

March–May 2014

BY THE TIME I RETURNED, THE GOVERNMENT WAS ON THE offensive, diplomatically speaking. A three-man team of South Sudanese officials was touring the region trying to sell the fabricated story of the coup to other African leaders, in an attempt to reinforce Kiir's legitimacy and undermine his opponents. Inside the country, the government continued to organize anti-foreigner and anti-UN rallies from the shadows. It was a full-court press to solidify the narrative against the new common enemy.

I'd also returned to Juba just in time for the start of the "treason trial": the proceedings against the political detainees who had sided with Riek Machar in his political moves against Kiir and who were subsequently accused of leading the invisible coup—yet another effort by the government to bolster its version of events. In a rare concession, the government had released seven of the political detainees in January but claimed it had sufficient evidence to charge seven others with treason (four in detention and three in absentia, including Machar himself, who was believed to be somewhere in the bush near the Ethiopian border). Following months of diplomatic haranguing that these key political players be released to participate in peace talks, a special tribunal court had been established to try them, but by whom and under what authority remained unclear. The judiciary had never been renowned for its independence, so expectations in the diplomatic community were low, but the trial promised to be an event to watch.

It began March 12 in a courtroom in the judiciary complex in the capital city. The court was located near the Juba Teaching Hospital and a few blocks from the prison, just off a roundabout on the eastern side of town. The facility was modest, giving the impression not of a national courthouse but more of the small, rural district courthouses one might find in any number of towns across the continent. The parking lot was mostly dirt and broken pavement, lined by a series of pale yellow buildings: one longer building housing offices and then three or four courtrooms. The grounds were sparse, dotted with a few trees and some scrub. This wasn't a landscaped facility. It felt abandoned, appropriately reflecting the government's opinion of justice and the rule of law.

The courtroom where most of the treason trial took place was round, with high ceilings and yellow walls. Despite its height, the room felt too small for the event and the crowd that attended it. The room was packed with hard wooden benches, and experienced observers knew to bring cushions to sit on during the long hearing days. The judges sat on a raised platform front and center, and each sported a sash similar to what you might see in a beauty contest—green for the chief justice on the panel and red for the others. The four sitting defendants were cordoned off to the right, looking serious and professional in suits and ties during the early proceedings. They would all get more comfortable and casual as the trial progressed. Pagan Amum, the ousted SPLM secretary-general, appeared to be their de facto leader. The defense team and prosecution sat in a crowded line in front of the judicial panel. A wooden barrier separated the gallery from the legal teams, and lanky cameramen crowded up just behind it nearly every day.

From day one, the weakness of the government's case was clear, but that seemed no reason to stop the charade. The lead prosecutor offered into evidence a series of items that did little to support the claims that the accused had committed any crime: their own written

and exculpatory statements, the December 6 press statement criti-
cizing the president, photos of unidentified dead bodies in Juba, a
certificate from a hospital documenting 258 deaths, an indecipher-
able audio recording, and a flag the prosecution claimed to be part
of the conspiracy (similar to the South Sudan flag but with a cow in
the center in lieu of a star, presumably to reflect the animal's importance to the country's largest ethnic groups). Many international diplomats expressed dismay that Kiir would proceed with such a flimsy
basis for a case. A lack of evidence wasn't unique in my experience
with the country's weak justice system, but the highly public nature
of the case did make it stand out more. By day two, the prosecution
had chosen a different tack and was looking simply for ways to stall.
The judges unenthusiastically agreed to a week's delay to allow the
government to attempt to bring the seven released detainees back to
Juba to stand trial. The prosecution came back empty-handed, seeking further delay, but the patience of the judicial panel was wearing
thin. The trial would go on.

Day after day, witness after witness, I showed up, usually with
Chol, and we would find our way up to the front of the crowd and
listen. I took copious notes, as our audience in Washington and the
special envoy's team in Addis eagerly awaited our report each day.
Other diplomats would come and go, finding the long days somewhat tedious, but I'm a legal and political nerd. This was all high-
drama, live entertainment to me.

The prosecution at no point started to build a credible case against
the accused, though, so it began to feel more like watching a weak
sports team get crushed. No prosecution witnesses backed up the
coup story or could link the four accused with the outbreak of violence in any way. After a couple of weeks, the prosecution's scheduled
witnesses simply stopped showing up.

Nearly a month after the start of the trial, the accused were given
an opportunity to speak. I knew from experience that this would be
a lengthy affair. The South Sudanese love to talk, and Pagan was particularly loquacious. For four and a half hours, he described in excru-
ciating detail the press conference, his arrest, why he was absent from

the National Liberation Council meeting on December 14, the entire history of the SPLM, and the origins of the South Sudanese flag and national anthem (including his role in both). Pagan complained of being held without charge for a month and without trial for three. He asserted that this trial was a test case the whole world was following, and he pleaded with the court to deliver justice after all.

The accused all provided their statements in subsequent days, and over the next two weeks the trial proceeded in fits and starts. Progress was slow, and neither a guilty finding nor a not-guilty finding was politically tenable under the circumstances. Someone was trying to work out a third option, but who and what, we didn't know.

With all eyes and press on the treason trial, Riek Machar, the alleged instigator and subsequent leader of an armed resistance, was sitting in Nasir, a small town on the Sobat River about twenty miles from Ethiopia. It was Machar's home territory. Sven, the EU ambassador, flew there for a brief visit. In a meeting with ambassadors from other Western countries and a couple of staffers like me, he told us that the market was thriving and the town was in good condition, compared with the destruction in Malakal. I listened intently, taking notes for what was sure to be a short cable back to Washington. Sven's firsthand view from Machar's bush base was unique at the moment. It hadn't been easy to get a feel for Machar's position and thinking.

According to Sven, Machar was just sitting in his hut when they arrived, reading *Why Nations Fail*. He was only guarded by about ten soldiers, and the town wasn't fortified like Malakal. Sven said Machar seemed calm and confident, but also isolated, with little connection to the outside world. Was this part of a clever and strategic waiting game, or had Machar become a madman in the woods?

Back in Juba, a hopeful grassroots effort was also underway to try to build a national reconciliation framework, outside the auspices of the peace talks in Addis. On April 5, three separate national bodies (allegedly independent in nature) launched the National Platform for Peace and Reconciliation. Western diplomats had long been skeptical that the separate reconciliation initiatives had any hope of success. The Committee for National Healing, Peace, and Reconciliation; the

South Sudan Peace and Reconciliation Commission; and the Special-
ized Committee on Peace and Reconciliation of the National Legislative Assembly—all three had vague and overlapping mandates—were
established by the government and had not much to show for their
efforts. A lack of enthusiasm for this new initiative was unsurprising.
It was, however, one of the few initiatives attempted by South Sudanese religious and community members (much of civil society in
South Sudan stemmed from churches) to work with affected citizens
across the country, and some of the initiative's leaders were widely
respected. I attended the launch out of curiosity.

The event was held at Freedom Hall and it drew a crowd of about
two hundred people. As the US representative, I was ushered to a
section set aside for diplomats and found an unfortunate seat in the
front row. A few ambassadors had joined, but most embassies also
sent their B team, so I was primarily in the company of friends. As
with many similar events I'd attended, it began very late and with
a prolonged period of song and dance. It was the same traditional
dance group we'd seen many times. We knew the drill. When some
of the dancers started to approach the front row for the obligatory
drag-a-foreigner-to-the-stage opportunity, I focused intently on my
notebook, scribbling a description of the scene to feign an important busy-ness until they settled on a victim closer to the middle of
the room. She unenthusiastically obliged, faking a smile and shaking
her hips awkwardly. Dancing then concluded, and a military band
filled the air with patriotic-sounding tunes before Archbishop Deng
began his lengthy speech on the aspirations of the National Platform,
emphasizing that the effort would be independent and driven by the
South Sudanese people. I breathed a sigh of relief with the start of the
actual meeting, knowing my performance throughout the day would
be limited to looking thoughtful and interested each time the local
press and state television cameras spanned the section of "important
foreign people."

After Archbishop Deng concluded his remarks, several other no-
tables spoke. The event continued for four hours with no break, but it
was mostly an optimistic and hopeful event in the spirit of the topic,

reconciliation, until the government took the stage. Minister of Cabinet Affairs Martin Elia Lomuro spoke rather incoherently about the church's responsibility to lead "spiritual governance" and the moral responsibility of "all of you people" to find peace. It wasn't a particularly useful message, but it was sufficiently hard to understand that it posed little damage to the overall tone of the day.

And then Vice President James Wani Igga took the stage. An Equatorian selected by Kiir after Machar was sacked, Igga was surprisingly petit for a South Sudanese, but what he lacked in size, he made up for in enthusiasm. For an hour and a half, Igga spat out fighting words and blame, hammering down on the evils of Riek Machar. His message so contradicted the entire purpose of the event that one of my counterparts sitting near me whispered that maybe he'd mistakenly brought the wrong speech or gone to the wrong venue.

Igga spoke of "rivers of blood" and condemned the "failed coup." He droned on about how Riek had "divorced" three other political partners over the years and had now "divorced" Salva Kiir. "Any husband who has divorced four wives, you know it is not the wives who are bad but it is the husband!" he exclaimed. The military band then struck up music as if on cue. Igga turned to an irate explanation of how Machar's forces began the fighting on December 15, growling, "He wants power now and now!" He then shifted focus to the peace talks, complaining about international interference and lamenting the push for additional parties to the talks, which also seemed directly contradictory to the message of the day. Igga closed by dispassionately reading a statement from President Kiir, who was supposed to headline the event. The statement said something about the importance of reconciliation and the National Platform's independence from the government, but it mattered not at this point. The closing message of the day had already been delivered: take your reconciliation and shove it.

IT WAS LATE April, six weeks after the start of the treason trial, when the minister of justice unexpectedly announced in a press conference that the four detainees would be released the follow-ing day. The president had pardoned them, he said, "for the sake of peace." The entire ordeal evaded clear legal definition, because even the minister's statements were contradictory. He claimed at times that the detainees had been pardoned, and in the next sentence that the charges had been dropped. Later, he said that the court would stay the proceedings—all three being distinctly different outcomes with different legal, practical, and political implications. I suspected a deal had been struck behind the scenes that no one would reveal.

I was in the courtroom with Mike the following morning. Since the news emerged, we'd been in close communication with the wives of the detainees regarding their very real fears about their husbands' safety. Government representatives had made the same veiled threat on more than a few occasions to the wives and to diplomatic repre-sentatives: Wouldn't it be terrible if we released them and angry citi-zens took matters into their own hands? Chiefs of mission across the diplomatic community hoped that the presence of foreign witnesses would help mitigate the chance of reckless government action, so we were there in force for the final day.

The courtroom was as crowded as I'd seen it, with a palpable air of nervous anticipation. The diplomatic set had been in constant com-munication about how we could facilitate the next steps. The security of these detainees represented far more than the individuals at this point. Having been detained at the very outset of the violence, none of them had played any role in the ongoing fighting. They repre-sented the future of peace talks, of political participation, of the gov-ernment's tolerance of nonviolent opposition. The government had indicated it would allow the four to leave the country, and the heads of diplomatic missions vocally encouraged it. Kenya had agreed to take them in.

The court was called to order, and with little fanfare or elaboration the chief justice announced the detainees' release. The room erupted in celebration. The four men promptly exited the courtroom through a side door, where a crowd met them in the courtyard. I called back to the embassy to pass on the news to Larry, a senior diplomat who had come to Juba in March to fill in for Ambassador Page as chargé d'affaires while she was on leave for a few weeks in the United States. I had the phone to my ear as Mike and I rushed out to the courtyard. "The crowd has lifted them up on their shoulders. I can see Ezekiel up front." Ezekiel was the dual-national American detainee, so we were tracking him particularly closely. "I'll be honest, for a guy who was just released from detention, he doesn't look particularly happy," I shouted through the phone over the cheers in the crowd. Ezekiel's eyes were wide and darted around the courtyard. He'd be an easy target from there. He seemed to be thinking that too.

"We need to go," Mike said, sensibly noting that the jubilation could turn ugly quickly or an armed loyalist could decide to render a different verdict on the crowd. I was torn but knew he was right.

It was mostly a triumphant moment. I would rather have seen a not-guilty verdict, but even so it was a victory for justice and a hard knock for the government's coup story. Within moments, our security officer had ushered us to our car. The former detainees were also loaded into an SPLA van in short order to be taken to the NSS offices to collect their belongings. Afterward, all four and their wives came to our residence to meet with our chargé d'affaires and other foreign chiefs of mission. It was a public showing, for whatever it was worth, to demonstrate that the Western world was keeping a watchful eye.

Despite this, Kiir ultimately decided not to let his enemies leave the country yet. The government offered them each two security personnel "for protection," and they settled in for a different kind of detention until it suited Kiir to let them go. Since Kiir had lost his gamble in the courts, exercising some continued power over his political opponents was probably a minor consolation.

THE END OF the treason trial offered a small win in an otherwise bleak atmosphere of ongoing violence and increasing humanitarian crises. The government's obstruction of the UN's work and humanitarian relief more broadly continued unabated. Private pressure from diplomats failed to make headway, and the situation became so grave that friendly Western embassies, including the United States, released a public statement expressing concern over the disruption of critical relief supplies. The modest statement was carefully constructed; it didn't even assign blame for atrocities or interference, but no matter. The government made clear once again that it would tolerate no criticism, no matter how gentle, indirect, or true. The chiefs of mission were convoked to the Ministry of Foreign Affairs, where a deputy foreign minister admonished them harshly with cameras present to ensure public consumption—that was the audience, after all. The government's concern over its image yet again trumped its concern for the well-being of its citizens.

As the position of Kiir's government continued to harden, threatening what little progress had been made in peace talks in Addis, the US government started to warm up to the idea of consequences. The debate in Washington had been ongoing for months, just as it has been in the embassy. Much of the staff favored bold action, strongly worded public condemnation, and aiming directly at the top. We also pushed for further cuts to government assistance (most support to the military had been suspended by this point, but very little other support had been affected). Leadership—whether in the embassy, State Department headquarters, or White House—was generally more measured and deliberate, their worries about losing our influence and access a steady refrain. Four months into the war we had failed to prevent, launched by a partner who had long failed to heed our warnings or advice and who had allowed his cabinet officials to routinely insult us, I couldn't see what purpose that influence was serving.

I was thrilled when I heard from the special envoy's office that the Obama administration was considering sanctions. Washington asked the embassy to provide recommendations for individuals to consider, along with evidence of their relevant offenses. It seemed we might have finally broken the spell, finally be willing to recognize and punish bad acts committed by those we'd helped to put and keep in power. I pored over the reports I'd compiled and met with counterparts at UNMISS and other embassies who also had been tracking human rights abuses. I worked with military and intelligence colleagues to identify commanders in different areas where atrocities had occurred. Our colleagues in the human rights bureau at State made suggestions and cross-referenced what we had with what advocacy groups in Washington were tracking. One advisor in the special envoy's office took particular interest in Michael Makuei Lueth's inflammatory approach, so we all contributed examples of his particular offenses. Since they mostly consisted of words, however, it was a tricky space to navigate for the free-speech-loving USA. We sent specific names and incidents to the special envoy's office, which took the lead working with the National Security Council and the Treasury Department. Sanctions weren't prison, but they would be some form of accountability and send a message that our tolerance had limits.

In April, President Obama signed the executive order authorizing the sanctions. The order was sweeping, applying to anyone who was complicit in threatening the peace and security of South Sudan, including those responsible for human rights abuses, targeting of civilians, recruiting child soldiers, attacking UN missions or peacekeeping operations, or obstructing humanitarian assistance. It applied as well to anyone who led any group whose members had engaged in the relevant activities, but no individuals had yet been sanctioned under the order. Authorizing sanctions was the first step in applying pressure. The United States was finally saying it publicly: we've been urging you to bring peace or there will be consequences, and we mean it.

Most contacts in the South Sudanese government didn't have much to say about the order at this stage, but civil society representatives inside and outside the country applauded the move, telling me and others in the embassy that everyone was hopeful it would create the pressure needed to bring real results in the struggling peace talks.

As usual, Makuei couldn't help but comment, soon unleashing a public tirade blaming foreign intervention for obstructing peace in the country and claiming the order was evidence that the United States supported the rebels. Then, he went even further, personally circulating a fabricated speech he claimed Ambassador Page had

given at a university in the United States, in which she allegedly offered support for the rebels and called their fight a just war. It was
a brazen step even for Kiir's hard-liners, and a poorly written one
at that. It would have been laughable but for the seriousness of the
charge. For Ambassador Page, someone who had given so much of
her career to this cause, it was a horrible affront. It also seemed badly
miscalculated. In my view, Ambassador Page had not been tough
enough on the government in the lead-up to the war. In fact, this was
usually where the two of us had conflicted. Yet, for her tireless and
genuine efforts to help them succeed, this was how Kiir and his administration repaid her.

This was unsurprising to me, as I'd never seen South Sudan, or
this government, in its hopeful times. When I'd arrived, it was already on the precipice. I found it hard to believe, though, that some
of these signs hadn't been there all along. But hope can be blinding.
I wondered if I, too, would have found it so hard to accept that this
was who they were if I had known these players as long as the ambassador had—if I'd worked closely with them to secure peace and the
possibility of a future for this country.

With Ambassador Page still in the United States, Larry immediately sought a meeting with the Ministry of Foreign Affairs to protest the action, but he was met with indifference. The undersecretary
acknowledged the speech was obviously false but suggested the government wasn't to blame for rogue acts by ministers who followed
their own line. "But he's the government spokesperson!" Larry replied indignantly. The undersecretary simply shrugged.

The US government's willingness finally to consider consequences
mollified the sting of having to sit quietly in meetings, enduring insults from South Sudanese officials complicit in their country's destruction. I'd also been working on another tool at my disposal: the
annual trafficking in persons (TIP) report. The Trafficking Victims
Protection Act of 2000 established the TIP office at State and mandated annual reports on trafficking in every country in the world.
Most officers considered it a tedious task. A human rights officer
would typically dedicate a few weeks to answering dozens of specific

questions from the TIP office in Washington, which would then draft the report based on those inputs:

> *Have the profiles and methods of traffickers changed? Does the country have laws against sex trafficking and forced labor? What are the penalties? Has anyone been prosecuted for these crimes? Does the government provide assistance to victims?*

This report went further than other reports required by Congress by assigning rankings (Tier 1: good; Tier 2: risky; Tier 3: bad). The TIP office, in consultation with the relevant embassy and regional bureau, makes the final call on a country's ranking, and a Tier 3 ranking has consequences. If a country has shown no progress addressing or attempting to address the worldwide scourge of human trafficking, it risks losing certain non-humanitarian assistance.

South Sudan, not surprisingly, had made no strides in addressing trafficking generally for years, but as a new country addressing wide-ranging challenges, it was given some leeway and special consideration. The TIP report, however, also has an entire section on child soldiers, part of the 2008 Child Soldiers Prevention Act, which has implications for any support or assistance to a country's military in particular.

It's a highly flawed system. The rankings are subjective and relative, and many diplomats disapprove of the automatic nature of the assistance cuts. At the same time, it's an active effort to connect the assistance we provide to some basic human rights standards, which I believed reflected a sensible long-term view. In passing these laws, Congress had decided some offenses were so grave that they should merit automatic consequences. Not providing aid to countries that use child soldiers seemed like a simple thing we could all agree on, but in South Sudan, we seemed capable of justifying any accommodation.

Under great pressure from the United States, and with our military assistance to the country under threat, the SPLA had made some efforts to demobilize child soldiers in the past, but we'd received many reports of new child-soldier recruitment on both sides since the war began. Some reports estimated as many as nine thousand children were affected. The chief of the UN International Children's Emergency Fund (UNICEF) in Juba told me it was again a widespread practice, and that children as young as twelve had been seen in SPLA uniform carrying weapons. I didn't need to take her word for it, though. I'd seen checkpoints at roundabouts in Juba not far from the embassy manned by teenagers toting AK-47s too large for their small stature. It was like the government was daring anyone to call them out on it. A colleague from a European embassy told me she stopped one day when she saw a particularly young-looking soldier. He told her he was fourteen and said the SPLA was welcoming young recruits in town since older men were being sent to fight. With so many defections, apparently they were taking whoever they could get.

The TIP tier system was pretty forgiving, but after two years on the Tier 2 watch list, South Sudan was on track for an automatic downgrade to Tier 3 unless the TIP office sought a waiver. The president ultimately had to sign off on any waivers, but we issued them pretty readily, the idea being that we can only help countries eliminate child soldiers if we're working with them on security-sector reform.* Cutting off security assistance would prevent that help. This idea only works, though, if the country you're working with recognizes that having child soldiers is an actual problem, and South Sudan clearly didn't seem to.

It had been over a month since I'd submitted our inputs to the TIP office for this year's report. I had low expectations, but with the uptick in press reports on child soldiers and the news that Washington was looking into sanctions anyway, I thought there was a shot that we might use this tool. The first feedback I got from the TIP office came with a few questions for follow-up and suggested that the situation would merit a downgrade. I wasn't looped in on subsequent

---

* In 2018 and 2019, the Trump administration would take the opposite approach with TIP waivers, using them as one of many methods to cut aid across the board, with little consideration of the potentially negative policy implications.

conversations in Washington, though, and Special Envoy Booth had objected to the decision. The next email I saw came from the special envoy's office, and the office's director, Lucy, was copied.

"Lizzy, in order for South Sudan to avoid automatic downgrade to Tier 3, the government needs to submit a written action plan stating how they plan to address TIP in the future. This should be sufficient to get a waiver."

It wasn't unexpected, but then came the kicker: "Can you draft up a plan to give to the MFA so they can submit it?"

I could stomach letting South Sudan off the hook again, but the idea that we would do the government's homework was simply too much to take. I took a deep breath and replied with the most dip-lomatic version of "hell no" I could muster. It went something like this: "I disagree with this decision but understand if Washington has decided to take this approach. However, given my deep under-standing of the situation regarding renewed active use of child sol-diers, I cannot in good faith draft this plan myself. I hope you can understand."

Within seconds of hitting send, James appeared next to my desk, his even temper knocked off-balance for a change. "Lizzy, you can't write an email like that! Someone could forward it!" James knew that, in the department, "corridor reputation" was the basis on which people secured good future postings, or didn't. He didn't want me to burn professional bridges, and this type of email could earn me a reputation as a troublemaker.

"So? A half-dozen people were copied on that email. Do you think I'm trying to hide my position?" I was more heated than I normally would be with James, but the hypocrisy of the whole exercise was get-ting under my skin. I took a deep breath and adjusted my speech to a less hysterical pitch. "I get it if other priorities prevail. I know I'm supposed to defer to the bigger picture, but I disagree here, and I'm not going to be complicit with it."

James had just returned to Juba, so after nearly four months of working relatively independently, I had an immediate boss again. It took some getting used to. I understood his concern, but I felt in the right, though I conceded that I probably should have given him a heads-up.

He was still standing at my desk when Lucy replied moments later. "I understand this is a complicated issue. Can we all set up a call to discuss?" I respected Lucy, and I suspected part of her respected my response, but it was her job to implement Special Envoy Booth's decisions.

Lucy heard me out, but I knew the call wasn't a merits-based discussion. She offered to have someone else draft the plan. They'd work it through the South Sudanese Embassy in Washington. It was a good call, I thought, since the Foreign Ministry here would probably spit on whatever we gave them, harangue our audacity, and tell us to mind our own business, at which point we'd need a new plan to fake their participation and commitment.

Clearly, our appetite for consequences wasn't picking up as quickly as I'd hoped.

THROUGHOUT APRIL, OTHER US government refugees returned to Juba. More than a dozen staff returned from Nairobi, and the closure of the Juba Support Unit coincided with the one hundredth and final "Juba unrest sitrep," the daily brief provided to Washington from the field.

War was no longer a crisis but the new normal, although that month saw an uptick in violence in a way we hadn't seen since the very start. In Bor, several hundred Dinka youth, interspersed with SPLA soldiers and other armed men, marched on the UNMISS compound, blew open the gate with a rocket-propelled grenade, entered the compound, and attacked the IDPs. This was precisely the kind of violence Ken had tried to prevent when he stopped Makuei's armed men from entering months before. Dozens of unarmed civilians were killed, and some UNMISS peacekeepers were injured attempting to repel the attack. The diplomatic community, myself included, was rather surprised they managed to fire back at all. Unsurprisingly, the state news broadcast that night claimed the incident was caused by

UNMISS personnel opening fire on peaceful demonstrators. The press offensive against the UN didn't let truth get in the way of a good opportunity.

Inside the compound at the time were two protection officers for Nonviolent Peaceforce, a plucky international organization that goes to the most dangerous places on earth and deploys civilians to help locals stay safe. At first, I found the group's approach of unarmed civilian protection naive, but I became a convert, impressed by concrete, local accomplishments under dire circumstances. And the protection officers did it all bravely, as proved by Derek and Andres, the Nonviolent Peaceforce officers in Bor that day. When the base came under attack, they sheltered in a mud hut with fourteen women and children. During hours of siege, armed militiamen entered the hut three times and stuck rifles in their faces. They were even threatened with an axe. The gunmen commanded Derek and Andres to leave, saying they would kill them if they didn't. They only wanted the women and children, they said. Derek and Andres knew that they meant it—the lives of these women and children would be lost if they complied. So they didn't. They refused. They told the gunmen they were unarmed, but they were there for protection. They had nothing but their presence to offer. Eventually, the gunmen left for good, and all the lives in the hut were spared. The protection officers' presence in that hut wasn't planned, but it was what they trained to do and the reason they were there. And it worked. Their example gave me a needed boost of hope in humanity.

Bentiu, farther north toward the border and near critical oil fields, was also attacked and again taken by rebel forces. Dinka and Darfuri civilians were targeted and killed. As the fighting was underway, I worked with Washington to identify which American citizens were still in the area. We heard from a South Sudanese American man who needed assistance getting out safely. He was in Bentiu temporarily to help with his family's business. Working with a humanitarian organization there, we were able to get him out during a pause in the fighting a few days later. It took him a while, but once he made it to Juba, he came to the embassy. He'd lost everything but his passport and had been shot in the hand, so I helped him organize his travel back to America.

He and I sat in the embassy's entryway on the long wooden bench. I had to get a few more details from him to organize his trip, but I was also curious about the situation in Bentiu since I hadn't talked to many people directly who'd experienced a rebel attack. "When the rebels moved into town, I had gathered with forty-seven other people in the house of a local businessman I knew. Rebels, groups of them, kept coming to the house demanding money and cell phones. At about 11 a.m., the rebels returned and demanded we leave the house, so they could give it to one of the rebels in command. The soldiers then told us to go to the mosque, but shortly after we started walking there, they demanded we sit down, in a line, in the middle of the street. And then, they began shooting us."

It was a dramatic and alarming story, but as he told it, he wasn't excited. There was just a sadness in his voice and a disbelief, like he wouldn't believe it himself if he didn't bear the scars and multiple fractures where he was shot.

"I pulled out my passport and held it up, pleading with the soldiers that I was American, not on either side of the conflict. One of them took my passport and studied it, said 'okay,' and handed it back to me. Some of the soldiers then took me to the hospital."

I asked, "Did they take anyone else there?"

"No," he replied, looking down. "All of the others I was with, all of them were killed."

His story confirmed that the rebels, too, were nonchalant about war crimes and terrorizing civilians. Irrespective of who started the fight, the two sides' styles and misdeeds would be hard to differentiate—they'd learned from the same playbook, after all. It was a good reminder for me that while I was sickened by the government's heinous actions and callous approach toward its citizens, I wasn't rooting for the rebels either. What I didn't want was for the United States to legitimize the actions of either of the fighting parties, and I feared our ongoing relationship with the government was doing just that. I was rooting for peace, justice, and accountability, and neither of the armed groups were offering that. This particular man, though, might have been lucky that he hadn't been under attack by government troops this time. Under the influence of the government's ongoing anti-Western campaign, government troops might not have seen an American passport as a reason to spare him.

It was after meeting him that my nightmares picked up again. I'd had them off and on throughout the conflict. They were different scenarios: sometimes I was in danger, and sometimes I simply couldn't help others who were. Sometimes I was in Juba, and sometimes I was in Malakal or Bor. But now they came every night like clockwork. I would wake up at 3 a.m. in a sweat. It was always in the streets of Bentiu, and I was always trapped with other civilians, and I always thought I was going to die.

SECRETARY OF STATE John Kerry visited Juba in early May, purportedly to deliver a harsh message, although some of us in the embassy were concerned it would be received differently. We didn't send Kerry to visit just anyone, after all. James recommended the ambassador assign me to take notes in the big meeting between Secretary Kerry and President Kiir. As the political chief, it was James's prerogative to attend the meeting, and an honored slot for any political officer, but he thought I'd earned it. The ambassador vetoed the idea, however. It was too important to be trusted to the junior in the political office. Instead, I was relegated to setting up the token civil society meeting and "all other tasks, as required." The S visit was always a heavy lift, all hands on deck, because every move was meticulously planned and every minute accounted for, from wheels down to wheels up just a few hours later. My event was the last one, just before Kerry would say a few words to the embassy staff in the cafeteria and head back to the plane. Those two slots were easily shortened or cut should the main events get delayed or run long. I'd been in and out of the meeting room—a prefab trailer we'd done our best to spruce up—for a couple of hours. Most of the Foreign Service is populated with type-A personalities, but S's travel staff took it to a whole new level.

The advance staffer tried to mask his shock when he first laid eyes on the trailer meeting room. "Yeah, I don't think S has been somewhere quite like this before." The comment indicated the broader challenge of bringing a cabinet-level official to a war-zone facility that didn't garner the generous budgets of Iraq and Afghanistan.

We'd managed to get a set of tabletop and standing flags from both countries. I thought he should be impressed, all things considered. "This is what we've got. Feel free to rearrange it if you'd like," I said, trying to muster greater concern about flag and camera placement.

Our five civil society guests were required to come in two hours early to ensure they got through security and were in place well ahead of Secretary Kerry's arrival. I was managing other logistics and putting out fires the whole time, but I couldn't leave them unaccompanied inside the embassy grounds, so I was hovering between the overly air-conditioned trailer and the sweltering heat outside in ten-minute increments. While inside, I made small talk about the peace efforts and what topics Kerry might ask them about. All were happy to be there, although two of them had no idea who Kerry was and were very curious why someone important was called a secretary.

I reiterated many times, "I know it's tempting, but we're on a very tight schedule. No time for photos. His staff has been extremely clear about that. Please don't ask."

Kerry and his entourage arrived only a little late, and the meeting went smoothly, except for the predictable request for a photo just as he was attempting to extract himself gracefully from the meeting. But I had to give it to the civil society activist who made the request: "Mr. Secretary, thank you so much for your time. But you and I are both so tall, we must have a photo." Kerry's staff gave me death stares, but I took my cue from S, who politely obliged, although he did insist the rest of the civil society participants join too.

Immediately after the photo, Kerry was ushered next door to the crowded cafeteria to give inspiring remarks to his expansive State Department team in Juba. We still had a small number of Americans, but the overall embassy operation ran on the work of local staff, and several dozen were gathered there so he could thank them for their ongoing work in difficult and dangerous circumstances. It was one of those great moments when you can really reflect on being part of a much bigger and more important global effort, and I missed it. I had to escort our meeting participants to the embassy entrance and sign them out. I sprinted back across the dusty parking lot uncomfortably in my wilted pantsuit, but arrived just as Kerry had finished his remarks and was making his way back out through the crowd to the motorcade. I didn't even make it in for a handshake.

Nonetheless, I enjoyed some of Ajani's rum punch at the wheels-up party by the pool, and messages circulated shortly thereafter about a job well done. In the coming days, though, it was unclear if the visit had had the intended effect. We heard from some close government contacts that top officials interpreted the visit as a high-level demonstration of support for Kiir and recognition of his legitimacy, in contrast to the rebels. Ambassador Page assured us the tough message to Kiir had been clear, but I wasn't in the meeting, so I couldn't be certain. This government heard what it wanted to hear and little else.

WHEN THE FIRST sanctions were announced a few days later, it was a disappointment. Marial Chanuong was sanctioned on the government side. He was a bad man, no doubt about it, and deserving of punishment. He had been the commander of the Presidential Guard when it led the attacks in Juba in December. But he had no assets in or need for travel to America, and no one pretended he had conducted the attacks of his own volition. His orders came from somewhere else. Peter Gadet, the rebel commander who led attacks on civilians in Bentiu in April, was sanctioned on the rebel side. He similarly had no affected property or interests. A UN contact who knew Gadet told me he literally laughed at the idea that banks in America would have any impact on him, as he fought in the bush. It came across as a symbolic move, more of a warning than a punitive measure—enough to piss off the government but not enough to hinder those responsible for the war or those capable of bringing peace. I learned later that the

White House and the special envoy's office really were ready to go bigger this time (sanctioning more individuals, though not higher-ranking ones), but the Treasury Department had to sign off on every sanction. Their office for global sanctions had a giant workload and a tiny staff. With no regional expertise, their threshold for approving sanctions was hard to meet, and pinning them down even to review applications was a difficult task. On sanctions, at least, capacity was an even bigger impediment than political will.

On May 9, Salva Kiir and Riek Machar were back in Addis Ababa. They signed another cease-fire agreement, or at least they signed another document "re-dedicating" themselves to the first one signed, and promptly violated, in January. Some in Washington attributed this breakthrough to pressure brought about by Kerry's visit, but it seemed another effort by the warring parties to simply buy time. Even the greatest advocates of the peace process found it hard to be optimistic. The disdain between them was visible. They couldn't even shake hands. They could barely stand being in the same room and, in fact, were not until that very moment. These two men had reached no middle ground. All they had agreed to was to sign something so the international and regional leaders would let them escape the luxury hotel and get back to their war.

President Kiir dispelled any contrary expectations during a May 11 press conference in Juba, where he slammed the countries involved in the peace process, Westerners in particular. "We thought these were our friends," he said. "But then on 15 December, we realized that these people were not the friends of South Sudan."

On May 22, the US government took another stab at using high-level personal diplomacy to influence Kiir in a better direction. Gayle Smith, senior director at the National Security Council and a special assistant to President Obama, arrived in Juba. Smith was a legend. After twenty years as a journalist and NGO worker, covering some of the continent's most dangerous wars and worst humanitarian crises, she knew many of the rebels and former rebels (including South Sudan's current president) personally from their days in the bush. Smith had later cofounded the Enough Project, which combined in-depth field research with highly potent advocacy in Washington and beyond. The organization's reach into successive administrations and Congress had been impressive, though it, too, had suffered a delayed reaction to the bad acts of the independence heroes it had supported so fervently in the fight against Khartoum.

But I had high hopes for Smith. I'd heard she was tough, a straight shooter. This was no career diplomat. She was an operator. I was looking forward to seeing her in action. Lucky for me, being a minion for a senior director wasn't above my pay grade, so I got to be her control officer, which meant I planned out, executed, and accompanied nearly every step of her visit. Since she was pretty chill, she traveled without staff, which meant I'd be liaising directly with her throughout the trip.

Ambassador Page knew I was excited to have this role, so she invited me to join the two of them for dinner. They'd known each other well for years, and it was evident that this was two friends getting together rather than a staged event. I was giddy to be included. Despite my misgivings about some of Ambassador Page's positions, I still admired her and all she'd accomplished in her career, and I expected that this was an opportunity to see a truly authentic version of her. Maybe more exposure was what I needed to better understand what drove the decisions she made.

It was a casual evening, and Page and Smith opted to stay at the residence, choosing the open-air area by the bar instead of the fluorescent lighting of the Tukul. When we met, the sun hadn't quite set, but it was nearly dark by the time the wine was poured. I mostly kept my mouth shut, just soaking in the war stories and reminiscences of two impressive women who had fought and worked for peace and justice for decades in far-flung lands because they genuinely cared. In doing so, they had reached the pinnacle of their fields. I knew I had hours of work to do back in my container, emails to catch up on, schedules to update and distribute, emergency queries to reply to, and cables to clear. But I let myself enjoy the moment, in near darkness at a rickety table, wondering if I had what it took to have a career like theirs. These women were tough and determined. Throughout long and varied careers in foreign affairs, they'd seen some of the worst of humanity, and they'd used the opportunities available to them to fight back. They'd taken setbacks in stride and stayed the course, working their way up to positions of greater influence, never giving up on the idea that they had a role to play to make things better. This was what diplomacy was about: persisting in the long game, relentlessly using whatever tools you have to continually work toward greater peace and prosperity.

The next morning, we had little on the schedule but a tentative time for a meeting with President Kiir. For visits like this, Kiir was the main event, and everything else was penciled in until that meeting was done. I was excited to be joining this time. I'd met Kiir and been on the phone taking notes before, but this was my first time in the room. We waited the requisite time at J1, the presidential palace, before we were invited in. The wait for Smith wasn't too long, considering. Kiir greeted us all warmly. If you knew this man personally, I supposed it would be hard to imagine his being responsible for so much destruction.

Kiir didn't really know me but generously welcomed me all the same, his large hands enveloping mine. (By this point, I was fairly well known in the high-level South Sudanese political circles, mostly as "Ambassador Susan's little girl," apparently. I knew this because, after introducing myself to a deputy minister once, he said, "Oh, right, you're Ambassador Susan's little girl.") The office was palatial, and faux gilded, with enormous overstuffed furniture. We sat in a large seating area far across the spacious room from Kiir's desk. I took a seat on one side of a giant couch, my feet several inches off the floor as I tried to find a comfortable and appropriate manner to sit. It was a serious occasion, but the environment seemed almost comical in its scale. I felt like Alice in Wonderland.

I was farther from Kiir than Ambassador Page and Smith, as was appropriate, but Kiir could be a low talker and his speech wasn't clear, so the positioning was unfortunate for a notetaker. I inched forward throughout the meeting until I was barely perched on the edge of the couch, dramatically leaning forward, stretching my ear as far in Kiir's direction as I was able to without collapsing. At this point, I still really thought this meeting was going to matter, so I took my task seriously.

Smith opened by asking Kiir sincerely how he was doing. "I do not know if I am okay or not," he replied, sounding genuine. I knew they'd known each other for years, but somehow I was not expect-ing the sentiment of two old friends reuniting. Smith applauded the May 9 agreement as a positive step, but Kiir quickly dismissed it as forced. He got defensive when she raised concern about the cycles of violence, squarely blaming Machar and claiming total innocence on the part of the government. The theme of the meeting was set. Kiir wouldn't moderate. Smith tried to explain that no one cared about blame, only about peace and avoiding the famine that would become inevitable if fighting continued. Kiir invoked Machar's attacks in 1991, at which point Smith seemed to realize the meeting was going downhill fast. She said civilians weren't just fleeing the rebels, hoping to get him to admit that his side, too, was causing problems, but he punted. "It's because the uniforms are the same," he suggested.

I was waiting for her to call him out on his bullshit, as she'd prom-ised she would do, but it didn't come. The tone remained friendly and understanding, on our side at least, and Kiir continued to flaunt the same blame game the government had championed for months.

At the end of the meeting, Smith asked for a few minutes alone, and Ambassador Page and I left the room. Outside in the waiting area, I quietly expressed my surprise at how friendly the meeting was. "She'll be more direct in the one-on-one. That's how it's done. It's not effective embarrassing him in front of others," Page told me, though it seemed the ambassador wasn't overly excited about how the meeting went either.

During her conversation with Kiir, Smith delivered President Obama's invitation to the US-Africa summit occurring in Wash-ington, DC, in August. It was the first event of its kind, and Africa watchers everywhere were excited the White House was putting so much emphasis on the continent, although the question of who was invited was a contentious one. Several heads of state considered too controversial due to oppression or violence against their own citizens were deliberately left off the list. We were surprised Kiir wasn't. Smith told Kiir the invitation was conditional and would be revoked if no progress was made toward ending the conflict.

I wondered about her delivery. I hoped she had stayed true to her commitments and was harsher and more direct in the private session. But unless the tone was dramatically altered from that in the earlier meeting, I expected the threat was not as persuasive as she imagined it to be.

18

Leaving Juba

June–July 2014

ON JUNE 2, PRESIDENT KIIR SPOKE AT THE OPENING CERE-
mony of the National Legislative Assembly, lauding the great plans he
had for the country, from food security and agricultural renewal to a
hydroelectric power project. He briefly mentioned the peace process
and Riek Machar, only to highlight that Machar was continuing to be
the cause of division in the country. He dismissed recent calls for federalism as part of Machar's ploy, reaffirming his own plans to maintain a stranglehold on power. This was a direct jab at the Equatorian
community, which had, for the most part, tried to stay out of the fray.
But in recent weeks, the three governors in the Equatorian states had
more proactively spoken out, not in favor of the rebels, but in favor
of federalism in an effort to secure more autonomy. Their collection
of smaller ethnic groups held no responsibility for the conflict and
power struggle but suffered all the same.

Otherwise, the speech and the event generally suggested a return
to normalcy, a determination to get to the status quo regardless of the
violence ongoing across other parts of the country and the continued
fear, and self-segregation, of the Nuer community in Juba.

A few days later, the State Department officially lifted the embassy's ordered departure status. This, too, portended assumptions
of normalcy, though in reality it was a practical matter. Ordered

departure status was intended to be a temporary emergency state, with a maximum possible duration of six months, and it had been almost six months to the day since it began. The embassy would allow a few more evacuees to return, but the situation actually changed very little. The real difference, to me, was the message it sent. Terminating ordered departure status was the bureaucratic equivalent of deeming the country at war as the new normal.

Those who opposed President Kiir didn't accept the new normal, though. Within days of his speech, local media reported a wave of public resignations and defections, including more than a dozen from the National Legislative Assembly. Kiir didn't seem to be fooling everyone.

On June 12, the latest round of peace talks in Addis Ababa came to a close with remarks from the special envoy for the East African regional trade organization that was hosting them, the Intergovernmental Authority on Development. Even while confirming that donor countries had spent $17.4 million in less than five months on sporadic talks leading to two failed cease-fire agreements, the ambassador expressed IGAD's "appreciation" to President Kiir and Machar. I found this nauseating, given the obvious failure of the talks, and I expected much of the funding for the boondoggle came from US coffers.

I wasn't the only one disturbed to learn how much had been spent on keeping the warring parties comfortably housed and fed in luxury hotels in Addis, to no particular end. Everyone in the embassy had been talking about it since the figure hit the local press. It caught us just as we were suffering through the annual chore of planning the embassy's Fourth of July event. After the ordered departure, we were back to "normal embassy" status, and an Independence Day party was standard fare. It showcased for the host country our enduring democracy and was an opportunity to give something back—one of the hottest tickets in town—to contacts across the government and community who had facilitated our efforts throughout the past year.

The distaste of hosting a flashy patriotic event in a country torn apart by civil war and humanitarian crisis was not lost on most of the embassy staff. Contrary to what our status might suggest, the situation in the country was unusual, so someone suggested we take a different approach. "Instead of an embassy party, couldn't we use that money to host a meal at the IDP camp? The ambassador could take part in handing out food or relief materials to IDPs and use it as an opportunity to highlight the ongoing suffering in the country. Seems like not only a better use of the funds but also a good public diplomacy opportunity." A few other similar ideas emerged, but the theme was to avoid having a party at any cost.

We took it to the rest of the members of the senior staff—more or less the emergency action committee, but slightly expanded now that ordered departure was off. All of the staff supported the idea, so we raised it with the ambassador, but she seemed skeptical, suggesting that the party was a required event. I asked Jessie, the desk officer in the special envoy's office, if she could find out what was possible. She learned that the funds came from a special budget earmarked only for representational events. "If there were no party, the money would just go back to Treasury," she said in an email, adding that she'd discussed it with Lucy, the office director, who suggested ambassadors could use the opportunity to deliver a pointed address to a captive audience. She ended the email, "Let's hope that's the case in Juba!" The team wasn't pleased. I think most of us would have preferred to send the money back to Treasury, but the ambassador insisted the show go on, so we all did our best to make it a successful but modest affair, held on the grounds of the residential compound.

The event began early, as we planned to end it at 7:30 p.m. sharp to allow everyone time to get home before their respective curfews. The timing of the city curfew had been the subject of some debate recently. For months, 11 p.m. had been the official time, but some government officials had suggested, both publicly and privately, that it was being moved up in advance of July 9, South Sudan's independence day, to ensure no one used the occasion to create trouble. When that would happen, no one seemed to know, but most diplomatic missions had earlier curfews anyway, out of caution.

Securing participation for evening events had been a challenge for some months now.

Ambassador Page's remarks were solemn. She thanked everyone for joining and noted that she'd be brief, given the curfews. She then harkened back to more celebratory times in the country and lamented the ongoing humanitarian crisis and grave suffering of the people of South Sudan, who deserved so much better. The solemnity of the speech was appropriate for the occasion. *Wouldn't it be nice if any of South Sudan's leaders were focused on the same concerns?*

It was standard to allot the host country an opportunity to address the event, so Kiir's spokesperson took to the podium. His comments were confusing and hard to follow, and they contained no serious message. He said clearly, however, that there was no 8 p.m. curfew in Juba, adding enthusiastically that curfews were only for criminals. The crowd laughed awkwardly, to which he replied, "Are any criminals present here?" His speech began to trail off, and someone stepped up to politely take the microphone from him, thanking him for joining the event. Guests promptly began moving toward the exit. It was an awkward conclusion to an event that was awkward from its inception. The generous buffet was still full, and the staff wanted to donate the leftovers to the IDP camps, but the catering contract prohibited donation. Reluctantly, someone decided to use the leftovers to feed three large hogs dropped off earlier in the day by General Mamur, an Independence Day gift to the Marines, he had said. Everyone left feeling somewhat disgusted.

On July 8, the curfew question was answered, sort of. Minister of Interior Aleu Ayienyi Aleu announced that an 8 p.m. curfew was in place in advance of the country's third independence anniversary. He added, "It is only witches who move at night. They steal and kill our people. . . . Shoot them."

After a year in Juba, that this was a public statement from a government minister was less shocking than it should have been. Local media reported it widely, indicating that local authorities had been issued a "shoot-to-kill" order for any curfew violators. The Ministry of Foreign Affairs and others scrambled by sundown to have the inspector general of police hold a press conference denying the curfew change as well as the shoot-to-kill order, but it was too late. The news had gone viral around the globe, causing alarm in capital cities and diplomatic missions alike. The embassy promptly shifted our own curfew to 8 p.m., and I got clearance from Washington to issue a warning for American citizens too. Government officials were annoyed, telling us that it wasn't necessary and complaining that the US government was again stoking fear where there need be none. But we had no reason to trust that cooler heads in the security services would prevail. The damage was already done.

MY YEAR IN South Sudan was coming to a close, but the war clearly was not. Instead of focusing on the suffering of its people and doubling down on the peace effort, the government of South Sudan had reinvested in war, having just spent $14.5 million on new weapons from China. And why not? We were feeding their people, after all. The rebels were following suit, as both sides prepared for another peace-less season.

As news emerged about President Kiir's invitation to the US-Africa summit, international organizations and individuals spoke out publicly and privately about the message it sent, noting the continued impunity for crimes during the war and Kiir's stubborn refusal to seek peace. An advocacy group focused on ending mass atrocities organized a letter-writing campaign, and more than twelve thousand activists sent letters to President Obama and Secretary Kerry opposing the invitation. Nuer communities across the globe organized a petition calling on President Obama to rescind the invitation, but it had become clear that Washington had no intention of following through on the threat Gayle Smith had personally delivered. Predictably, the event produced stomach-turning media moments, such as Secretary Kerry squarely blaming Machar for the broken peace deal, and a cheery photo op with Kiir, President Obama, and the First Lady at the White House.

I was ready to leave Juba, ready to be free of the sense of responsibility to do something and the total helplessness to do anything. But the idea of moving on was deeply depressing too. We'd failed the people of this country, we'd failed our own priorities, and I'd failed to do anything meaningful to change it. I'd put so much of myself into the work over the past year, but for what? To move on? Could I really just close this chapter, leave while the cycle of violence and impunity marched on?

My sentiments were shared by a half dozen other colleagues who were also seeing their tours come to an end. For those like James, who began their work here in more optimistic times, it was even more wrenching. At least I had never witnessed the place at such a promising moment. Ambassador Page had been here before and during independence, but her three years as ambassador, too, were ending. I could only imagine that her disappointment vastly exceeded my own.

It had been a tremendously difficult year, but there was a bond among those of us who'd seen it through together. Some had been here throughout the year. Others, like me, were exiled for a few weeks, but a core group was about to say goodbye, leaving the embassy to an entirely new staff, almost 100 percent turnover that summer, and we couldn't help but think that none of the new team would understand this place the same way. None of them saw Juba before the war began. None of them saw our embassy before that either. None of them understood that this new normal was anything but. It was a massive loss of institutional memory—and of outrage at South Sudan's leaders and at how little we, the US government, had really done.

A few USAID officers who had just returned would be extending, but they seemed poised to jump right in where they had left off six months ago, resuming development projects across the country with increased budgets, as though nothing had changed. They saw their development efforts as distinct from the political situation, arguing that the show must go on for the benefit of the people. But the people were victims in a war, and we lacked the access needed to verify the effectiveness, or unintended consequences, of our efforts and funds.

IT WAS FRIDAY afternoon, and I would depart Juba the next day. I was frantically wrapping up my check-out list. I clicked "send" on a seventeen-page handover memo for my successor. I was still clinging to the belief that my work was important, critical even, but it was hard to keep believing when no one in Washington or the embassy seemed overly concerned that my position would go empty for weeks before my successor's arrival.

I didn't know what the new officer would do, if anything, regarding the issues I'd focused on and the contacts I'd developed. I didn't know what the embassy team would prioritize, or even how US policy toward the country might progress. Since before the war began, though, I'd felt strongly that accountability had been one of the gravest and most consequential oversights. The war had only reaffirmed this view. I'd followed the issue closely since my first day here, and I'd uncovered a pattern—easy to see if you looked for it, but easy to ignore if you didn't. I hoped that if I laid it all out in writing, it would not be so easy for the US government to continue avoiding this issue. The memo was my last attempt at championing the same call to action I'd made for months: we must start addressing impunity.

I outlined the South Sudanese government's half-assed efforts at accountability before the war began. I talked about how international pressure to address SPLA human rights violations in Jonglei state was met with claims of arrests and prosecutions that quickly dissipated when our attention moved on to the next crises. I laid out the post–December 15 accountability initiatives, also announced with great fanfare in the face of international pressure, and how none of them had amounted to any action at all. Since January, the government had announced five separate initiatives, none of which had progressed in any way, including two different military investigative committees and a human rights investigative committee led by a former judge. None ever released conclusions or findings.

My report argued that the government of South Sudan had long proven it was not seriously seeking accountability, so outside forces would be needed to do so. It addressed the current status of the African Union's Commission of Inquiry (AU/COI), which was set up by the African Union very early in the conflict and tasked with investigating human rights violations and recommending steps for accountability, reconciliation, and healing. This effort had been both lauded as an "African solution for an African problem" and derided as a thinly veiled effort to stave off action by the International Criminal Court, but its capacity limitations suggested it could offer little of value even if it wanted to. Its recently released interim report was merely a rehashing of publicly available information. My report concluded that the AU/COI, like the South Sudanese government efforts, was not likely to deliver results.

For the third time, my report recommended in writing to Washington that we facilitate investigations and collect evidence as soon as possible, to ensure evidence was not lost, preserve a wide range of options for future transitional justice efforts, and signal to the warring parties that their crimes would not be forgotten this time. We were pouring money into this country still. Surely we could spare some for a legitimate accountability effort.

James, Mike, and Ambassador Page knew how strongly I felt about accountability, and they kindly scrambled to help me clear my final cable quickly. It was the last report I sent from Juba before logging off on my final day. Emily in the human rights bureau called it my swan song. Even then, though, I had no illusions that the message would finally be heard and heeded, but it was important for me to make the case one last time. Maybe it was just the obituary of my assignment to Juba.

ON JULY 24, the so-called peace talks resumed as I was en route back to America. I had a layover in Amsterdam's Schiphol airport. I fought the urge to continue poring over books and articles on South Sudan—old habits die hard. Instead, I picked up Michela Wrong's book on Eritrea, *I Didn't Do It for You* (I wasn't quite ready to leave the continent behind entirely). The first few pages felt painfully familiar.

Far from learning from the continent's mistakes, Eritrea had turned into the stalest, most predictable of African cliches. . . . For the journalists, diplomats, academics and aid workers who follow Africa, this felt like a personal betrayal, because it had destroyed the last of their hopes for the continent. . . . Somewhere along the line, it wasn't yet clear where, the True Believers must have missed the point. They had failed to register important clues, drawn naive conclusions, misinterpreted key events. The qualities we had all so admired obviously came with a sinister reverse side. Had we mistaken arrogant pigheadedness for moral certainty, dangerous bloody-mindedness for focused determination?

Her book was nearly a decade old. Just then, I felt very stupid for thinking that our role in South Sudan could have been any different, for the naive thought that I might have been able to shape another outcome.

19

Quieting the Voices
of Opposition

DIPLOMATS ARE TASKED WITH RESOLVING ISSUES AND smoothing over conflicts. The culture of diplomacy, and of the State Department, is not one of conflict. Career Foreign Service Officers are problem solvers, so we naturally shy away from anything causing tension. Create no issues where no issues need be. We are rule followers who live squarely within a hierarchical bureaucracy. Dissent does not come readily.

At the same time, frustration is a professional hazard long associated with the diplomatic corps. Presidents as varied as Franklin D. Roosevelt, John F. Kennedy, and Richard Nixon all found common ground in dismissing the Foreign Service with rude and at times amusing epithets ("striped-pants boys," "a bowl of jello," and "sons of bitches," respectively).* Foreign Service Officers have long endured insults and abiding derision, as their well-considered analysis and recommendations, grounded in regional and local expertise, have

---

* Hannah Gurman, *The Dissent Papers: The Voices of Diplomats in the Cold War and Beyond* (New York: Columbia University Press, 2012), 20. Gurman's book provides a thorough and well-researched history of dissent in the modern State Department.

been routinely dismissed for the inconvenience they impose on domestic situations or, simply, for inertia's sake.

The State Department has been fighting demoralization for at least a century. And yet, like the good soldiers they are, the diplomatic officers march on, drafting reams of reporting on intricate issues from countries across the globe that only manage to enrapture analysts in the basement of CIA headquarters at Langley.

The profession isn't all dreary all the time, but this is a common facet. For the most part, the careerists have accepted it, and political leadership has endeavored to keep it this way. The system ensures that dissent—voicing opinions that oppose the prevailing Washington view—remains an underused resource, to the peril of our national security interests.

While conformity has a long history in the State Department, the McCarthy era in the 1950s further undermined what little sense of agency and independence civil servants had. At the behest of Senator Joseph McCarthy and his hunt for communist sympathizers, the State Department, like so many others, purged employees who didn't follow the party line or who offered a whiff of disagreement.* This period enhanced what had already been a culture of compliance, increasing self-censorship by career diplomats who knew rocking the boat on policy risked one's reputation and professional advancement. Suffice it to say, this time did not see robust or honest debates of policy options.

Things began to change, though, when the Vietnam War heated up in the 1960s, as reporting officers in Vietnam grew frustrated with the disconnect between the reality they were seeing and their superiors' messages for Washington. Lars Hydle, who was a consular and political officer in Saigon in the late 1960s, captured the dilemma in

---

* The website of the American Foreign Service Association (AFSA) includes a section on dissent, www.afsa.org/state-dissent-foreign-service. The page includes a September 2017 article, "The State of Dissent in the Foreign Service," by Harry Kopp, published in the *Foreign Service Journal*, which offers a good overview and history of the dissent channel, some of which is recounted here, but in brief.

an oral history project for the Association for Diplomatic Studies, stating in an interview that the political section "was basically trying to make the South Vietnamese government look as good as possible. . . . Reports were continually massaged and changed around to make them seem less bad than they were." He said his superiors warned him that negative reports had to be suppressed or they could be leaked to the press "and used against the policy."* A tactic and sentiment I could recognize so many years later.

How did the Vietnam War go so terribly wrong for us? How did we make such massive strategic errors over and over again? As it turns out, lying to yourself leaves you ill-prepared to effectively address foreign policy challenges. This is the cost of closing your eyes and systematically suppressing dissenting views.

If an institution doesn't reward truth, discourages it even, it will not receive it. The White House didn't want honesty to detract from its policies, so neither the State Department nor the military provided it. For quite some time, we were making policy decisions based on wishful thinking and reports designed to reaffirm our existing positions.

The costs of this strategy were becoming clear to both the American public and the rank-and-file foreign policy professionals. Protests rocked the country, and a sense of hopelessness spread throughout the State Department too. Unable to pierce the bureaucracy above them in order to convey the truth, officers either fell in line or quit. There were 266 resignations from the Foreign Service in 1968 alone, mostly junior officers.** Then, in 1970, some State Department personnel tried another tack. Fifty Foreign Service Officers, along with two hundred other State Department employees, sent a statement to the secretary opposing the bombing campaign in Cambodia. The culture of compliance was beginning to crack under the pressure of widespread dissent. The department needed to establish a way to

---

* Kopp, "State of Dissent." This article quotes the interview, the full text of which can be found here: https://adst.org/OH%20TOCs/Hydle,%20Lawrence%20H .toc.pdf.

** Kopp, "State of Dissent."

release that pressure, and so, in 1971, the much heralded Dissent Channel was born. This official avenue for expressing dissent inside the department had the dual benefits of appearing to encourage dissenting views and keeping them safely contained inside the walls of the institution.

Today, the Dissent Channel is memorialized in the Foreign Affairs Manual, the State Department's regulations. Section 2 FAM 070 states:

> *It is Department of State policy that all U.S. citizen employees, foreign and domestic, be able to express dissenting or alternative views on substantive issues of policy, in a manner which ensures serious, high-level review and response.*

The office in charge of managing the receipt and distribution of Dissent Channel communication is the secretary's policy planning staff, known by the acronym "S/P," which was established essentially to be the secretary's own think tank, an office with the time and mandate to think big thoughts about policy analysis. Its role in the Dissent Channel sounded good but has since become something more like an administrative shepherding function. S/P circulates incoming Dissent Channel messages to the secretary, the deputy secretary, the deputy secretary for management, the undersecretary for political affairs, the executive secretary, and other senior officers as required, such as the relevant regional bureau's assistant secretary. S/P is also required to provide a substantive reply to the drafter within a specified time period. At the very least, someone is stuck with the inconvenience of drafting a reply, though it is mostly informed (and probably written) by the bureau or office that has likely already dismissed the dissenting view.

The Dissent Channel seemed to play its role well in subsequent years. Dissent, where it existed, was well contained. There are a few notable exceptions. *The Blood Telegram: Nixon, Kissinger, and a Forgotten Genocide* by Gary J. Bass tells the dramatic story of one of the first dissent cables that lambasted the US government's failure to denounce or intervene in the genocide in Bangladesh, due to our close relationship with the perpetrators in the Pakistani government. Archer Blood, our consul general in East Pakistan (present-day Bangladesh), had sent many cables to Washington calling for public condemnation of the atrocities, to no avail. In April 1971, his staff sent a dissent cable, which Blood endorsed, calling for action "to salvage our nation's position as a moral leader of the free world."* The dissent was dismissed and Blood recalled to Washington.

In 2018, George Washington University's National Security Archive published a few dozen dissent cables, mostly from the 1970s and early 1980s, secured through a Freedom of Information Act (FOIA) lawsuit.** This collection provides an interesting read of strong internal views about some rather unflattering moments in our foreign policy history. Before the university's FOIA efforts, tracking down information on prior dissents was extremely difficult. I know this because I tried. Even from inside the department, you can't search for them in the cable distribution repository. They are not findable because they are carefully guarded and distributed. The Dissent Channel serves the purpose of collecting dissenting views, which are meticulously documented and argued, and folding them up tidily and locking them away.

Since the State Department is hardly a hotbed of opposition and insubordination, most Foreign Service Officers take the routine dismissal of their views in stride. Better to do your best from inside the machine and otherwise keep your head down, the way we always have, whether through the distasteful George W. Bush war on terror years or the politicized Benghazi episode. Dissenting just isn't our thing, broadly speaking. But some of us can't help ourselves, I guess. I gave it a try, and I learned how it works, or doesn't, inside

---

* Kopp's article discusses these details briefly, but the entire episode is captured in the book.

** The links to the documents can be found at "Department of State's Dissent Channel Revealed," National Security Archive, March 15, 2018, https://nsarchive.gwu.edu/briefing-book/foia/2018-03-15/department-states-dissent-channel-revealed.

the department. It's an uphill, discouraging battle, the apex of which is the Dissent Channel. It's nice we have it, I suppose. It means something, perhaps. It's a message of sorts. One could generously describe it as a type of departmental suggestion box, though it would be more accurate to picture it as a shredder.

20

The Last Resort

February–July 2015

BY FEBRUARY 2015, I'D BEEN A WATCH OFFICER IN THE OP-erations Center for six months, which meant I was one of the Foreign Service Officers manning the twenty-four-hour "watch" in the State Department's crisis center. It was the same Ops I had had on speed dial throughout the crisis in Juba. When I'd first arrived, I was greeted like an old friend. Officers who had staffed the Juba Task Force showed me the whiteboard where my phone number had been listed for weeks. To me, those staffing the Task Force and the officers on the watch floor had been faceless, nameless people on the other end of the line, but everyone here knew "Lizzy from Juba." It was surreal finally being on the other side.

I'd been excited for the tour in Ops. It was considered prestigious and competitive. It's a bit like a law student earning a coveted seat on the law review, complete with the kudos, résumé boost, and seemingly endless tedious work that someone meticulous needs to do on behalf of the institution. The reality of working there turned out to be less enthralling than I'd imagined, though that was probably Juba's fault. The year before, I'd been the one in the midst of the crisis, not the one supporting from afar. It was unusual that I'd had ample first-hand crisis experience as a third-tour officer. Most of my colleagues found the fast pace and proximity to emergencies exciting, but for me it all felt less consequential than Juba.

Ops was also a place with proximity to power, in the State Department world at least. The center is housed on the seventh floor of the Harry S. Truman Building in Foggy Bottom—"Main State"—just down the hall from the corridor known as Mahogany Row, which houses the secretary's office, though the two areas could hardly be mistaken for neighbors. Mahogany Row, with its high ceilings, antique rugs, and stately decor, feels precisely like the kind of place where important diplomatic work is conducted. The watch floor of Ops, on the other hand, looks like the inside of a bunker, well into the end of times. At any time day or night, officers are stationed at computer terminals in rows facing each other, with several television screens on the wall streaming different news channels and a series of digital clocks identifying time zones around the world, the most important of which is "S": wherever the secretary is at that moment. In the back of the room sit a handful of other computer terminals for crisis management support officers—civil servants with regional expertise who work regular day jobs tracking ongoing and potential crises around the world—and staff task forces as needed. Other watch officers mull in and out of the remaining terminals, preparing for the next shift or wrapping up from the last.

The watch is primarily staffed by Foreign Service Officers like me, serving thirteen-month tours on a punishing and ever-changing shift schedule. The shifts last eight hours, beginning at 6:30 a.m., 2:30 p.m., and 10:30 p.m., but with prep time and wrap-up time, one's workday can last anywhere from eight and a half hours to ten or more. When you're "in the chair," you're literally in the chair. Bathroom breaks are sequenced and must be announced before leaving the floor. You check the blue light near the door to make sure the one shared toilet isn't already occupied, and shout "Going blue!" to alert your colleagues that you've pulled out of the call order momentarily. A note above the toilet reminds you to be speedy. Meals are eaten at your terminal, and since the watch is in action twenty-four hours a day and is in a classified area, the office gets cleaned extremely rarely, which makes for a pretty gross environment. The mouse—or likely many mice—that frequented the floor, at times running across terminals and keyboards, we called Ralph. The small one that was caught in a mousetrap behind one of the monitors, we deemed "son of Ralph."

The hours are difficult, but the worst part of the schedule is that officers only serve two days on each shift time at a time—typically starting with two early shifts, then two afternoon shifts, and finishing with two overnight shifts. Unlike in Juba, though, work really is done when you leave the office. You can't take it with you, and someone else literally takes your chair when you go. Your time off is yours, and I had significantly more of it in Ops than I'd ever had before. But the changing shift schedule was punishing. I was jet-lagged the entire year.

I didn't have much energy to do things, but I had ample time to think. Months after my departure from Juba, South Sudan still occupied my mind, appearing in my nightmares, keeping me awake, looming in my head on slow overnight shifts as I found myself searching for the latest Juba cable traffic. I found it hard to think about anything else, and, as friends attested, I found it hard not to talk about it too often.

It was February when I decided to do something about it. I emailed Oliver to tell him I was working on a dissent cable. We'd shared many conversations about our shared dismay at US foreign policy in South Sudan. I needed to know if this was a crazy idea.

Oliver was conflicted, suggesting that because the real impediment to progress, as he saw it, had been the White House, a dissent cable inside State wouldn't serve much purpose. But then he read the draft and replied: "It made me happy." He said he'd consider signing on and helping revise the draft. He thought we should pull in more people as signatories. I had validation and a partner in crime, and suddenly it all felt less futile. This made me happy too.

Titled "U.S. Should Change Course on South Sudan: From a Short-Term Focus on Elites in Addis to a Long-Term Focus on Sustainable

Peace," the cable laid out the argument in five sections and concluded with specific recommended actions. It lambasted empty threats as having damaged US credibility, calling specifically for sanctions on President Kiir and Riek Machar (for fomenting violence and failing to negotiate in good faith) and a UN arms embargo. It also recommended making our support to the ongoing peace process contingent on concrete steps toward peace and inclusion of other stakeholders, arguing that our massive financial support had legitimized and perpetuated a process that had been compromised, since the regional countries steering it, like Uganda, were using the negotiations as a proxy for their own ambitions. By validating this effort, which was doomed to fail, we were hindering the possibility of other, better efforts. The dissent argued that even if the negotiations could succeed, whatever came of them would be a partial solution among elites, returning the country to its precarious prewar political state without addressing any of the underlying grievances that had made the level of violence possible. The document outlined how our effort to maintain our close relationship with the South Sudanese government had come at a tremendous cost, and our commitment to the country's leaders had not been reciprocated. It called for a further reduction in our technical assistance to the federal government, which included support to the Central Bank, Ministry of Finance, and Ministry of Petroleum. This had long been justified as critical activity necessary to keep the economy afloat, but it had had the unintended consequence of helping the government fund its war, which included the perpetuation of violence against civilians.

The dissent wrapped up with the issue most dear to me. The final section called for proactive efforts to ultimately ensure accountability, recounting that decades of impunity remained possibly the greatest driver of conflict in the country. We recommended that the monitoring and verification mechanism that had been established as part of the original peace agreement be repurposed to collect and preserve evidence of prior and ongoing human rights abuses and atrocities. The mechanism had been staffed and funded primarily by the United States, but an absence of political will, in both the South Sudanese government and the regional governments that could have pressured it, had left the mechanism powerless. The teams were tasked with reporting on violations of the peace agreement, but their reports were never made public, and none of the violations they reported were ever met with consequences. If the monitors were powerless to halt the violence now, perhaps they could at least prove useful in laying the groundwork for effective transitional-justice efforts in the future.

Oliver and I started reaching out to others who we knew had long shared similar concerns. Several agreed to sign on enthusiastically. Meanwhile, I reached out to S/P to find out more about the dissent process and to let them know what we were working on. Jon was the S/P staffer who covered Africa, and he'd covered South Sudan and Sudan in different capacities for years. He was sympathetic to our position, but he thought the dissent unnecessary since similar views were regularly considered. But this had been the case for some time, and these considerations had brought little change. In my mind, there was plenty of room for whatever tools might be able to shake up the conversation.

On the mechanics of the process, Jon had little information to offer, as he hadn't handled a dissent cable yet in his tenure in S/P. He referred me to the regulations and also encouraged me to speak with Special Envoy Booth about our plans and position, in keeping with the spirit of using the Dissent Channel as a last resort.

By late March, we'd circulated and revised the document a half-dozen times to address concerns and issues of interest for our collection of signatories, and we were happy with where it was. I reached out to Special Envoy Booth with a short email capturing our thoughts in brief and welcoming an opportunity to discuss them in person if he was interested in meeting. I expected Booth wouldn't be wildly surprised. I'd staffed him repeatedly in the course of his many visits to Juba the previous year and never missed an opportunity to briefly and politely voice my opinion about the need for stronger action on accountability and following through on our threats. I was a junior officer, though, so I also didn't expect he had thought much of it.

Although it took some time to pin down a meeting date because of his travel schedule, the special envoy was more gracious and generous with his time than I'd anticipated. When the date came, he welcomed me to his office. I took a seat on a chair across from him, thanked him for his time and consideration, and then nervously stated our case. This self-inflicted exercise had been a labor of love and obsession, but suddenly it seemed more real and risky, though I couldn't figure what it was I was risking. My reputation? In the State Department, one's corridor reputation is a thing to live by. It didn't take much to be branded a problem child, and that could impact your ability to secure good postings for the rest of your career. But the position we were taking wasn't controversial. It was just stronger and more determined than that of many others working on South Sudan, all of whom lamented the state of affairs and agreed we should do something more, though they weren't sure what. Mostly, we risked annoying people higher up than we were by forcing them to take note. I supposed I'd take my chances there.

Booth thanked me for bringing the concerns of our group to him, but on specific points he pushed back repeatedly, gently defending the status quo, as I would have expected, and suggesting, as Jon had, that everything we raised concerns about was already being discussed, so a dissent simply wasn't needed. His bottom line was that we were already doing everything that could possibly be done.

Our main point of contention in the meeting, however, was on the question of why the United States hadn't followed through on its threats, whether of meaningful sanctions, an arms embargo, or rescinding simple diplomatic niceties such as invitations. I knew the matter of sanctions and an arms embargo had been debated feverishly within the US government. It was slow to come, nearly a year into the violence, but US ambassador to the UN Samantha Power had taken the lead in pushing the UN Security Council to impose sanctions against Kiir's government and an arms embargo. The initiative was on a path to approval, with even Russia and China (the Security Council's usual naysayers) appearing persuadable, until Susan Rice killed it. Rice had suggested that it was wrong to undermine a democratically elected government's ability to defend itself, and that Uganda would ignore the embargo anyway. The Security Council had settled for a nonbinding statement urging Kiir and Machar to embrace peace.

Given Kiir's bad acts, Rice's position was indefensible, but at least it made sense. Booth's explanation, on the other hand, was nonsense. It was evident he had been defending this stance for a long time, and he'd grown frustrated with having to do so. As though it was the most logical argument imaginable, Booth explained to me that we couldn't follow through on the threats because they were our only leverage, and once we followed through with the threatened actions, we wouldn't have them to threaten anymore.

"Then what's the point of the threats if we aren't willing to follow through, and they know that?" I asked honestly. His reply was circular: that we needed to keep the leverage of making the threat but couldn't use it or we would lose the option. I was genuinely confused and made him walk me through the circle twice more, reluctantly realizing I'd heard him correctly.

We were stuck and nearing an hour, so I thanked him warmly for his time and consideration. Booth welcomed the opportunity to respond to the dissent before we moved forward with it formally. I told him we'd revise the document to reflect some new information he'd shared with us about what specifically the United States had been doing on the negotiations side and would send him the draft. After Oliver and I went through a few more rounds of edits to make sure our criticisms and recommendations were clearly articulated and acknowledged the ongoing efforts, I sent the new version to Booth.

After a couple of weeks, I received the written reply from Special Envoy Booth. It was, as expected, mostly shallow denials and robust defenses of the status quo. It was thorough, though, and took our argument point by point. His rebuttals deflected but didn't persuade, mostly just restating, in a variety of terms, that we've considered this, but it wouldn't work.

I learned from staff in his office that they were looking seriously at policy changes, but instead of shifting away from IGAD's peace talks, those changes would involve doubling down by adding representatives from additional countries as official members of the mediation process, including the United States, the United Kingdom, Norway, and a handful of other African countries. The idea would keep IGAD in the lead but dilute everyone's individual power in order to reduce the influence of biased actors. I didn't see how this provided meaningful change to a failed peace process, but I did envision a higher overall price tag.

We revised the dissent to carefully address the rebuttals from the special envoy's office. On May 3, I submitted it to S/P.

> Please find attached a dissent memo regarding our policy toward South Sudan. The co-author and I both previously served at Embassy Juba. We appreciate your consideration.

We were owed a reply within thirty to sixty days, so we settled in for the long wait. Overnight shifts got a little duller again, since I didn't have a side project to mull over in the quiet hours. Oliver predicted that the response would be some combination of dismissive and defensive. "We should keep in mind that there has surely never been a dissent cable for which the response has been 'you're exactly right and we are shifting U.S. policy accordingly,'" he told me, ever the rational one. "It shouldn't make us feel any less good about having pointed out shortcomings and expressed our frustrations with years of failed policy." I quietly wondered if taking this last possible policy step would help me finally move on.

On June 30, Oliver and I received the response by email from S/P:

> Attached you will please find the response to your Dissent Channel message on South Sudan policy.

Oliver's prediction was spot-on. I took some comfort in the fact that the response was five pages long. It was dismissive, sure, but someone had to put a lot of thought and effort into dismissing it.

Oliver sent our brief reply, as usual demonstrating a masterful ability to relay clear and strong messages in the fewest words possible:

Thank you for the response. We continue to disagree with the claim that USG has leveraged its leadership role to the greatest extent possible, and we reiterate our concern that years of hollow threats have contributed to the atmosphere of impunity in which South Sudanese leaders now operate. That said, we appreciate the thoughtful response and want to express our thanks to all those involved.

My email to our working group of cosigners was, as usual, less pithy and diplomatic:

I wanted to let you all know that we have received the official response from S/P. Unfortunately, I cannot circulate it as it is very clearly marked "for Addressees only," and Oliver and I are the only addressees. That said, you are not missing out. It is very much what we were expecting and reads very much like (in fact, word for word in many places) Booth's original response. This is including references to specific language that we took out of the final version (unimpressed, I am).

It is for the most part defensive of our current stance, suggesting we are doing everything realistically possible without addressing in detail most of what we recommend, other than vague dismissals (ex. "we are actively exploring whether the arms embargo discussion can be reopened in New York" without addressing the fact that we were the ones who stopped that discussion, and saying the US has taken the lead in the sanctions discussion without saying why we haven't sanctioned anyone worth sanctioning).

So, long story short, this chapter is over. I am grateful again for the role you all played. At least at the end of the day, we know we have done everything we could to influence this effort. Thank you again for all the work you all put in to help us put this argument on the record.

"FOR ADDRESSEES ONLY." It felt like a dull bureaucratic version of a James Bond moment, and a curious one. Why the limited distribution? It seemed unnecessarily cagey. The document wasn't searchable in our system. No one beyond the very limited distribution list inside the department would ever see it. How exactly was the Dissent Channel supposed to foster real debate if its use was so limited and distribution so controlled?

On the day we received the response, the headlines included an NBC report: "South Sudan's SPLA Raped, Burned Girls Alive: United Nations Report." Someone had leaked the full UN report to me and it was horrific, capturing widespread and systematic abuse of children by government forces, lest the children become adults who sought revenge later in life. It was not that I thought the opposition forces were any better. They had come from the same military for the most part. It was just that I couldn't stomach the idea that this was being done systematically by the forces of a government we openly legitimized and supported.

A few days later, Susan Rice would release a statement on South Sudan's independence blaming both sides but also finally stating plainly that the South Sudanese government had "abdicated its responsibilities" and "squandered its legitimacy." But it was too little too late and would be followed by no meaningful action.

I remained dumbfounded by our failures, but I'd done everything I could. The Dissent Channel was the last resort. I'd taken it, and it didn't matter. Just as designed, this entire chapter had been folded up and locked away.

In 2018, after he had left the department, Jon would pen an extensive report while working with the Simon-Skjodt Center for the Prevention of Genocide: *From Independence to Civil War: Atrocity Prevention and US Policy toward South Sudan*. It was more thorough, covering the patterns for an additional three years, but otherwise closely mirrored our dissent's arguments, criticisms, and recommendations. He highlighted, however, that there had been no effort "to challenge core assumptions and relationships and standard ways of doing business." His report continued, "It is difficult to imagine, in other parts of the world, that policy toward an ostensibly high-priority country would go unchallenged like this." He chalked it up to "the fog of war" being a "legitimate challenge." As the saying goes, "hindsight is 20/20," he said.

He failed to acknowledge the formal use of our only dissent mechanism to offer such a challenge, the one he had personally witnessed and helped shepherd through. *Some of us saw through the fog of war, and we told you so.*

21

All Your Friends Are False, All Your Enemies Real

October 2015–September 2016

IN OCTOBER 2015, THE AFRICAN UNION'S COMMISSION OF IN-
quiry on South Sudan released its final report. The report was extensive, more than three hundred pages, and shockingly frank,
particularly as little had been expected of it. The AU/COI had been
concluded a year earlier, but securing the report's public release was
a battle.

The commission found no evidence of a coup but had found evidence that the killings were organized on the part of the state. With
regard to the violence that began the war:

> *The evidence gathered by the Commission suggests that there were
> killings committed by elements of security forces from 16th Decem-
> ber 2013 in residential areas.... The Commission was informed
> that Juba was subdivided into four operation sectors.**

> ...

---

* *Final Report of the African Union Commission on South Sudan* (Addis Ababa:
AU Commission of Inquiry on South Sudan, 2014), para. 464, www.peaceau
.org/uploads/auciss.final.report.pdf.

> *Roadblocks or checkpoints were established all around Juba and house to house searches were undertaken by security forces. During this operation male Nuers were targeted, identified, killed on the spot or gathered in one place and killed.**
>
> . . .
>
> *The evidence thus suggests that these crimes were committed pursuant to or in furtherance of a State policy.***

The United States welcomed the decision to release the report and pledged $5 million to promote justice and accountability. The money was marked for a hybrid court that was still not operational four years later.

SINCE MY DISSENT had been unceremoniously packed away, I had focused on moving on. I adopted a dog and named it Juba. Like his namesake, Juba was conflicted and suffered from some deeply ingrained trauma. Six weeks later, he was hit by a car and killed. It felt like a sign.

I stopped talking about South Sudan entirely. I didn't seek out news of the war or the flailing peace process. I hung out with friends who had no connection to the country, who hadn't lived and worked there. I started running again. I signed up for a marathon. I finished my assignment in Ops and began Somali language training in preparation for my upcoming assignment. I devoured every book I could find on the country—unlike South Sudan, there were few, so it didn't take long. I threw myself into language training, listening to Somali news broadcasts daily. My focus shifted entirely, and it helped. The nightmares went into remission, and before I realized it I was sleeping through the night. Not living on a shifting shift schedule helped too.

I arrived in Nairobi for my position as political officer in the Somalia Mission in May 2016. Shortly thereafter, I had to revisit it all

---

* *Final Report*, para. 810.
** *Final Report*, para. 812.

again. Juba was heading toward violence at a level not seen in the capital since the conflict began, and it was preceded by an incident the US government had awkwardly tried to downplay.

Tension had been boiling in Juba since Machar had returned in late April to take up his position as vice president in a Transitional Government of National Unity outlined in the latest iteration of the peace agreement. This had been viewed as a huge development in the peace process, but it had translated to little more than symbolic meetings thus far. Machar had delayed his return due to concerns about his safety, since he felt the limited allotment of soldiers he was allowed to bring with him was not sufficient. He'd been lambasted as a spoiler for doing so, but his concerns would soon be validated.

On July 7, skirmishes between some of Machar's forces and Kiir's Presidential Guard were reported in Juba, so Ambassador Mary Catherine Phee, who had succeeded Ambassador Page to lead the embassy, reached out to several staff who were at dinner in town and asked them to hurry back to the compound. Seven American diplomats piled into the armored two-car convoy for the short trip back to the embassy.* As they passed by the presidential palace, Presidential Guards ordered them to pull over, yelling at the car and flaunting their AK-47s. One of the guards tried to force open one of the vehicle doors. Diplomatic vehicles aren't required to stop at checkpoints or to open doors on demand, so this was a clear provocation. The South Sudanese driver knew the protocol: it was a dangerous situation, so get out. He hit the gas, and the second car followed while the Presidential Guard forces began to fire on both. The departure was chaotic as the drivers swerved their way out. In the getaway, two other separate groups of government soldiers nearby also sprayed the vehicles with bullets. The vehicle carrying the embassy's deputy chief of mission was badly damaged, with two tires blown out, coming to a stop ironically on CPA Road, the street named after the Comprehensive

---

* Details for this account come from Colum Lynch, "Dinner, Drinks, and a Near-Fatal Ambush for U.S. Diplomats," *Foreign Policy*, September 6, 2016, https://foreignpolicy.com/2016/09/06/dinner-drinks-and-a-near-fatal-ambush -for-u-s-diplomats/.

Peace Agreement that had laid the foundation for South Sudan's independence with significant American support. Luckily, the Americans were now out of sight of the gunmen. Marines were dispatched from the embassy to retrieve the passengers in the disabled car.

The State Department spokesperson later told CNN, "We do not believe our vehicles and personnel were specifically targeted and have no indication that the security forces were instructed to fire on our vehicles. However, we condemn this attack on U.S. embassy personnel," adding that no one had been injured because the vehicles were armored.* The armor was a saving grace, but even I knew that those vehicles would only hold off close-range AK fire for so long. This had come very close to being a horribly bloody incident.

Publicly, State officials claimed the soldiers wouldn't have known who was in the vehicles. Privately, we all knew that was absurd. The vehicles were clearly marked with large laminated American-flag decals on the front windshields, and everyone in town knew what the diplomatic "11" number plates meant. Was the attack on our vehicles ordered? Probably not, but how else would you expect the armed forces to act when the government openly maligned the United States and accused it of supporting the rebels. That same evening, across town in the Tomping neighborhood, other government soldiers fired on a UN vehicle that wasn't armored. A senior UN official was shot in his thigh, hand, and arm.

I heard from colleagues who had been in Juba with me, and we collectively lamented the US government's ongoing unwillingness to call out South Sudan for such brazen acts. Other State Department colleagues who heard the story emailed to ask if it could possibly be true. "Sadly, it is," I replied.

As it turned out, Machar's security instincts were spot on. On July 8, while he was at the presidential palace meeting with Kiir, fighting broke out between Machar's and Kiir's protective forces and violence spread across the city, with government forces utilizing helicopter

---

* Elise Labott, "Shots Fired at US Embassy Vehicles in South Sudan," CNN, July 8, 2016, www.cnn.com/2016/07/08/politics/south-sudan-us-embassy/index.html.

gunships and heavy artillery that hadn't been available in the early days of the war. The city suffered from exactly the kind of slaughter an arms embargo would have limited. Hundreds were killed. Both sides blamed each other for the start of the violence, but Machar's forces were massively outnumbered and outgunned, and they were in enemy territory. They wouldn't have begun a suicide mission. The only real question was how high up the plot to take out Machar went. Unsurprisingly, Machar didn't stay in Juba to find out. He fled south on foot.

The violence continued for several days, and Embassy Nairobi set up a support task force to prepare for expected evacuations. As the resident expert on evacuating Juba, I was put on standby for possible travel into the country and spent a lot of time on the phone with the latest Juba Task Force in Ops to provide guidance and context. In the end, it was a short-term crisis, and things returned to normal in relatively short order, but information slowly trickled out about a brutal attack on Terrain Camp, a hotel complex that had long housed many expats, including contractors working on US government projects. It happened on July 11. The victims were many of our own people—people brought to South Sudan on the US government's dime to work on State Department and USAID projects, people we had put in harm's way. Reports varied, but it was said that between fifty and one hundred government soldiers attacked the facility, beating and torturing the inhabitants for hours, gang-raping several Western women, and executing John Gatluak Nhial, a Nuer journalist.

Press reports stated that government forces had already pushed the rebels from the city when the attack on Terrain Camp occurred. Soldiers reportedly beat an American for about an hour and told him, "You tell your embassy how we treat you." Several other captives were asked specifically if they were American. One woman said she was raped by fifteen men after they broke into a safe house where about twenty people had tried to hide. From the start of the attack, people inside the compound called multiple people at the US Embassy and the UN, but no one came to their aid. The UN peacekeepers refused to send anyone. The embassy's response was to contact the South Sudanese government and seek its intervention. A State Department spokesperson said later, "We were not in a position to intervene." After several hours, it was the South Sudanese government that sent a different group of its soldiers to stop the group already there perpetrating the attack.

Western and even regional press focused mostly on the violence directed at Westerners. Since government forces had been brutally attacking South Sudanese civilians en masse for years at this point, the violence directed at Westerners in the capital city was the most shocking element of the Terrain Camp attack. Many US government officials are still haunted by our failure to help those people who were living and working there on our behalf. But the greatest tragedy was surely the loss of John Gatluak Nhial.

John was a natural at journalism and fearless, in one of the most dangerous countries for journalists in the world. As he once put it, "Being a journalist in South Sudan is risking one's life, but I have dedicated myself to serving my community through radio as a watchdog, informing them about what the politicians are doing once the citizens elect them to power." John pursued the stories other reporters feared. One of the first controversial stories he tackled was the theft of USAID rice and cooking-oil shipments, meant for returning Sudanese refugees, by corrupt government officials. Local officials warned John not to write the story, as did fellow reporters. His response was simple. "We have a responsibility to tell the truth. It's not a matter of whether we should do the story or not. It's only a matter of how to cover it properly."

When war erupted in 2013 and ravaged John's community in Leer, he stayed to keep the local radio station on air for as long as he could. When government soldiers went on the offensive and destroyed the radio station and every living thing around it, John was evacuated with other staff, friends, and family to Juba, where he initially resided at the UN's IDP camp. By 2016, John was still living in Juba under dangerous conditions. After being detained by government authorities, his employer relocated him to Terrain Camp only days before the attack, hoping it would be a safe haven for him. John was captured and lined up with others. One of the commanding soldiers shouted "Nuer!" and John was shot twice in the face and four more times as he lay on the ground.

John wanted to do something good for his people, for all South Sudanese, regardless of tribe. One of his last social media posts was a simple picture that said, "I love Dinka," which was a radical thing for a Nuer to publicly state at the time. It was his openness and his truth that made him a threat to the government.

Shortly before his murder, John developed and led a network of community radio stations and helped establish a South Sudanese NGO to manage and advocate for them. John also represented his country at the 2014 African Leaders Forum in Washington, DC. As a dear friend of mine and a mentor of John's put it, "John loved a challenge and was an extremely hard worker. He was an old soul, kind and gentle. I don't even have the words to describe how remarkable John was as both a journalist and a person. Nor do I have the words to truly articulate how much I, and his country, will miss him."

Some low-level soldiers would ultimately be tried and convicted following massive international pressure (which tends to step up effectively when the victims include expatriates), but no one in a position of authority would pay any price for what was obviously not some random mistake or a matter of disorderly troops. The attack on Terrain Camp shook the community of expatriates who had lived in or worked on South Sudan.

What was most shocking to me, though, was not the attack. It was that it took over a month for it to hit the news, and that the US government waited until then to publicly acknowledge or condemn it.

On August 15, US ambassador to the UN Samantha Power released a statement condemning the attack and the government's pattern of allowing impunity for violence. In an apparent attempt to head off criticism, the statement mentioned that the US Embassy responded to distress calls throughout the attack, though it neglected to explain why the embassy hadn't done anything beyond urging the government to take action. The statement offered a harsh rebuke of the perpetrators but suggested a disconnect between the perpetrators and the government, so we once again pulled our punch. It ended with the usual equivocation: "The parties to the conflict must immediately cease attacks against innocent civilians and recommit to settle the conflict and leave the South Sudanese to live in peace at last."

After the fighting in Juba had concluded, President Kiir publicly issued a plea for Machar to return to take up his position as vice president within forty-eight hours or, he said, he would be compelled to fill the position with someone else in order to keep the peace agreement implementation on track. A UN spokesperson warned that any replacement would have to be chosen by the opposition in order to be consistent with the peace agreement, but Kiir had made clear he would put in place General Taban Deng Gai, a former opposition negotiator who had since broken ranks with Machar. Anyone following the conflict knew Gai had been chosen as a stooge and that the peace process would be effectively dead with his appointment.

Secretary of State John Kerry came to Nairobi a couple of weeks later to try to revamp peace efforts. Since I knew the players and the context well, I was tapped to staff him for the meeting. It seemed I couldn't escape Juba even if I tried. Secretary Kerry was joined by foreign ministers from across the region, and both Special Envoy Booth and Ambassador Phee were also there. We were in a large conference room at a Nairobi hotel. The long rectangular table sat in the middle of the room adorned with tiny flags, and two rows of additional chairs sat behind either side. South Sudan had sent an excessively large delegation that took one entire side of the table, across from single representatives of several other countries. I shuddered when I saw Michael Makuei Lueth enter the room, with his usual swagger and permanent look of condescension. If anyone was to blame for stoking anti-American violence, it was this man.

The meeting lasted hours. My seat was too far away to hear some of the quieter talkers, so I was yet again awkwardly perching at the far edge of my seat and leaning in unnaturally. My hand was cramping. The dialogue was heavily dotted with the usual platitudes, and the South Sudanese delegation returned fire with the expected denials and deflections. High diplomacy indeed. The most interesting thing I'd heard thus far was the Sudanese minister asking the South Sudanese delegation if they could please change the name of their army, still dubbed the Sudanese People's Liberation Army, since they weren't liberating Sudanese people anymore.

Toward the end, though, Kerry made what seemed like a profound gaffe. He said, in so many words, that the United States was done with Machar, suggesting that since Machar had left the vice president position vacant, Kiir was empowered to replace him. With just a few words, Kerry had legitimized Kiir's naked power play, making Machar the fall guy in return for literally fleeing for his life after the government's attempted hit job on the other half of the Transitional Government of National Unity.

I was not the only one shocked by Kerry's words. Special Envoy Booth and Ambassador Phee seemed to almost fall off their chairs. But this was no gaffe. As it turned out, this was an intentional move, indicative of the serious disconnect between Secretary Kerry's position and that of the special envoy's office and the embassy. Kerry had come to adopt the stance of the National Security Council and the White House, and the gap between the prevailing position in Washington and that of those in the field was only widening. I expected National Security Advisor Susan Rice was behind it, continuing to defend the pro-Kiir stance. She had President Obama's ear on all foreign policy matters, and I knew she had routinely overruled State. While I got where she was coming from, I still couldn't fathom why. After all that had happened at Kiir's hands, I couldn't believe anyone was still backing this guy, even her.

We were handicapped in the field, far removed from the decisionmakers in Washington. It was a structural defect that caused harm in both directions. We didn't understand decisions coming out of Washington, and Washington didn't understand why they were such bad ideas. The disconnect seemed to increase with each administration, as the White House brought more and more policymaking and implementation in-house, led by political appointees. This trend had been on the rise since President Eisenhower in the 1950s, but Susan

Rice's ability to single-handedly direct foreign policy in the Obama years still surprised me.

Only five weeks after two separate intentional attacks on American citizens and diplomats by South Sudanese government forces, America took the lead once again in anointing Kiir's destabilizing acts with legitimacy.

22

Resignation

2016–2017

THE SUN WAS RISING OVER THE INDIAN OCEAN, BATHING THE rough waves off the coast of Mogadishu in a soft glow, masking the jagged rocks and coral beneath the surface. The waters here are so lethal that this two-mile stretch of beach, which marks the eastern boundary of Mogadishu's international military base, has no security wall or fence. Standing on the balcony of the dining hall at the Bancroft International Campus, home away from home for US diplomatic personnel in Somalia, I stared out across the deceptively glassy surface in disbelief.

Hillary Clinton had just lost Florida.

We were hosting the first election watch party in Mogadishu in a quarter century, as the United States slowly normalized diplomatic relations with Somalia, and the writing was on the wall. Donald Trump would be the next president, and the nature of US engagement with the world would be disrupted, perhaps irreparably so. It was hard to tell who was more upset—the American diplomats or our Somali guests. Trump had singled out the Somali people as avid terrorist supporters during his campaign. We were all concerned about what his election would mean for our futures, for America's relationship with Somalia and with the world. Our future president had made it clear he had little patience with or interest in diplomatic solutions, multilateral action, or playing well with others, generally speaking. But, as a US official, I couldn't share my concerns. So as the news rolled in, I took slow, deep breaths and bit my tongue.

After escorting the last guest to the security gate around 10 a.m., I sprinted past the housing trailers and scrubby landscape back to the bunker in the rear of the compound—our office and living space in Mogadishu. I pushed through the large back security door, passed through the makeshift gym inside the external blast wall, and into the interior. As my eyes struggled to adjust from the bright equatorial sun to the fluorescence of our windowless container, they filled with tears.

Raymond, the public affairs officer, brought me a coffee mug of whisky, a welcome gift after a sober event, and gave me a hug. Ambassador Stephen Schwartz entered the room. "I hope those are spiked," he muttered. "They're straight, sir," I replied.

A half-dozen security officers milled about at computers, pretending to work but mostly just watching the large TV screen affixed to the wall above our work space as election coverage continued. Ambassador Schwartz had gently warned us to be cautious in our political conversations in mixed company. As career diplomats, we were tasked with nonpartisan positions, but every US diplomat I knew had strong views about the consequences of this election. I scanned the room as I sipped my whisky, wondering about these security officers, knowing that some of them were pleased with the result, wondering how it was possible that they could see this so differently.

Candidate Trump had applauded strongmen, derided allies, and promised to abandon our greatest recent diplomatic achievements. His sweeping condemnation of the Islamic faith played into the hands of our enemies and undermined our foundational religious freedom. Trump's view of the world and our place in it was transactional, and a powerful military seemed to be his answer to all questions beyond our borders. Many of his stated foreign policy positions were anathema even to the Republican establishment, yet the party was falling in line with its new leader. It was unclear if anyone or anything would act as a check on Trump's whims.

My fear of Trump wasn't a matter of partisanship. His administration wouldn't represent mere political differences with what I believed. His election called into question the very foundation of what it was we—our country's diplomats—were doing across the globe. What did we stand for now?

For well over two hundred years, the State Department had led US foreign affairs, promoting our national interests overseas. Our mission statement captured our understanding of what this meant: "To shape and sustain a peaceful, prosperous, just, and democratic world and foster conditions for stability and progress for the benefit of the American people and people everywhere."* (Notably, this mission statement would soon change, deleting the reference to "people everywhere," along with "just" and "democratic.")

Trump's view was not aligned with this mission. That much was clear. But as the new reality began to set in over the coming days, I reflected on the fact that our foreign policy approach had never really aligned with this mission.

Trump wasn't an aberration. He was merely the unapologetic reflection of what we'd already become.

America was cocky before Trump.

America had double standards before Trump.

America's shining city on a hill was a fiction long before Trump.

Repeatedly, our leaders had selectively invoked American values while turning a blind eye to gross abuses and injustice when convenient.

I saw this most clearly while I was stationed in South Sudan under the Obama administration. I watched us squander considerable leverage even as we were expending hundreds of millions of dollars in the country. We had touted our foreign policy success, bathed in the victorious glow of this new nation we had helped bring into being, generously pouring money and support into its government, all while conveniently looking past the government's steady creep toward ethnically oriented authoritarianism. We had

---

* https://2009-2017.state.gov/s/d/rm/rls/perfrpt/2015/html/249683.htm.

not shaped or sustained peace, prosperity, or justice. We had not fostered democratic or stable conditions. We had little to show for our efforts but a propped-up regime that abused its own people and robbed the country blind. We missed repeated opportunities to change course.

We settled for selling the idea of success, even to ourselves, because the work of building a durable and just nation out of the ashes of conflict is hard, uncertain, and clearly not our forte.

When I first arrived in Juba, I didn't realize this. And then I did. I saw it firsthand. Our human rights stance was all talk. We failed to admit when atrocities were occurring, lest we be expected to act. This was even more true when the perpetrators were our "friends," or when admitting the bad acts of our friends would reflect poorly on our prior (and future) foreign policy choices. We were willing to overlook human rights abuses merely to save face. We gave the benefit of the doubt to some of the most heinous people on earth. In the field, this seemed to be driven by misguided hope. In Washington, it was expedience or inertia.

But it was all becoming clear. Complex foreign policy decisions were made on an electoral timeline. Americans fear imminent foreign threats? Go to war. Americans are now over those threats and focused on a poor economy? Bring the troops home. The cyclical nature of the public's interest in foreign policy unfortunately did not align with compelling foreign policy concerns. The hard work of soft power was falling by the wayside. Hoping for the best had become an acceptable policy response.

And, for all of this, there were consequences, for us and for the people who suffered under those we empowered.

I had struggled with this during and after my time in South Sudan, but I stuck it out, hoping we could become the great country we claimed to be if people like me kept trying to make it so. From inside the government, maybe I could help steer us toward a foreign policy grounded in the values that we claimed were our foundation. We were still talking as if they were, after all.

I'd been hopeful that our foreign policy under Hillary Clinton would allow for that change I was seeking. I hoped it would be one grounded in the values of human rights and justice, and that her administration would have no problem standing up to the bad guys—most of them at least. I was fully aware from Trump's rhetoric during the campaign that he would do none of those things, and any incremental progress we had made in recent years toward a more just, strong, and effective foreign policy would not only be lost but actively reversed.

I held on for a while, trying to help manage the disaster from the inside where I could. I tried to reassure counterparts from other diplomatic missions that things wouldn't be that bad, that career diplomats still managed much of the machinery of our foreign policy and would help us stay the course. I helped my ambassador author a cable back to Washington outlining the disastrous effects the Muslim travel ban would have on our counterterrorism partnership with Somalia and our own activities in the country. I watched hopefully as Congress, on both sides of the aisle, rejected Trump's attempt to cut the State Department budget by 37 percent. I was pleased when 121 US military generals and admirals wrote congressional leadership also making the case, including the well-known quote from Secretary of Defense James Mattis: "If you don't fully fund the State Department, then I need to buy more ammunition." I looked for reasons to be hopeful, frequently shouted into my pillow, and sat on the rocks by the Indian Ocean and stared.

Our direction from Washington, which had already been minimal, dissipated entirely, as dozens of State Department leadership positions went unfilled. Some people began to think Secretary of State Rex Tillerson was dangerously clueless in how he ran the organization, but I suspected this former ExxonMobil executive knew exactly what he was doing. His landmark oil deal with Russia had foundered due to sanctions pushed by the State Department. He had nothing to gain from robust civilian foreign affairs.

Critical projects ground to a halt, stalled due to our inability to find anyone in Washington willing or empowered to give approvals. The military's activities in Somalia continued to expand with less and less meaningful oversight, and the Somali government slowly lost confidence in what our diplomats had to say.

A draft dissent cable against the travel ban began circulating widely around the State Department and overseas posts only a few weeks after Trump took office. "We are better than this ban," it said. Colleagues were reading it and debating whether to sign on. Unsurprisingly, the draft was leaked to the press. Sean Spicer, Trump's press secretary at the time, was asked about it and replied with a poorly veiled threat, saying of the department's civil servants, "They should either get with the program or they should go."

I got an email from a colleague from my Foreign Service orientation class. She knew I had written a dissent cable and asked my thoughts about this one. I was torn. Of course I opposed the travel ban, but so did nearly everyone at every level of the department. Our mission had replied appropriately, I believed, by submitting a regular cable—not a dissent, because it went forward with the approval and signature of our ambassador, intended to inform those to whom he reported. To me, the effort to use the Dissent Channel in this case seemed misdirected. The draft appeared geared toward a public audience from the start.

I understood why more than one thousand State Department employees ultimately signed on to the document, and I didn't blame them, but I also didn't see how it helped. Amid the relentless news coverage and constant hallway chatter about the ban, I couldn't help but think about my own experience with dissent, and I couldn't be sure that leaking the document was a bad call in the end. These were people who longed to be heard, and the Dissent Channel would have efficiently quashed any hope of that.

But if dissenting was hopeless, what hope could I look to in the department?

I started talking to friends and mentors about the possibility of resigning. At first, the response was usually, "I certainly wouldn't blame you, but wouldn't it be better to stay and try to change things from the inside, where you can have influence?" But I'd learned first-hand that opposition from the inside was futile here, even in normal times, and we were not in normal times. These weren't policy debates about how to achieve the same ends. I might have disagreed mightily with our strategy in South Sudan, but I knew we all wanted the same peaceful outcome and all genuinely cared about the issue. Under the Trump administration, I had no such reassurance. These weren't disputes over policy, but rather over what our values were, what our priorities were, what we stood for at the most basic level.

So why am I still here? Day after day, week after week, the question plagued me. By summer, the same mentors and friends who had encouraged me to wait it out, to change things from the inside, were starting to change their tune. Hopelessness had set in. The only people who continued to urge me to stay were people who had already left themselves. *Easy to say from out there,* I thought. I didn't think leaking information was appropriate, but I knew I could only stay silent for so long. In the end, the decision was an easy one. It wasn't just the headline issues, like the Muslim travel ban, budget cuts, or unqualified political appointees. Every day there were small changes in language, how the administration spoke to or about our allies or our foes, how we addressed democracy, what we said (or didn't say) about human rights, where our leadership traveled to, and where it didn't. It swelled from a small discomfort into an unstoppable force, built out of dozens of dangerous moves. I didn't believe we even wanted to be a force for good anymore, and I didn't think we were acting in our own self-interest either. I couldn't in good faith defend the policies of the administration, so I had to leave to have the freedom to speak my piece.

And so, a year into the Trump presidency, I resigned. In my letter to then–secretary of state Rex Tillerson, I stated the facts as I saw them:

Over the past 10 months, our government has failed to demonstrate a commitment to promoting and defending human rights and democracy. President Trump's dismissive attitude toward human rights was no surprise following his campaign, but your [Secretary Tillerson's] May 3 remarks to Department staff shocked many as you called into question the utility of advancing human rights when it proves inconvenient. As a foreign policy professional, I understand better than most that we must balance competing interests, but human rights and democracy are fundamental elements of a safer world for our people.

I went on to humbly recommend Secretary Tillerson follow me out the door.

BY THE TIME I resigned, South Sudan's five-year war had left a staggering death toll for a small country. Nearly four hundred thousand people were believed to have perished, more than 3 percent of the country's total population. More than two million had been displaced inside the country, with another two million living as refugees beyond the borders. I watched from the sidelines as little shifted in the US approach to the country and the conflict, wondering what more I or anyone could have done to change that direction, wondering what inside the State Department or the foreign policy establishment would have to be different to enable that change to happen.

With my resignation, I lost any opportunity to continue trying to change things from the inside. But outside the department? I haven't given up on that yet. The costs of a transactional and short-sighted foreign policy are too high to ignore.

So where, then, and how?

I've learned a few things in my time in the Foreign Service. I've learned that our career diplomats are only as effective as the political leadership allows them to be, and that swaying political leadership is necessary to change our foreign policy direction. I know that political leadership pays attention to public opinion. I know the American public knows little about South Sudan, our foreign policy in Africa, or our foreign policy generally speaking.

I've also learned that civilians around the world have a tremendous capacity for forgiving the United States. Our values still resonate with people across the globe. I think of the dozens of refugees and victims who looked to me, to us, with hope, believing that America could help them establish these values too. For all the mistakes we've made, and there are many, the world still recognizes something unique in the promise of America. It is still ours, if we choose it.

I believe we can recover, but not by simply seeking a return to a pre-Trump world. It will require a deliberate national discourse on what actually makes America great. What are the values that set us apart? How must we put them into practice?

South Sudan provides a roadmap of what happens when we lose sight of that. Now that I've told this story, will people listen? Is change possible? Can we live up to our potential, and, in doing so, help shape a safer, more prosperous world?

I don't know yet, but I'm willing to try.

Acknowledgments

I've been the beneficiary of a lifetime of tremendous opportunity and support. This book would not exist without the efforts and support from colleagues, family, and friends across four critical stages in particular.

In South Sudan, I faced challenges I couldn't have imaged. Many of the people who supported, encouraged, protected, and educated me along the way appear in the pages of this book, but not all. I've had to change some names and leave out some stories for reasons of safety and security. I've had opportunities to thank some of those people in person. Some I never will. Without the herculean work of Gio Gore in our humble consular section, I might have given up on the job long before the war began. Suzanne Grantham was always ready to offer invaluable support, solutions, and much-needed humor. Ajani Husbands, Byron Hartman, and Lori Enders were rock stars during the crisis. Alicia Dinerstein and Adrienne Galanek were both mentors and dear friends. Mike McCarthy's continued guidance and confidence in me were also invaluable. I recall sitting in his office in Juba, one of the many times he had to deliver the news that my argument was not going to win the day. He told me anyway, "Don't ever lose that passion," and I carry that message with me still.

James Liddle taught me a tremendous amount about South Sudan and the State Department. I'm very grateful for his patience, his investment in the country and our mission, and his professional support. Thanks to Rob McKee for the beers, security tips, and the ongoing input and support in Juba and thereafter. I'm grateful also to Boxcar, for advice, support, encouragement, and help on more occasions than I can list here. I offer a special thanks to all the South Sudanese who entrusted me with their personal stories. Their confidence in America's capacity to do good in the world inspires me to continue to try to help our country live up to its promise.

I went through a difficult period after leaving Juba in 2014. I might have lost my mind in State Ops but for the patience and support of my epic Ops team: Catherine Schweitzer, Brendan Rivage-Seul, Ian Arzeni, Phil Dimon, Sonia Kim, and Jenny Olson. I look forward to an Orca reunion again soon.

I am deeply indebted to Oliver Mains for coauthoring the dissent. It might not have led to the changes we were championing, but I've learned that's no reason to stop speaking out. My gratitude goes also to those colleagues who bravely added their names, support, and input to our submission: Jessie Huaracayo, Alicia, Adrienne, and David McCloud.

I was humbled by the extensive support and encouragement I received from so many colleagues when I decided to resign from the State Department. Thanks to Caitlin Conaty for going many rounds of edits with me to ensure my resignation letter captured perfectly the message I wanted to share. Special thanks to Jessie Evans for holding my hand as I navigated the transition from government life and the media chaos that ensued (not to mention making all those long days and nights in Mogadishu eminently more enjoyable). To Jessi Wolz, one usually has to pay a therapist for the kind of reaffirming, confidence-building, you-can-do-it support you offered me so often. I'll also be forever grateful to Dan De Luce, who saw a bellwether in my resignation and saw fit to launch my letter to the world with his article in *Foreign Policy*.

To my Naivasha family, what would I have done in that strange, unmoored first year of living alone—with no affiliation, no black passport, no badge to give me meaning and value, full of uncertainty about the future—if I hadn't been embraced by the wonderful quirky community that filled my heart with warmth, my evenings with picturesque sundowners, and my mind with incredible stories when it was exhausted from writing my own? Lynne Coyte, I'd have been far hungrier, thirstier, and high-strung without you.

I took another leap in 2019 and moved to Vermont, where I wrote most of the rest of this book, and I was met again with a welcoming community that I now call home. The support and friendship of my dear neighbor Irene Smead made this transition particularly smooth.

I am fortunate to have a story to tell, and even more so for having the support of amazing professionals to help me tell it. I am deeply indebted to my agents, David Kuhn and Nate Muscato at Aevitas Creative, for taking a chance, believing in the project, and giving me the confidence and the opportunity to do it. I am exceedingly grateful to Colleen Lawrie, my wonderful editor at PublicAffairs, whose vision for the book exceeded even my own, and whose direction made the bigger vision possible. My sincere thanks to the entire PublicAffairs team for bringing this book to life.

I am grateful to my brilliant friend Barrett Hightower for many careful rounds of reading, editing, and brainstorming. I am indebted to Emily Renard, not only for her insightful feedback on the manuscript, but also her tremendous professional and personal support and camaraderie. There would be no book without my sister Signe, my first reader of every draft, a skilled editor and cheerleader, the one who pushed me past my comfort zone to all the best material—often the hardest but most important things to face and to write. Signe has been with me every step of the way, and for that and so much more, I am exceedingly grateful.

I am deeply grateful to my partner Dan for his unending patience and for the support that made it possible for me to take the time I needed to write this book. A shout-out as well to my dog Boogie. No one has been with me throughout more of the writing process than my ever-faithful furry companion.

My sister Hilary has been my partner in crime on so many adventures across a lifetime, but I am particularly grateful for her love and support on my return to Washington after my year in Juba. Our repertoire was limited, but sister dinners got me through. What a gift to have a sister only a mile and a half away.

The final words of this book I wrote in San Francisco, breaking out of a slog of writer's block in my uncle's sunlit apartment overlooking the bay. The break came just when I needed it, but there is never a bad moment for some quality time with Uncle Luke.

To Mom and Dad, you both drive me crazy in your own special ways, but I would not be the person I am today—with all the contradictions, strengths, and weaknesses that entails—without either of you. I'm grateful for all of it.

Bibliography

Most of the information in this book has come from my own personal experience and consultations with those with whom I shared it. Where I have relied on external sources to provide additional historical and political context, I have so noted in the text and in footnotes. Sources I relied on extensively or that are particularly relevant to the subject matter are listed below.

Bass, Gary J. *The Blood Telegram: Nixon, Kissinger, and a Forgotten Genocide.* New York: Alfred A. Knopf, 2013.

Brooks, Rosa. *How Everything Became War and the Military Became Everything.* New York: Simon & Schuster, 2016.

Final Report of the African Union Commission of Inquiry on South Sudan. Addis Ababa: AU Commission of Inquiry on South Sudan, 2014. www.peaceau. org/uploads/auciss.final.report.pdf.

Gurman, Hannah. *The Dissent Papers: The Voices of Diplomats in the Cold War and Beyond.* New York: Columbia University Press, 2012.

Hutchings, Robert, and Jeremi Suri, eds. *Foreign Policy Breakthroughs: Cases in Successful Diplomacy.* New York: Oxford University Press, 2015.

Maddow, Rachel. *Drift: The Unmooring of American Military Power.* New York: Broadway Books, 2012.

Van Buren, Peter. *We Meant Well: How I Helped Lose the Battle for the Hearts and Minds of the Iraqi People.* New York: Metropolitan Books, 2011.

Index

KAREN PIKE

ELIZABETH SHACKELFORD was a career diplomat in the US State Department until December 2017, when she resigned in protest of the Trump administration. During her tenure with the Foreign Service, Shackelford served in the US embassies in Poland and South Sudan, the US Mission to Somalia, and Washington, DC. For her work in South Sudan during the outbreak of civil war, Shackelford received the Barbara Watson Award for Consular Excellence, the State Department's highest honor for consular work.

Her resignation letter to Secretary of State Rex Tillerson, first shared by *Foreign Policy*, went viral. Since her departure, Shackelford has advocated for greater civilian oversight and leadership in foreign affairs and increased local democratic activism. Born and raised in Mississippi, she now lives in Rochester, VT.